Teen Health Series

Abuse and Violence Information for Teens, Third Edition

Abuse and Violence Information for Teens, Third Edition

Health Tips about the Causes and Consequences of
Abusive and Violent Teen Behavior

Including Facts about the Types of Abuse and Violence,
the Warning Signs of Abusive and Violent Behavior, Health
Concerns of Victims, and Getting Medical Help and Staying Safe

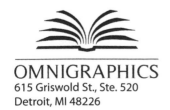

OMNIGRAPHICS
615 Griswold St., Ste. 520
Detroit, MI 48226

Bibliographic Note
Because this page cannot legibly accommodate all the copyright notices, the Bibliographic Note portion of the Preface constitutes an extension of the copyright notice.

* * *

OMNIGRAPHICS
Angela L. Williams, *Managing Editor*

* * *

ISBN 978-0-7808-1743-2
E-ISBN 978-0-7808-1744-9

Library of Congress Cataloging-in-Publication Data
Names: Williams, Angela L., 1963- editor.

Title: Abuse and violence information for teens : health tips about the causes and consequences of abusive and violent behavior : including facts about the types of abuse and violence, the warning signs of abusive and violent behavior, health concerns of victims, and getting help and staying safe / Angela L. Williams, editor.

Description: Third edition. | Detroit, MI : Omnigraphics, Inc., 2019. | Series: Teen health series | Includes bibliographical references and index. | Audience: Ages 13 | Audience: Grades 7-9 | Summary: "Provides basic consumer health information for teens about risk factors, consequences, and prevention of various types of abuse and violence. Includes index, resource information and recommendations for further reading."-- Provided by publisher.

Identifiers: LCCN 2019027356 (print) | LCCN 2019027357 (ebook) | ISBN 9780780817432 (library binding) | ISBN 9780780817449 (ebook)

Subjects: LCSH: Youth and violence--United States--Juvenile literature. | Youth and violence--United States--Prevention--Juvenile literature.

Classification: LCC HQ799.2.V56 A25 2019 (print) | LCC HQ799.2.V56 (ebook) | DDC 303.608350973--dc23

LC record available at https://lccn.loc.gov/2019027356

LC ebook record available at https://lccn.loc.gov/2019027357

This book is printed on acid-free paper meeting the ANSI Z39.48 Standard. The infinity symbol that appears above indicates that the paper in this book meets that standard.

Printed in the United States

Table of Contents

Preface

Part One: Types of Abuse

Part Two: Violence and the Teen Experience

Part Three: Recognizing and Treating the Consequences of Abuse and Violence

Part Four: Prevention, Staying Safe, and Your Legal Rights as a Victim

Part Five: If You Need More Information

Preface

About This Book

Teens experience violence in many forms, including bullying, fighting, hazing, dating violence, sexual abuse, domestic violence, and even homicide. According to a report from the Centers for Disease Control and Prevention (CDC), teen violence is a leading cause of death for young people and results in more than 475,000 nonfatal injuries each year. Nearly 1 in 5 high-school students are reported being bullied on school property in the year 2018. Each day, about 14 young people are victims of homicide, and about 1,300 are treated in emergency departments for nonfatal-assault-related injuries. The physical and emotional scars resulting from these experiences can endure a lifetime.

Abuse and Violence Information for Teens, Third Edition discusses contributing factors and warning signs for the most commonly experienced types of abuse and violence. Facts about seeking medical care and mental-health services for the physical and emotional consequences are included. A section on prevention and safety suggests ways to protect teens against violence and offers guidelines for staying out of harm's way. In addition, information about the legal rights of a victim of sexual assault is provided, and the book features a statistical summary of abuse and violence, resource directories, and information on how and where to report child abuse.

How to Use This Book

This book is divided into parts and chapters. Parts focus on broad areas of interest; chapters are devoted to single topics within a part.

Part One: Types of Abuse talks about the primary forms of abuse such as domestic violence, child abuse, and neglect. It discusses adverse childhood experiences and the impact of childhood trauma on well-being. It explains other forms of sexual abuse such as sibling and elder abuse, stalking, incest, and victimization of persons with disabilities. It also discusses the role new technologies play in child pornography and sexual exploitation.

Part Two: Violence and the Teen Experience explains teen exposure to violence, crime, and abuse. It discusses the possible risk factors and warning signs for youth violence, including electronic aggression and substance abuse. It talks about teen dating violence, bullying, hazing, gang-related activity, and hate crimes. The part concludes with facts about the effects of school violence exposure, teen firearm violence, self-injury, teen suicide, and violence against the lesbian, gay, bisexual, and transgender (LGBT) community.

Part Three : Recognizing and Treating the Consequences of Abuse and Violence outlines the impact of sexual abuse on the physical, mental, and psychological health of the victims. It explains what to do after a sexual assault, including seeking mental-health services, and discusses the long-term consequences of child abuse and neglect. It also discusses teen depression, posttraumatic stress disorder, trauma-focused interventions for youth psychotherapies, and therapeutic approaches for victims of sexual assault and abuse.

Part Four: Prevention, Staying Safe, and Your Legal Rights as a Victim discusses how domestic violence and abuse can be prevented and treated. It also explains preventing violence at schools and promoting protective factors for children exposed to domestic violence. It talks about conflict resolution, suicide prevention, and how the child welfare system works. It concludes with information about the legal rights of a victim of sexual assault.

Part Five: If You Need More Information includes a statistical summary of abuse and violence, resource directories, and information on how and where to report child abuse.

Bibliographic Note

This volume contains documents and excerpts from publications issued by the following U.S. government agencies: Administration for Children and Families (ACF); Centers for Disease Control and Prevention (CDC); Child Welfare Information Gateway; CrimeSolutions. gov; Federal Bureau of Investigation (FBI); National Center for Posttraumatic Stress Disorder (NCPTSD); National Criminal Justice Reference Service (NCJRS); National Institute of Justice (NIJ); National Institute of Mental Health (NIMH); National Institute on Aging (NIA); National Institute on Drug Abuse (NIDA) for Teens; National Institutes of Health (NIH); National Oceanic and Atmospheric Administration (NOAA); Office of Adolescent Health (OAH); Office of Juvenile Justice and Delinquency Prevention (OJJDP); Office on Women's Health (OWH); U.S. Department of Education (ED); U.S. Department of Health and Human Services (HHS); U.S. Department of Justice (DOJ); U.S. Department of Veterans Affairs (VA); and Youth.gov.

It may also contain original material produced by Omnigraphics and reviewed by medical consultants.

The photograph on the front cover is © Sabphoto/Shutterstock.

Medical Review

Omnigraphics contracts with a team of qualified, senior medical professionals who serve as medical consultants for the *Teen Health Series*. As necessary, medical consultants review reprinted and originally written material for currency and accuracy. Citations including the phrase "Reviewed (month, year)" indicate material reviewed by this team. Medical consultation services are provided to the *Teen Health Series* editors by:

Dr. Vijayalakshmi, MBBS, DGO, MD

Dr. Senthil Selvan, MBBS, DCH, MD

Dr. K. Sivanandham, MBBS, DCH, MS (Research), PhD

About The *Teen Health Series*

At the request of librarians serving today's young adults, the *Teen Health Series* was developed as a specially focused set of volumes within Omnigraphics' *Health Reference Series*. Each volume deals comprehensively with a topic selected according to the needs and interests of people in middle school and high school. Teens seeking preventive guidance, information about disease warning signs, medical statistics, and risk factors for health problems will find answers to their questions in the *Teen Health Series*. The *Series*, however, is not intended to serve as a tool for diagnosing illness, in prescribing treatments, or as a substitute for the physician/patient relationship. All people concerned about medical symptoms or the possibility of disease are encouraged to seek professional care from an appropriate healthcare provider.

If there is a topic you would like to see addressed in a future volume of the *Teen Health Series*, please write to:

Managing Editor

Teen Health Series

Omnigraphics

615 Griswold St., Ste. 520

Detroit, MI 48226

A Note About Spelling And Style

Teen Health Series editors use *Stedman's Medical Dictionary* as an authority for questions related to the spelling of medical terms and *The Chicago Manual of Style* for questions related to grammatical structures, punctuation, and other editorial concerns. Consistent adherence is not always possible, however, because the individual volumes within the *Series* include many documents from a wide variety of different producers and copyright holders, and the editor's primary goal is to present material from each source as accurately as is possible following the terms specified by each document's producer. This sometimes means that information in different chapters may follow other guidelines and alternate spelling authorities. For example, occasionally a copyright holder may require that eponymous terms be shown in possessive forms (Crohn's disease vs. Crohn disease) or that British spelling norms be retained (leukaemia vs. leukemia).

Part One
Types of Abuse

Chapter 1

Primary Forms of Abuse

There are four commonly recognized forms of child maltreatment: neglect (including medical neglect), physical abuse, sexual abuse, and psychological maltreatment. These may be found separately or in any combination. For fiscal year 2010, the breakdown of substantiated maltreatment for child victims is as follows.

- 78.3 percent neglect

- 17.6 percent physical abuse

- 9.2 percent sexual abuse

- 8.1 percent psychological maltreatment

- 2.4 percent medical neglect

- 10.3 percent other, such as abandonment or threats of harm to the child

Note that the sum of these percentages is more than 100 percent because children may have experienced more than one type of maltreatment.

About This Chapter: Text in this chapter begins with excerpts from "Types of Maltreatment," Administration for Children and Families (ACF), U.S. Department of Health and Human Services (HHS), October 2, 2013. Reviewed August 2019; Text under the heading "Child Abuse" is excerpted from "Child Abuse," MedlinePlus, National Institutes of Health (NIH), June 19, 2017; Text under the heading "Physical Abuse" is excerpted from "Physical Abuse," Office on Women's Health (OWH), U.S. Department of Health and Human Services (HHS), September 13, 2018; Text under the heading "Sexual Assault" is excerpted from "Sexual Assault," Office on Women's Health (OWH), U.S. Department of Health and Human Services (HHS), March 14, 2019; Text under the heading "Emotional and Verbal Abuse" is excerpted from "Emotional and Verbal Abuse," Office on Women's Health (OWH), U.S. Department of Health and Human Services (HHS), September 13, 2018.

There is no single, universally applied definition of child abuse and neglect. While legal definitions describing the different forms of child maltreatment, as well as guidelines for reporting suspected maltreatment and criminal prosecutions, are found mainly in state statutes, the guidelines for accepting reports, conducting an investigation, and providing interventions may vary not only from state to state, but from county to county.

Despite these differences, there are some commonalities. The Child Abuse Prevention and Treatment Act (CAPTA) provides minimum federal standards for states to use when defining physical child abuse, child neglect, and sexual abuse if states choose to receive federal funds under the CAPTA state grant program. Under CAPTA, child abuse and neglect means:

- Any recent act or failure to act on the part of a parent or caretaker that results in death, serious physical or emotional harm, sexual abuse, or exploitation

- An act or failure to act that presents an imminent risk of serious harm

This definition refers specifically to parents and other caregivers. Under this definition, a child generally means someone under the age of 18 or someone who is not an emancipated minor. In sexual abuse cases, a child is someone who is under 18 or the age specified by the state's child protection law where she or he lives, whichever is younger.

Child Abuse

Child abuse is doing something or failing to do something that results in harm to a child or puts a child at risk of harm. Child abuse can be physical, sexual or emotional. Neglect, or not providing for a child's needs, is also a form of abuse.

Most abused children suffer greater emotional than physical damage. An abused child may become depressed. She or he may withdraw, think of suicide, or become violent. An older child may use drugs or alcohol, try to run away, or abuse others.

Child abuse is a serious problem. If you suspect a child is being abused or neglected, call the police or your local child welfare agency.

Physical Abuse

Physical abuse is using physical force that injures you or puts you in danger. Physical abuse can happen in dating or married relationships, but it can also happen outside a relationship. No one—not a spouse, romantic partner, or family member—has the right to physically abuse you.

There are many types of violence and abuse. Some of these signs are signs of physical abuse or domestic violence. Some are signs of emotional and verbal abuse or sexual abuse.

Signs of abuse include:

- Being jealous, controlling, or angry
- Demeaning you
- Physically hurting or threatening to hurt you or loved ones
- Forcing you to have sex or other intimate activity

If you think someone is abusing you, get help. Abuse can have serious physical and emotional effects.

(Source: "Am I Being Abused?" Office on Women's Health (OWH), U.S. Department of Health and Human Services (HHS).)

Sexual Assault

Sexual assault is any type of sexual activity or contact that you do not consent to. Sexual assault can happen through physical force or threats of force or if the attacker gave the victim drugs or alcohol as part of the assault. Sexual assault includes rape and sexual coercion. In the United States, one in three women has experienced some type of sexual violence. If you have been sexually assaulted, it is not your fault, regardless of the circumstances.

Emotional and Verbal Abuse

You may not think you are being abused if you are not being hurt physically. But emotional and verbal abuse can have short-term and long-lasting effects that are just as serious as the effects of physical abuse. Emotional and verbal abuse includes insults and attempts to scare, isolate, or control you. It is also often a sign that physical abuse may follow. Emotional and verbal abuse may also continue if physical abuse starts. If you have been abused, it is never your fault.

Chapter 2

Domestic Violence or Abuse

What Is Domestic Violence?

The term "domestic violence" includes felony or misdemeanor crimes of violence committed by a current or former spouse or intimate partner of the victim, by a person with whom the victim shares a child in common, by a person who is cohabiting with or has cohabited with the victim as a spouse or intimate partner, by a person similarly situated to a spouse of the victim under the domestic or family violence laws of the jurisdiction receiving grant monies, or by any other person against an adult or youth victim who is protected from that person's acts under the domestic or family-violence laws of the jurisdiction.

In an emergency, victims of domestic violence should call 911 or contact state or local law enforcement officials, who can respond to these crimes.

How Do I Know Whether I Am Being Abused?

Intimate-partner violence, or domestic violence, can be difficult to see if it starts little by little, if your partner says they love you, or if they support you financially. Domestic violence can include forced sex, physical abuse, and emotional abuse, such as cruel words or threats. It can happen between married people, to a couple who lives together or apart, or to a same-sex couple. Abuse is never okay.

About This Chapter: Text under the heading "What Is Domestic Violence?" is excerpted from "Domestic Violence," U.S. Department of Justice (DOJ), August 3, 2014. Reviewed August 2019; Text beginning with the heading "How Do I Know Whether I Am Being Abused?" is excerpted from "Signs of Domestic Violence or Abuse," Office on Women's Health (OWH), U.S. Department of Health and Human Services (HHS), September 17, 2018.

You may be experiencing domestic violence if your partner:

- Controls what you are doing

- Checks your phone, e-mail, or social networks without your permission

- Forces you to have sex when you do not want to

- Controls your birth control or insists that you get pregnant

- Decides what you wear or eat or how you spend money

- Prevents or discourages you from going to work or school or seeing your family or friends

- Humiliates you on purpose in front of others

- Unfairly accuses you of being unfaithful

- Destroys your things

- Threatens to hurt you, your children, other loved ones, or your pets

- Hurts you physically (e.g., hitting, beating, punching, pushing, and kicking), including with a weapon

- Blames you for her or his violent outbursts

- Threatens to hurt herself or himself because of being upset with you

- Threatens to report you to the authorities for imagined crimes

- Says things like, "If I cannot have you, then no one can"

What Are the Signs of Domestic Violence or Abuse in Same-Sex Relationships?

If you are in a same-sex relationship, many signs of domestic violence are the same as they are for an abusive heterosexual relationship. Your partner may hit you, try to control you, or force you to have sex. But you may also experience additional signs of abuse, including:

- Threatening to "out you" to your family, friends, employer, or community

- Telling you that you have to be legally married to be considered a victim of domestic violence and to get help

- Saying women are not or cannot be violent

- Telling you the authorities would not help a lesbian, bisexual, transgender, or other gender-nonconforming person

- Forcing you to "prove" your sexuality by performing sex acts that you do not consent to

Regardless of your gender identity or sexual orientation, no one has the right to physically hurt you or threaten your safety.

What Can I Do If I Am Being Abused?

Your safety is the most important concern. If you are in immediate danger, call 911.

If you are not in immediate danger, consider these options:

- **Get medical care.** If you have been injured or sexually assaulted, go to a local hospital emergency room or urgent care center. You need medical care and may need medicines after being injured or raped.

- **Call a helpline for free, anonymous help.** Call the National Domestic Violence Hotline at 800-799-SAFE (800-799-7233) or 800-787-3224 (Toll-Free TDD). The hotline offers help 24 hours a day, 7 days a week, in many languages. Hotline staff can give you numbers for other resources, such as local domestic-violence shelters. If you are deaf or hard of hearing, there are resources available for you. The National Coalition of Anti-Violence Programs (NCAVP) has a hotline to help lesbian, gay, bisexual, transgender, or questioning (LGBTQ) victims of violence. Call 212-714-1141 for 24-hour support in English or Spanish.

- **Make a safety plan to leave.** Domestic violence usually does not get better. Think about a safe place for you to go and other things you will need. Staff at the National Domestic Violence Hotline can help you plan.

- **Save the evidence.** Keep evidence of abuse, such as pictures of your injuries or threatening e-mails or texts, in a safe place the abuser cannot get to.

- **Find out where to get help in your community.** Look up local resources for a list of local places to get help.

- **Talk to someone.** Reach out to someone you trust. This might be a family member, a friend, a coworker, or a spiritual leader. Look for ways to get emotional help, such as a support group or mental health professional.

- **Look into a restraining order.** Consider getting a protection order.

If you are the victim of domestic violence, know that you are not alone. There are people who want to help you and who are trained to respond.

What Can Happen If I Do Not Get Help?

Domestic violence often results in physical and emotional injuries. It can also lead to other health problems, reproductive-health challenges, mental-health conditions, such as depression and suicide. Women affected by intimate-partner violence are also more likely to use drugs or alcohol to cope.

Domestic violence can even end in death. Women who live in a home with guns are five times more likely to be killed. More than half of women murdered with guns are killed by intimate partners.

How Common Is Domestic Violence against Women?

Domestic or intimate-partner violence is a very common type of violence against women:

- Domestic or intimate partner violence happens in all types of relationships, including dating couples, married couples, same-sex couples, former or ex-couples, and couples who live together but are not married.

- Intimate-partner violence happens more often among younger couples.

- Almost half of American Indian and Alaskan Native women, more than four in 10 African American women, and more than one in three white and Hispanic women have experienced sexual or physical violence or stalking by their intimate partner.

- Nearly 23 million women in the United States have been raped or experienced attempted rape in their lifetimes.

- More than 33 million women—including one in three African American and White women and one in four Hispanic women—have experienced unwanted sexual contact, other than rape, by an intimate partner.

- Women who identify as lesbian experience as much or more physical and sexual violence as heterosexual women by an intimate partner. Women who identify as bisexual experience intimate-partner violence more often than heterosexual women.

How Can I Help End Violence against Women?

Violence against women hurts the whole community. Learn ways you can work to help end violence against women in your community. Here are some suggestions:

- **Call the police** if you see or hear evidence of domestic violence.

- **Learn about bystander intervention**. You can help prevent sexual assault from happening.

- **Support a friend or family member** who may be in an abusive relationship.

- **Volunteer** at a local domestic-violence shelter or other organization that helps survivors or works to prevent violence.

- **Teach your children** early on that they are the ones who decide who gets to touch them and where. Consider teaching them the proper names for the parts of their body at a young age so that they can clearly communicate about their bodies. Teach children that it's their choice whether they want to hug or kiss others, even family.

- **Raise children to respect others.** Teach children to treat others as they would like to be treated. Talk to your children about healthy relationships and the importance of treating their dating partners and others with respect. Teach them that consent from a dating partner is a clear "yes" for sexual activity.

- **Lead by example.** Work to create a culture that rejects violence as a way to deal with problems. Speak up against messages that say that violence against or mistreatment of women is okay. Do not be violent or abusive yourself.

- **Become an activist.** Participate in an antiviolence event like a local Take Back the Night march. Support domestic-violence services and violence-prevention programs by donating your time.

- **Volunteer in youth programs.** Become a mentor. Get involved in programs that teach young people to solve problems without violence. Get involved with programs that teach teens about healthy relationships and healthy masculinity and femininity.

- **Ask about antiviolence policies and programs at work and school.** At work, ask about policies that deal with sexual harassment, for example. On campus, ask about services to escort students to dorms safely at night, emergency call boxes on campus, campus security, and other safety measures. Ask about any bystander intervention training programs that may be happening on campus or at work.

(Source: "Help End Violence against Women," Office on Women's Health (OWH), U.S. Department of Health and Human Services (HHS).)

How Are Gender and Sexual-Minority Women Affected by Domestic Violence?

Gender and sexual-minority women, such as lesbian or bisexual women, may be more likely than heterosexual women to experience domestic violence. Two in five lesbian women and three in five bisexual women experience intimate partner violence at some point in their lifetimes.

Researchers think women who identify as something other than straight or cisgender (people whose biological sex matches their gender identity) may experience higher levels of domestic violence. But there is not yet enough research on all types of gender and sexual-minority women to know for sure.

Chapter 3

Understanding Child Abuse and Neglect

How Is Child Abuse and Neglect Defined in Federal Law?

Federal legislation lays the groundwork for state laws on child maltreatment by identifying a minimum set of actions or behaviors that define child abuse and neglect. The Federal Child Abuse Prevention and Treatment Act (CAPTA), as amended and reauthorized by the CAPTA Reauthorization Act of 2010, defines child abuse and neglect as, at a minimum, "any recent act or failure to act on the part of a parent or caretaker which results in death, serious physical or emotional harm, sexual abuse or exploitation (including sexual abuse as determined under section 111), or an act or failure to act which presents an imminent risk of serious harm" (42 U.S.C. 5101 note, § 3).

Additionally, it stipulates that "a child shall be considered a victim of 'child abuse and neglect' and of 'sexual abuse' if the child is identified, by a state or local agency employee of the state or locality involved, as being a victim of sex trafficking (as defined in paragraph (10) of section 7102 of title 22) or a victim of severe forms of trafficking in persons described in paragraph (9)(A) of that section" (42 U.S.C. § 5106g(b)(2)).

Most federal and state child protection laws primarily refer to cases of harm to a child caused by parents or other caregivers; they generally do not include harm caused by other

About This Chapter: Text under the heading "How Is Child Abuse and Neglect Defined in Federal Law?" is excerpted from "What Is Child Abuse and Neglect? Recognizing the Signs and Symptoms," Child Welfare Information Gateway, U.S. Department of Health and Human Services (HHS), April 2019; Text beginning with the heading "What Are Child Abuse and Neglect?" is excerpted from "Preventing Child Abuse and Neglect," Centers for Disease Control and Prevention (CDC), February 26, 2019.

people, such as acquaintances or strangers. Some state laws also include a child's witnessing of domestic violence as a form of abuse or neglect.

Types of Neglect

Although state laws vary regarding the types of neglect included in definitions, summarized below are the most commonly recognized categories of neglect:

- **Physical neglect:** Abandoning the child or refusing to accept custody; not providing for basic needs like nutrition, hygiene, or appropriate clothing
- **Medical neglect:** Delaying or denying recommended healthcare for the child
- **Inadequate supervision:** Leaving the child unsupervised (depending on the length of time and child's age/maturity), not protecting the child from safety hazards, not providing adequate caregivers, or engaging in harmful behavior
- **Emotional neglect:** Isolating the child, not providing affection or emotional support, or exposing the child to domestic violence or substance use
- **Educational neglect:** Failing to enroll the child in school or homeschool, ignoring special education needs, or permitting chronic absenteeism from school

(Source: "Acts of Omission: An Overview of Child Neglect," Child Welfare Information Gateway, U.S. Department of Health and Human Services (HHS).)

What Are Child Abuse and Neglect?

These important public-health problems include all types of abuse and neglect of a child under the age of 18 by a parent, caregiver, or another person in a custodial role (such as clergy, a coach, a teacher) that results in harm, potential for harm, or threat of harm to a child. There are four common types of abuse and neglect:

- **Physical abuse** is the intentional use of physical force that can result in physical Examples include hitting, kicking, shaking, burning, or other shows of force against a child.

- **Sexual abuse** involves pressuring or forcing a child to engage in sexual acts. It includes behaviors, such as fondling, penetration, and exposing a child to other sexual activities.

- **Emotional abuse** refers to behaviors that harm a child's self-worth or emotional well-being. Examples include name-calling, shaming, rejection, withholding love, and threatening.

- **Neglect** is the failure to meet a child's basic physical and emotional needs. These needs include housing, food, clothing, education, and access to medical care.

Child abuse and neglect result from the interaction of a number of individual, family, societal, and environmental factors. Child abuse and neglect are not inevitable—safe, stable, and nurturing relationships and environments are key for prevention. Preventing child abuse and neglect can also prevent other forms of violence, as various types of violence are interrelated and share many risks and protective factors, consequences, and effective prevention tactics. Using a public-health approach, we can prevent child maltreatment before it starts.

How Big Is the Problem?

Child abuse and neglect are common. At least 1 in 7 children have experienced child abuse and/or neglect in the past year, and this is likely an underestimate.

Children living in poverty experience more abuse and neglect. Rates of child abuse and neglect are 5 times higher for children in families with low socioeconomic status compared to children in families with higher socioeconomic status.

Child maltreatment is costly. In the United States, the total lifetime economic burden associated with child abuse and neglect was approximately $124 billion in 2008. This economic burden rivals the cost of other high-profile public-health problems, such as stroke and type 2 diabetes.

What Are the Consequences?

Children who are abused and neglected may suffer immediate physical injuries, such as cuts, bruises, or broken bones, as well as emotional and psychological problems, such as impaired socioemotional skills or anxiety.

Child abuse and neglect and other adverse childhood experiences (ACEs) can also have a tremendous impact on broader lifelong health and well-being outcomes if left untreated. For example, exposure to violence in childhood increases the risks of injury, future violence victimization and perpetration, substance abuse, sexually transmitted infections, delayed brain development, reproductive-health problems, involvement in sex trafficking, noncommunicable diseases, lower educational attainment, and limited employment opportunities.

Chronic abuse may result in toxic stress and make victims more vulnerable to problems, such as posttraumatic stress disorder (PTSD), conduct disorder, and learning, attention, and memory difficulties.

Protective factors may lessen the likelihood of children being abused or neglected. Protective factors have not been studied as extensively or rigorously as risk factors. Identifying and understanding protective factors are equally as important as researching risk factors.

Family Protective Factors

- Supportive family environment and social networks
- Concrete support for basic needs
- Nurturing parenting skills
- Stable family relationships
- Household rules and child monitoring
- Parental employment
- Parental education
- Adequate housing
- Access to healthcare and social services
- Caring adults outside the family who can serve as role models or mentors

Community Protective Factors

- Communities that support parents and take responsibility for preventing abuse

(Source: "Risk and Protective Factors," Centers for Disease Control and Prevention (CDC).)

How Can We Prevent Child Abuse and Neglect?

Child abuse and neglect are serious public-health issues with far-reaching consequences for the youngest and most vulnerable members of society. Every child is better when she/he and her/his peers have safe, stable, nurturing relationships and environments. The Centers for Disease Control and Prevention (CDC) has developed a technical package to help communities take advantage of the best available evidence to prevent child abuse and neglect.

The strategies and approaches in the technical package represent different levels of the social ecology with efforts intended to impact individual behaviors as well as the relationship, family, school, community, and societal factors that influence risk and protective factors for child abuse and neglect. They are intended to work together and to be used in combination in a multi-level, multi-sector effort to prevent violence.

- Strengthen economic supports to families

- Change social norms to support parents and positive parenting

- Provide quality care and education early in life

- Enhance parenting skills to promote healthy child development

- Intervene to lessen harms and prevent future risk

Chapter 4

Adverse Childhood Experiences/ Impact of Childhood Trauma on Well-Being

Adverse Childhood Experiences: An Overview

"Adverse childhood experiences" (ACEs) is the term used to describe all types of abuse, neglect, and other potentially traumatic experiences that occur to people under the age of 18 years.

Adverse childhood experiences have been linked to factors such as:

- Risky health behaviors

- Chronic health conditions

- Low life potential

- Early death

As the number of ACEs increases, so does the risk for these outcomes.

Early Adversity and Lasting Impacts

The impacts of early adversity are long-lasting experiences such as:

- **Injury:** Traumatic brain injury (TBI), fractures, and burns

- **Mental health:** Depression, anxiety, suicide, and posttraumatic stress disorder (PTSD)

- **Maternal health:** Unintended pregnancy, pregnancy complications, and fetal death

---

About This Chapter: This chapter includes text excerpted from "About Adverse Childhood Experiences," Centers for Disease Control and Prevention (CDC), April 9, 2019.

- **Infectious disease:** Human immunodeficiency virus (HIV) and sexually transmitted diseases (STDs)

- **Chronic disease:** Cancer and diabetes

- **Risky behaviors:** Alcohol, drug abuse, and unsafe sex

- **Opportunities:** Education, occupation, and income

The presence of ACEs does not mean that a child will experience poor outcomes. However, children's positive experiences or protective factors can prevent children from experiencing adversity and can protect against many of the negative health and life outcomes even after adversity has occurred.

It is important to address the conditions that put children and families at risk of ACEs, so that we can prevent ACEs before they happen. The Centers for Disease Prevention and Control (CDC) promotes lifelong health and well-being through various strategies to assure safe, stable, nurturing relationships and environments for all children.

Childhelp National Child Abuse Hotline

Call or text 800-4-A-CHILD (800-422-4453). Professional crisis counselors are available 24 hours a day, 7 days a week, in over 170 languages. All calls are confidential. The hotline offers crisis intervention, information, and referrals to thousands of emergency, social service, and support resources.

(Source: "How to Report Suspected Child Maltreatment," Child Welfare Information Gateway, U.S. Department of Health and Human Services (HHS).)

Strategies and Approaches to Prevent Child Abuse and Neglect

- Strengthen economic support to families
  - Strengthen household financial security
  - Family-friendly work policies
- Change social norms to support parents and positive parenting
  - Public engagement and education campaigns

- Legislative approaches to reduce corporal punishment
- Provide quality care and education early in life
  - Preschool enrichment with family engagement
  - Improved quality of child care through licensing and accreditation
- Enhance parenting skills to promote healthy child development
  - Early childhood home visitation
  - Parenting skill and family relationship approaches
- Intervene to lessen harms and prevent future risk
  - Enhanced primary care
  - Behavioral parent-training programs
  - Treatment to lessen harms of abuse and neglect exposure
  - Treatment to prevent problem behavior and later involvement in violence

Chapter 5

Educational Neglect and Truancy

Defining Educational Neglect

Educational neglect occurs when a child frequently misses school because of the direct or indirect actions of caregivers. This type of neglect includes failure to enroll children in school or to implement an adequate homeschooling program if allowed by law, and failure to ensure that children attend school as required by law. In many cases of excessive absence from school, educational neglect is considered to occur only when the caregiver refuses to work with the school in attempts to improve the child's attendance.

Characteristics of Educational Neglect

Educational neglect takes many forms, and each case varies according to individual circumstances. Educational neglect situations typically include more than one characteristic. When caregivers do not regard school attendance as important, children may not be prepared to attend school each day (e.g., child is not fed and dressed in time for school). Young children are often dependent upon the caregiver to ensure regular school attendance, and caregivers may fail to accomplish this. Once an attendance problem is identified by the school, caregivers are typically contacted to participate in an intervention plan that will encourage children to attend school regularly. Educational neglect occurs when caregivers ignore attempts by the school to discuss and address the child's attendance problem and/or refuse to encourage or facilitate the child's school attendance. Caregivers may also fail to comply with special education or remedial instruction programs for the child when the child is not succeeding in school.

About This Chapter: "Educational Neglect and Truancy," © 2016 Omnigraphics. Reviewed August 2019.

Children are at risk of educational neglect when they experience a chaotic or disorganized home life. Some children suffer from the family's lack of sufficient financial resources and are responsible for caring for other children while the caregiver is at work. In many cases of educational neglect, other indicators of child abuse or neglect are also present.

Different Types of Educational Neglect

There are several different types of educational neglect. Caregivers may fail to enroll children in school or establish a homeschooling program where permitted by law. Educational neglect occurs when this failure to enroll causes the child to miss at least one month of school without valid reasons. Caregivers may also fail to seek adequate education for children with special needs, or fail to comply with recommendations for special education. If the child has been diagnosed with a learning disability, educational neglect intersects with healthcare neglect.

Risk Factors

While the presence of a risk factor does not mean that a child will be neglected, multiple risk factors are a cause for concern. Research indicates that many familial and societal factors, such as the following, place children at greater risk of being harmed or endangered by neglect:

- Poverty
- Single-parent status
- Dysfunctional family structure
- Lack of adequate support systems
- Lack of adequate family resources
- Mental-health concerns
- Substance-use disorders (SUDs)
- Domestic violence
- Parental childhood abuse

(Source: "Acts of Omission: An Overview of Child Neglect," Child Welfare Information Gateway, U.S. Department of Health and Human Services (HHS).)

School Truancy

Truancy is another type of educational neglect. A "truant" is generally defined as a child between the ages of six and 17 who is often absent from school without valid reasons. In addition to missing whole days of school, truancy can also apply to frequently arriving late or skipping classes. A distinction is often made between educational neglect and truancy. If a child misses school as a result of their own choices, that is generally considered truancy and not educational neglect.

Permitted truancy means that caregivers have been informed of the child's excessive absences and do nothing to resolve the problem. Habitual truancy applies to children between the ages of 12 and 17 who fail to comply with intervention plans developed and agreed upon by the school and caregivers, and who continues to miss school without valid reasons. Chronic truancy refers to children between the ages of 12 and 17 who receive a court order to attend school and continue to miss school without valid reasons.

Effects of School Truancy

School truancy affects children in many ways. Early effects include required participation in school-based intervention programs and increased monitoring by schools. If these programs are not successful, children may be referred to a government- or school-sponsored program in which a social worker or other caseworker attempts to resolve the truancy problem. Court intervention may be required, in which children and their parents must appear before a judge or other court official. At this stage, the court can set requirements for school attendance, often with strict consequences for noncompliance. A legal charge of truancy is a serious offense that can result in the child being removed from the home and placed under the jurisdiction of the court. Sometimes the court will order the family or caregiver to pay for the cost of intervention services for the child.

Longer-term effects of school truancy can also be quite serious. Missing many days of school usually results in poor performance when the child does attend classes. Children can then become discouraged and drop out of school entirely. Quitting school has been shown to greatly limit future career opportunities, while increasing the probability of engaging in criminal activity. Children who leave school are more likely to use alcohol and other drugs. Parents and caregivers also suffer the consequences of school truancy through lost income or work time to attend meetings, court hearing, counseling, or other intervention services.

Factors Responsible for School Truancy

There are many different factors that contribute to truancy. Some of the most common are issues associated with a troubled home life. This includes any problem that causes disruption at home, such as domestic violence, substance abuse, marital problems and divorce, a family that moves around a lot, or caregivers whose work schedules leave children frequently unsupervised. Medical issues with mental health or chronic illness of children or caregivers can also contribute to truancy. Children with learning disabilities sometimes find school too frustrating and discouraging, and choose not to attend for these reasons. A family history of school dropouts can lead to caregivers who do not value education.

Other potential causes of truancy are based on economic factors. Poverty may require caregivers to work multiple jobs, and older children may also be required to work to help support the family. A lack of transportation and/or affordable care for younger children also contribute to school truancy. The environment at school can also be a factor. Large schools, large class sizes, the behavior of other students, the attitudes of teachers and school administrators, and lack of individual attention can all result in truancy. Another issue in some schools is the lack of consequences for truancy, or inconsistent truancy policies.

References

1. "Educational Neglect," *Child Welfare Manual*, August 28, 2009.

2. "Educational Neglect and School Truancy: What Parents and Children Need to Know," Youth Assistance of Oakland County, n.d.

3. "Educational Neglect Statutes," Coalition for Responsible Home Education (CRHE), 2015.

Chapter 6

Sibling Abuse

The term "siblings" generally refers to biological brothers and sisters—children who share the same two parents—but in a broader sense it may also refer to any children who are part of a family unit. These include half-siblings, who share one common parent, and stepsiblings, who are not biologically related but who become part of a family as a result of marriage or partnership between their parents. Studies have shown that the risk of sexual abuse is usually more common between stepsiblings, but accurate statistics are difficult to compile about abuse between related individuals because of the powerful societal taboo against incest, which causes it to go underreported due to embarrassment, fear, denial, or lack of understanding.

Defining Sibling Abuse

When a child is victimized by a sibling, it is called "sibling abuse." Physical aggression—pushing, shoving, or more serious acts of violence—as well as bullying or harassment, are examples of sibling abuse. Unless serious physical harm takes place, parents may ignore this behavior, believing it to be a normal childhood activity. But sibling abuse can have severe consequences for survivors, often troubling them well into adulthood.

Classification of Sibling Abuse

Sibling abuse is a fairly broad term that can be classified into three types:

- Physical sibling abuse

- Emotional or psychological sibling abuse

- Sexual sibling abuse

About This Chapter: "Sibling Abuse," © 2016 Omnigraphics. Reviewed August 2019.

Physical sibling abuse. This is a very common form of sibling abuse, as arguments can often lead to physical fighting, pinching, slapping, or hair pulling. These conflicts may become abusive in the course of time and may escalate into violence or serious injury. Weapons, if used, may even result in fatal consequences. What begins as sibling rivalry, if not checked, may end up in tragedy within the family. One of the characteristic features of physical sibling abuse is that the perpetrator of the abuse is usually bigger and/or stronger than the victim, although this is not always the case. Physical sibling abuse is not gender-specific, and therefore, children of either sex may be the abusers.

Emotional/psychological sibling abuse. Physical sibling abuse is often quite evident, making it somewhat easier to take steps to protect the victim. However, emotional or psychological sibling abuse can be harder to detect. It is also very difficult to measure the impact of this form of sibling abuse. Quarrels between the adults in the family or acts of bullying at school can leave a deep impression upon the young mind. A child may also be emotionally abused by acts like belittling, demeaning, frightening, humiliating, name-calling, or threatening. Survivors of such abuse may become emotionally closed off, withdrawing from social contact and preferring to be alone. They tend to underperform both at school and home and to become aggressive in other areas of their lives. Identifying emotional abuse early can help head off future problems.

Sexual sibling abuse. Many types of sexual contact or related activity between siblings can be called "sexual sibling abuse." This can include such acts as using sexually toned language, exposing genitals to another sibling, inappropriate touching, deliberate exposure to pornography, and sexual assaults or rape. Sexual sibling abuse can occur between full siblings, half-siblings, or stepsiblings, although It is generally more common in the case of a half-sibling or

Importance of Sibling Relationships

Having a sibling provides children with a peer partner with whom they can explore their environments, navigate social and cognitive challenges, and learn skills. Sibling relationships can provide a source of continuity throughout a child's lifetime and can be the longest relationships that people experience. Unfortunately, though, many siblings may be separated upon removal and not have frequent contact while in care. However, for some siblings in care, their separation or infrequent visiting can cause those relationships to wither, sometimes to the point of permanent estrangement.

(Source: "Sibling Issues in Foster Care and Adoption," Child Welfare Information Gateway, U.S. Department of Health and Human Services (HHS).)

stepsibling. The general belief is that boys tend to be the perpetrators, but there is also considerable evidence of girls being abusers.

Risk Factors for Sibling Abuse

There are several factors that may increase the likelihood of sibling abuse, and it is vital that parents understand the root cause behind such behavior. Some factors that researchers have identified include:

- Parents absent from the home for long periods of time

- Lack of emotional attachment between parents and children

- Parents allowing sibling rivalry and fights to go unchecked

- Parents' inability to teach their children to deal with conflicts in a healthy manner

- Parents not intervening when children are involved in violent acts

- Parents creating a competitive environment by favoritism or frequently comparing siblings to each other

- Denial of the problem's existence, both by parents and children

- Overburdening children by giving responsibilities beyond their ability

- Exposure to violence from different environments, such as home, media, and school

- Parents failing to teach their children about sexuality and their personal safety

- Children who are witness to, or are victims of, sexual abuse

- Early access to pornography

Detecting Sibling Abuse

Sibling abuse may often be difficult to detect, especially when both parents are busy with their professional lives. Parents need to be alert to identify this behavior and take necessary action as early as possible. One symptom of sibling abuse is when one child is almost always the aggressor, while the other tends to be the victim. Other signs of sibling abuse include:

- A child avoids her or his sibling

- Noticeable changes in behavior, eating habits, and sleep patterns

- Frequent nightmares

- A child stages abuse in a play or reveals it in a story

- A child acts out in an inappropriate sexual manner

- Increase in the intensity of animosity between the siblings

Safeguarding Children from Sibling Abuse

Some steps that parents can take to help safeguard children from sibling abuse include:

- Discourage rivalry between siblings.

- Establish rules that will bar children from indulging in emotional abuse of their siblings, and stick to them so that children realize their importance.

- Give responsibilities to children based on their abilities, rather than overburdening them with tasks for which they are unprepared.

- Talk to children on a regular basis to gain their trust, and encourage them to ask for help from parents when they need it.

- Learn the art of mediating conflicts.

- Teach children that any kind of unwanted physical contact is inappropriate and should be reported to an adult.

- Build a healthy environment for sharing and talking about any issues, especially sexual issues.

- Be aware of children's media preferences to identify inappropriate videos, games, music, etc.

Dealing with Sibling Abuse

Acts like biting, hitting, or physical torture of a child by her or his sibling should not be taken lightly. Parents need to intervene and take necessary actions, including:

- Separate the siblings whenever they indulge in any kind of violence.

- When the situation is under control, discuss the behavior with all the members of the family, as well as the children involved.

- Listen patiently to understand the children's feelings.

- Restate what they say to clarify your understanding of the problem.

- Encourage the children to work together.

- Do not ignore, blame, or punish the child, but take a neutral stand and avoid favoritism.

- Be sure the children know the family rules, as well as the consequences of failing to follow them.

- Teach the children anger management techniques.

- Follow up by observing future behavior carefully.

- Seek professional help if the parents feel that things are beyond their control.

Sibling Abuse and Its Impact on Adult Life

Events or incidents of sibling abuse that take place during childhood may have long-term psychological effects whose impact may not be revealed until a later stage of life. Researchers have found that these effects may include:

- Alcohol and drug addiction

- Anxiety

- Depression

- Eating disorders

- Lack of trust

- Low self-esteem

Children who have been victims of sibling abuse tend to have feelings of insecurity and poor self-image well into adulthood. As much as physical abuse, emotional sibling abuse has a long-lasting impact. And the effects of this behavior do not only affect the victim. The abuser, too, has the potential to indulge in abusive relationships throughout her or his adulthood, making intervention critical for both individuals.

References

1. "Sibling Abuse Help Guide," LeavingAbuse, August 23, 2015.

2. Boyse RN, Kyla. "Sibling Abuse," University of Michigan Health System (UMHS), November 2012.

Chapter 7

Elder Abuse

Abuse can happen to anyone—no matter the person's age, sex, race, religion, or ethnic or cultural background. Each year, hundreds of thousands of adults over the age of 60 are abused, neglected, or financially exploited. This is called "elder abuse."

Abuse can happen in many places, including the older person's home, a family member's house, an assisted-living facility, or a nursing home.

Types of Abuse

There are many types of abuse:

- **Physical abuse** happens when someone causes bodily harm by hitting, pushing, or slapping.

- **Emotional abuse,** sometimes called "psychological abuse," can include a caregiver saying hurtful words, yelling, threatening, or repeatedly ignoring the older person. Keeping that person from seeing close friends and relatives is another form of emotional abuse.

- **Neglect** occurs when the caregiver does not try to respond to the older person's needs.

- **Abandonment** is leaving a senior alone without planning for her or his care.

- **Sexual abuse** involves a caregiver forcing an older adult to watch or be part of sexual acts.

About This Chapter: This chapter includes text excerpted from "Elder Abuse," National Institute on Aging (NIA), National Institutes of Health (NIH), December 29, 2016. Reviewed August 2019.

Money Matters

Financial abuse happens when money or belongings are stolen. It can include forging checks, taking someone else's retirement and Social Security benefits, or using another person's credit cards and bank accounts. It also includes changing names on a will, bank account, life insurance policy, or title to a house without permission from the older person. Financial abuse is becoming a widespread and hard-to-detect issue. Even someone you have never met can steal your financial information using the telephone or e-mail. Be careful about sharing any financial information over the phone or online—you do not know who will use it.

Healthcare fraud can be committed by doctors, hospital staff, and other healthcare workers. It includes overcharging, billing twice for the same service, falsifying Medicaid or Medicare claims, or charging for care that was not provided. Older adults and caregivers should keep an eye out for this type of fraud.

Who Is Being Abused?

Most victims of abuse are women, but some are men. Likely targets are older people who have no family or friends nearby and people with disabilities, memory problems, or dementia.

Abuse can happen to any older person, but often affects those who depend on others for help with activities of everyday life—including bathing, dressing, and taking medicine. People who are frail may appear to be easy victims.

What Are the Signs of Abuse?

You may see signs of abuse or neglect when you visit an older person at home or in an eldercare facility. You may notice the person:

- Has trouble sleeping

- Seems depressed or confused

- Loses weight for no reason

- Displays signs of trauma, like rocking back and forth

- Acts agitated or violent

- Becomes withdrawn

- Stops taking part in activities she or he enjoys

- Has unexplained bruises, burns, or scars

- Looks messy, with unwashed hair or dirty clothes

- Develops bed sores or other preventable conditions

If you see signs of abuse, try talking with the older person to find out what is going on. For instance, the abuse may be from another resident and not from someone who works at the nursing home or assisted living facility. Most importantly, get help.

Who Can Help?

Elder abuse will not stop on its own. Someone else needs to step in and help. Many older people are too ashamed to report mistreatment. Or, they are afraid if they make a report it will get back to the abuser and make the situation worse.

If you think someone you know is being abused—physically, emotionally, or financially—talk with her or him when the two of you are alone. You could say you think something is wrong and you are worried. Offer to take her or him to get help, for instance, at a local adult protective services agency.

Many local, state, and national social service agencies can help with emotional, legal, and financial problems.

Caregiver Stress—You Are Not Alone

Caring for an older person can be rewarding. It is also demanding, difficult, and often stressful work. The caregiver may need to be available around the clock to fix meals, provide nursing care, take care of laundry and cleaning, drive to doctors' appointments, and pay bills. Often, family caregivers have to give up paying jobs to make time for these new responsibilities.

It may be hard to keep a positive outlook when there is little hope of the older person's physical and mental condition improving. Over time, the demands and stress of caregiving can take their toll. A caregiver might not even know she or he is being neglectful or abusive.

If you are a caregiver, make sure you have time to rest and take care of your needs. You can ask a family member or friend to help out for a weekend, or even for a few hours, so that you can take some time for yourself. Some community service organizations provide caregivers a break, called "respite care." Caregiving support groups may also help. Exercise could even help with stress.

The Administration for Community Living (ACL) has a National Center on Elder Abuse (NCEA) where you can learn about how to report abuse, where to get help, and state laws that deal with abuse and neglect. Go to ncea.acl.gov for more information. Or, call the Eldercare Locator weekdays at 800-677-1116.

Most states require that doctors and lawyers report elder mistreatment. Family and friends can also report it. Do not wait. Help is available.

If you think someone is in urgent danger, call 911 or your local police to get help right away.

What Is the Long-Term Effect of Abuse?

Most physical wounds heal in time. But, any type of mistreatment can leave the abused person feeling fearful and depressed. Sometimes, the victim thinks the abuse is her or his fault. Protective services agencies can suggest support groups and counseling that can help the abused person heal the emotional wounds.

Chapter 8

Victimization of Persons with Disabilities

Individuals with disabilities are particularly vulnerable to crime for a variety of reasons, including but not limited to reliance on caregivers, limited transportation options, limited access to sign-language interpreters and assistive devices, and isolation from the community. While people with disabilities experience the same types of crime as people without disabilities, they may also experience unique forms of these crimes. For example, intimate partner violence victims with disabilities may be subject to denial of care or assistance, destruction of medical equipment, destruction of equipment for communication purposes, or manipulation of medications, in addition to more common controlling and abusive behaviors. These vulnerabilities not only increase opportunities for abuse and neglect, but they also make reporting victimization more difficult for victims.

Crime Trends

Between 2009 and 2015, individuals with disabilities were at least twice as likely to be victims of violent victimization as people without disabilities. In 2015, nearly 30 of every 1,000 people age 12 or older with a disability reported violent victimization, compared to 12 of every 1,000 people age 12 or older without a disability.

About This Chapter: This chapter includes text excerpted from "Crimes against People with Disabilities," National Criminal Justice Reference Service (NCJRS), April 24, 2018.

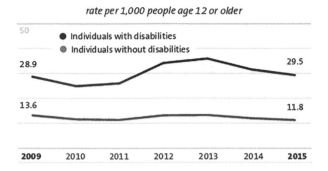

Figure 8.1. Violent Victimization

The rate of violent victimization among men and women with at least one disability was more than twice the rate for men and women without a disability.

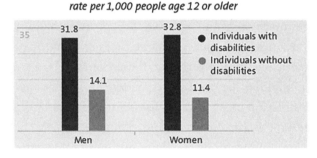

Figure 8.2. Violent Victimization by Sex and Disability

Nearly 11 of every 1,000 individuals with a single type of disability were victims of serious violent victimization. For individuals with multiple disabilities, 14 out of every 1,000 were victims of serious violent victimization.

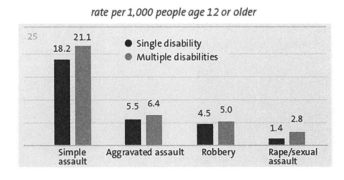

Figure 8.3. Violent Victimization by Crime and Number of Disabilities

Did You Know?

The National Crime Victimization Survey (NCVS) first included questions about disability victimization in 2007.

Between 2011 and 2015, 20 percent of crime victims with disabilities believed they were targeted because of their disability. People with multiple disabilities are more frequently victims of rape and sexual assault compared to victims with only one form of disability.

Between 2011 and 2015, 65 percent of rape/sexual assault victims with a disability had multiple types of disability.

People with a single disability were less likely to report their victimization to the police compared to people with multiple disabilities.

Data on Crimes against People with Disabilities

Between 2011 and 2015, nearly 60 of every 1,000 individuals age 12 or older with a cognitive disability reported they were victims of violent victimization. Of individuals aged 15 or older with an independent living, ambulatory, vision, or self-care disability, about 30 of every 1,000 individuals were victims of violent victimization, as were nearly 16 of every 1,000 individuals with a hearing disability.

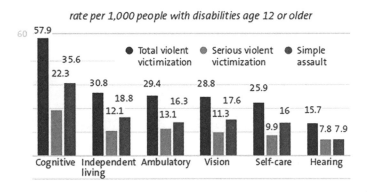

Figure 8.4. Victimization of People with Disabilities by Type of Disability and Victimization

Individuals with a disability who experience violent victimization are more frequently victimized by relatives, including parents and children, and acquaintances than victims without a disability. Almost 95 percent of individuals with a disability who were victims of violent crime could identify their perpetrator; 40 percent were victimized by an acquaintance, 30 percent were victimized by a stranger, and 15 percent were victimized by an intimate partner. (An acquaintance is defined as someone who was well or casually known to the victim, including caregivers.)

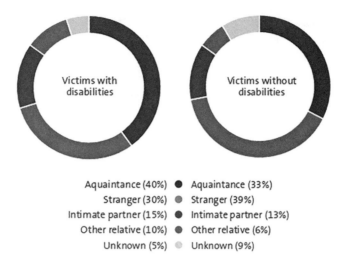

Aquaintance (40%) ● Aquaintance (33%)
Stranger (30%) ● Stranger (39%)
Intimate partner (15%) ● Intimate partner (13%)
Other relative (10%) ● Other relative (6%)
Unknown (5%) ● Unknown (9%)

Figure 8.5. Victim Relationship to Offender

Individuals with a disability were slightly more likely to report receiving assistance from nonpolice victim-service agencies compared to individuals without a disability. Overall, only a small percentage of violent crime victims receive victim services.

Figure 8.6. Victims Who Receive Services

In 2013, nearly 13 percent of children who were abused or neglected also had a disability. Of those, children with behavioral problems (24%) and those with emotional disturbance (19%) were most frequently victimized. One-third of victimized children with a disability also had an unlisted medical condition.

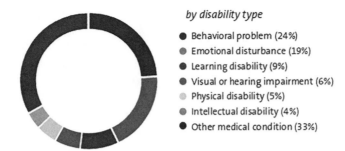

by disability type

● Behavioral problem (24%)
● Emotional disturbance (19%)
● Learning disability (9%)
● Visual or hearing impairment (6%)
● Physical disability (5%)
● Intellectual disability (4%)
● Other medical condition (33%)

Figure 8.7. Child Victims of Abuse and Neglect

Chapter 9

Abuse in Youth Sports

What Is Abuse?

The Child Abuse Prevention and Treatment Act (CAPTA) defines child abuse and neglect as, "any recent act or failure to act on the part of a parent or caretaker which results in death, serious physical or emotional harm, sexual abuse or exploitation" or "an act or failure to act which presents an imminent risk of serious harm." Any kind of physical, emotional, sexual maltreatment, neglect, or harassment that leads to harm is considered abuse. Abuse takes place in many startling ways in the world of youth sports.

What Is Emotional Abuse?

Any behavior that damages the sense of self-worth of a child is considered emotional abuse. Emotional abuse is the most common form of injury affecting youth in sports. It occurs when a parent, sibling, caregiver, guardian, or coach behaves negatively with a child. Some forms of emotional abuse are listed below.

- Forcing an otherwise unwilling child to participate in sports
- Yelling at a child for not performing well or losing
- Meting out punishment for mediocre performance or losing a game
- Ridiculing or criticizing moves on the field

About This Chapter: "Abuse in Youth Sports," © 2017 Omnigraphics. Reviewed August 2019.

- Ignoring, rejecting, or isolating a child

- Withholding love, support, and guidance

- Engaging in name-calling

- Being taunted or bullied by teammates

- Insulting a child for not meeting expectations

- Being intimidated by teammates or their guardians

- Hazing

Emotional abuse affects the development of children and triggers negative emotions, such as anger, anxiety, guilt, sadness, shame, envy, jealousy, fright, and disgust. Such children are emotionally vulnerable and are at a greater risk of developing psychiatric illnesses later in life.

What Is Physical Abuse?

Physical abuse happens when someone deliberately injures a child by hitting, shaking, throwing, biting, burning, scalding, suffocating, or drowning her or him. Sports training so intense that it cannot be borne by the body is considered physical abuse. Coaches who promote performance-enhancing drugs are also essentially engaging in physical abuse. Forcing athletes to participate in events despite injury and imposing sanctions that inflict pain for nonperformance are considered physical abuse as well.

Sexual Abuse in Sports

In sports and other youth activities, children and teens could be sexually abused by adults or peers. Sexual abusers in this setting often use their position of authority or trust to first gain the confidence of the victim and that of their parents or caregivers. Then they use this same authority to keep the child from reporting the abuse.

In youth sports, coaches will invariably come into close physical contact with students. Responsible coaches respect the privacy of their athletes and keep their physical interactions with their team minimal and nurturing. Abusers, on the other hand, will take advantage of the closeness to act, often without being discovered (e.g., kissing or fondling a student as a form of "praise," abusing students while traveling for a game or secretly filming students changing in locker rooms, etc.).

What Is Harassment?

Harassment of children involves threats, taunts, intimidation, and usage of homophobic, sexist, and racial slurs by others. Comments, behavior, and contact that are uninvited, unwelcome, offensive, and sexual in nature also constitute harassment.

What Is Neglect?

Neglect occurs when caretakers, parents, or guardians fail to meet the basic physical and psychological needs of children. In youth sports, children are neglected when supervisors or coaches fail to follow basic safety guidelines and use protective equipment. Forcing children to play and practice in adverse weather conditions without sufficient protection or hydration is also neglect. Requiring children to play in spite of being unwell or ignoring bullying by teammates can be considered neglect.

Coaches and administrators must also act responsibly to minimize risk for students. Injuries, such as concussions are a case in point. It would be better to have the player taken off the ground and sent for medical diagnosis than to convince her or him to "shake it off" and continue playing.

What Is Philosophical Abuse in Sports?

Following the rules of the game, treating everyone (teammates, coaches, opponents, referees, and fans) with respect, and giving you all on the field are the founding principles of sportsmanship. Most coaches and parents make sure children understand that sportsmanship always outweighs winning at all costs. However, when adults repeatedly want to know if they

What Is the Kind of Misconduct Seen in Sports Events?

Parents who verbally abuse or physically confront students and coaches at sporting events are becoming increasingly common. Surveys conducted recently indicate that a significant percentage of coaches have experienced parents behaving inappropriately, including yelling at or taunting children on the field, confronting referees, or physically attacking coaches or other parents.

For children of parents who act in the manner, regularly witnessing, or being the target, this behavior increases the chances of being diagnosed with anxiety or depression. It also increases the likelihood of them engaging in risky behaviors, such as aggression and delinquency.

won, what was the score, and punish or belittle the youth if they do not win, children acquire the false notion that self-worth is built only upon winning. The spirit of sportsmanship can be greatly beneficial to the psychological health of children and is worth making it a centerpiece of any sports program.

How Can Abuse in Youth Sports Be Prevented?

It is up to parents, coaches, and educators to teach children about what constitutes acceptable behavior in sporting circles and to protect them for abuse and exploitation. It is the responsibility of parents to understand the attitude of coaches who train and supervise their children.

It is important that organizations recognize the fact that children are vulnerable for abuse and it should be their top priority to prevent it. Organizations must develop programs to deal with child abuse in their day-to-day environment.

The Centers for Disease Control and Prevention (CDC) has defined six key components for the creation of an environment and culture in organizations that serve youth that can contribute to the prevention of child abuse. These include the following:

1. Screening and selecting employees and volunteers (to screen out offenders and individuals who carry the risk of abusing children from working with children)

2. Following guidelines on interactions between individuals (to understand how employees and volunteers should behave with youth and what constitutes appropriate behavior among youth themselves)

3. Monitoring behavior (to respond to risky behavior and reinforce positive ones)

4. Ensuring safe environments (to protect children from situations that are risky for abuse)

5. Responding to inappropriate behavior, breaches in policy, and allegations and suspicions of child sexual abuse (to counteract immediately and appropriately in cases of child abuse)

6. Training about child sexual abuse prevention (to educate stakeholders and provide them with the skills to respond and deal with issues of child abuse)

The programs must be assessed and reviewed periodically for effectiveness and changes should be incorporated if required for successful implementation.

Child abuse is a societal concern, and in the best interests of children, youth-serving organizations must unite to eradicate criminal behavior against children within their capacity.

References

1. "Emotional Abuse in Youth Sports," Focus Adolescent Services, n.d.

2. de Lench, Brooke. "Abuse in Youth Sports Takes Many Different Forms," MomsTEAM Institute, Inc., n.d.

3. "Child Abuse in a Sports Setting," National Society for the Prevention of Cruelty to Children (NSPCC), 2017.

4. Aron, Cindy Miller. "Mind, Body, and Sport: The Haunting Legacy of Abuse," The National Collegiate Athletic Association (NCAA), n.d.

5. "Definitions of Child Abuse and Neglect in Federal Law," Child Welfare Information Gateway, U.S. Department of Health and Human Services (HHS), n.d.

6. "Preventing Child Abuse in Youth Sports," SI Play, LLC., 2017.

7. "Kidpower Teams Up with Positive Coaching Alliance (PCA) to Stop Child Abuse in Youth Sports," Kidpower Teenpower Fullpower International, June 5, 2012.

8. "Preventing Child Sexual Abuse within Youth-Serving Organizations: Getting Started on Policies and Procedures," Centers for Disease Control and Prevention (CDC), 2007.

Chapter 10

Stalking

Stalking is any repeated and unwanted contact that makes you feel afraid, harassed, or unsafe. Someone may stalk you by following you or calling you often. About one in six women has experienced stalking in her lifetime. Women are twice as likely to be stalked as men. You can be stalked by a stranger, but most stalkers are people you know—even an intimate partner. Stalking may get worse or become violent over time. Stalking may also be a sign of an abusive relationship. Some stalkers harass you with less-threatening but still unwanted contact. The use of technology to stalk, sometimes called "cyberstalking," involves using the Internet, e-mail, or other electronic communications to stalk someone by sending unwanted e-mails or social media messages. Stalking and cyberstalking can lead to sleeping problems or problems at work or school.

What Are Some Examples of Stalking?

Examples of stalking may include:

- Following you around or spying on you

- Sending you unwanted e-mails or letters

- Calling you often

- Showing up uninvited at your house, school, or work

- Leaving you unwanted gifts

About This Chapter: This chapter includes text excerpted from "Stalking," Office on Women's Health (OWH), U.S. Department of Health and Human Services (HHS), September 14, 2018.

- Damaging your home, car, or other property

- Threatening you, your family, or pets with violence

What Are Some Examples of Cyberstalking?

Examples of cyberstalking include:

- Sending unwanted, frightening, or obscene e-mails, text messages, or instant messages (IMs)

- Harassing or threatening you on social media

- Tracking your computer and Internet use

- Using technology such as Global Positioning System (GPS) to track where you are

Are There Laws against Stalking?

Yes. Stalking is a crime. If you are in any immediate danger, call 911.

You can file a complaint with the police and get a restraining order (court order of protection) against the stalker. Federal law says that you can get a restraining order for free. Do not be afraid to take steps to stop your stalker.

Prevent Stalking

According to the National Intimate Partner and Sexual Violence Survey (NISVS), about 1 in 6 women and 1 in 17 men have experienced stalking in their lifetimes.

To prevent stalking, CDC promotes the importance of early prevention and support efforts, which can include:

- Empowering everyone to understand, recognize, and address stalking

- Mobilizing men and boys as allies in prevention efforts

- Creating and supporting safe environments within relationships, schools, and communities through programs and policies that reduce risk and promote healthy relationships

(Source: "Stalking: Know It. Name It. Stop It," Centers for Disease Control and Prevention (CDC).)

What Can I Do If I Think I Am Being Stalked?

If you are in immediate danger, call 911. Find a safe place to go if you are being followed or worry that you will be followed. Go to a police station, friend's house, domestic violence shelter, fire station, or public area.

You can also take the following steps if you are being stalked:

- File a complaint with the police. Make sure to tell them about all threats and incidents.

- Get a restraining order. A restraining order requires the stalker to stay away from you and not contact you. You can learn how to get a restraining order from a domestic violence shelter, the police, or an attorney in your area.

- Write down every incident. Include the time, date, and other important information. If the incidents occurred online, take screenshots as records.

- Keep evidence, such as videotapes, voicemail messages, photos of property damage, and letters.

- Get names of witnesses.

- Get help from domestic-violence hotlines, domestic-violence shelters, counseling services, and support groups. Put these numbers in your phone in case you need them.

- Tell people about the stalking, including the police, your employer, family, friends, and neighbors.

- Always have your phone with you so you can call for help.

- Consider changing your phone number (although some people leave their number active so they can collect evidence). You can also ask your service provider about call blocking and other safety features.

- Secure your home with alarms, locks, and motion-sensitive lights.

What Can I Do If Someone Is Cyberstalking Me?

If you are being cyberstalked:

- Send the person one clear, written warning not to contact you again.

- If they contact you again after you have told them not to, do not respond.

- Print out copies of evidence such as e-mails or screenshots of your phone. Keep a record of the stalking and any contact with police.

- Report the stalker to the authority in charge of the site or service where the stalker contacted you. For example, if someone is stalking you through Facebook, report them to Facebook.

- If the stalking continues, get help from the police. You also can contact a domestic-violence shelter and the National Center for Victims of Crime Helpline for support and suggestions.

- Consider blocking messages from the harasser.

- Change your e-mail address or screen name.

- Never post online profiles or messages with details that someone could use to identify or locate you (such as your age, sex, address, workplace, phone number, school, or places you hang out).

Chapter 11

Sexual Harassment

Harassment is any unwelcome behavior or comments made by one person to another. "Sexual harassment" is a term usually used to describe unwanted sexual contact or behavior that happens more than once at work, home, or in school. It includes any unwelcome sexual advances or requests for sexual favors that affect a person's job, schoolwork, or housing. Street harassment is behavior or comments that can be sexual but are not always and may target your sex, gender, age, religion, nationality, race, ethnicity, or sexual orientation.

What Is Sexual Harassment?

Sexual harassment happens when someone in your workplace, home, or school makes unwelcome sexual advances to you or requests sexual favors. It also includes verbal or physical behaviors that may affect your job, home, or education. These acts are sexual harassment when they are without your consent, or are unwanted, and interfere with your work or school performance or create a hostile or offensive environment.

Sexual harassment violates most work, housing, or school policies and may be illegal. Sometimes sexual harassment is also sexual coercion. Coercion is when you are forced in a nonphysical way into sexual activity. Sexual harassers can be anyone—women or men—and can be managers, coworkers, landlords, teachers, or other students. Sexual harassment does not mean you are in a sexual relationship with the person doing it.

About This Chapter: This chapter includes text excerpted from "Harassment," Office on Women's Health (OWH), U.S. Department of Health and Human Services (HHS), September 14, 2018.

Sexual harassment can occur in a variety of circumstances, including but not limited to the following:

- The victim, as well as the harasser, may be a woman or a man. The victim does not have to be of the opposite sex.
- The harasser can be the victim's supervisor, an agent of the employer, a supervisor in another area, a coworker, or a nonemployee.
- The victim does not have to be the person harassed but could be anyone affected by the offensive conduct.
- Unlawful sexual harassment may occur without economic injury to or discharge of the victim.
- The harasser's conduct must be unwelcome.

(Source: "Facts about Sexual Harassment," U.S. Equal Employment Opportunity Commission (EEOC).)

How Common Is Sexual Harassment?

The exact number of people who are sexually harassed at work, home, or school is not known. This is because many people do not report sexual harassment.

Surveys show that more than half of women have experienced sexual harassment at work. However, only one in four who experienced harassment reported the behavior to a supervisor or human-resources representative. Reasons for not reporting the behavior included fear that their supervisor would not believe them or would not help them. It also included fear of losing their job, especially if their supervisor was the person harassing them.

Studies of sexual harassment in housing are not common, but one study shows that sexual coercion by someone in authority, such as a landlord, is the most common type of sexual harassment experienced by women in rental housing. Recent studies also show that sex and gender minority women may have a harder time finding housing compared to other women.

What Are Some Ways That Women Can Be Sexually Harassed?

There are many different types of sexual harassment that happen at work, home, or school:

Verbal or Written Sexual Harassment

- Making comments about your clothing, body, behavior, or romantic relationships
- Making sexual jokes or comments

- Repeatedly asking you out on a date after you have said no

- Asking you to engage in sexual acts, such as kissing, touching, watching a sexual act, or having sex

- Requesting sexual photos or videos of you

- Threatening you for saying no to a sexual request

- Spreading rumors about your personal or sexual life

- Whistling or catcalling

- Sending online links or photos with explicit or graphic sexual content

Physical Sexual Harassment

- Being uncomfortably close to you

- Blocking you from moving or walking away

- Inappropriate touching

- Coercing you into sexual activity by threatening to hurt your career, grades, home, or reputation (this is a type of sexual assault) if you do not engage in sexual activity

- Physically forcing into sexual activity without your consent (rape and sexual assault)

Visual Sexual Harassment

- Displaying or sharing sexual pictures, texts (sexting), computer wallpaper, or e-mails

- Showing you her or his private body parts (called "flashing")

- Masturbating in front of you

Sometimes you may experience other types of harassment that may be difficult to document or prove but that can still be threatening. These can include someone staring at your body in a sexual way or making offensive sexual gestures or facial expressions.

What Can I Do to Stop Sexual Harassment?

As with all other types of abuse, if you are being sexually harassed, it is not your fault. You can take steps to alert others to the harassment and protect yourself from the person harassing you. Many types of sexual harassment are against the law. If you are being sexually harassed, try one or all of these actions:

- **Say "no" without saying anything else.** If a harasser asks you for dates or sexual acts, just say "no." You do not need to offer excuses such as "I have a boyfriend," or "I do not date people I work with." If you give a reason or an excuse, it gives the harasser a way to continue the conversation or to argue with you. Physically leave the situation if you can. If the person continues to ask you for unwanted dates or sexual behavior, report them to someone in authority whose job it is to help you stop the harassment, such as a human-resources manager.

- **Tell the person to stop the harassment,** if you feel safe enough to do that. If someone is harassing you by making sexual comments or showing sexual images, tell them that the comment or image is not okay with you. Saying "Stop it" and walking away is a good way to respond also.

- **Keep a record.** When you experience harassment, write down the dates, places, times, and any witnesses to what happened. Store the record in a secure place, such as your phone. If the harassment happened online, save screenshots or e-mails of the interactions.

- **Report it.** It can be difficult to talk about personal topics with someone at work or school, but you should tell your manager, human-resources department, local legal aid group, rental company, or school about the harassment. Describe the harassing experiences and explain that they are unwelcome and you want them to stop. If you can, it is best to make your report in writing so you can save a record of it. Keep copies of everything you send and receive from your employer, landlord, or school about the harassment.

- **Research your company's or school's complaint procedures.** Most employers and schools should have a specific procedure on how to respond to sexual-harassment complaints. If at work, get a copy of your company's employee handbook so you can use these procedures to stop the harassment. At schools that get federal funding, you can get a copy of the sexual harassment policy. Follow the complaint procedures and keep records of it.

- **File a government agency discrimination complaint.** You can take your workplace sexual assault case higher by filing a lawsuit in federal or state court, but note that you have to file a formal sexual harassment complaint with the federal Equal Employment Opportunity Commission (EEOC) first. To report sexual harassment in housing, call the U.S. Department of Justice at 844-380-6178 or e-mail fairhousing@usdoj.gov. You can also file an online complaint with the U.S. Department of Housing and Urban Development (HUD) or call your local HUD office. You can file an online school-based sexual harassment complaint with the U.S. Department of Education (ED).

What Is Street Harassment?

Street harassment is unwanted comments, gestures, and actions forced on someone in a public place without that person's consent. It may or may not also be sexual harassment. The harassment usually comes from strangers and is often directed at someone because of sex, gender, religion, nationality, race, ethnicity, or sexual orientation.

In a national survey, more than half of women reported experiencing street harassment. Women of color, lesbians, and bisexual women experienced street harassment more often than other women.

You may have experienced street harassment if anyone has ever:

- Whistled at or catcalled you

- Made negative comments about your sex, gender, religion, sexual orientation, or sexual identity

- Continued to ask for your name, phone number, or other personal information after you have said no

- Followed you or stalked you

- Showed you her or his private body parts (called "flashing")

- Masturbated in front of you

- Physically touched you in private areas

How Can I Respond to Street Harassment?

You may have only a few seconds to decide on the best way to react to someone harassing you or someone else. Because street harassment often happens between strangers in a public place, you may not have the same legal protection that you have for sexual harassment that takes place at work or school or in rental housing. But no one has the right to physically touch or hurt you. Physically hurting someone or touching someone else without their permission or consent is always illegal.

It is probably safest to leave the situation as quickly as possible. If you cannot physically leave the situation right away, you have some other options:

- **Ignore the person.** It can be difficult to ignore someone who is saying insulting or demeaning things, but talking or arguing may lead to physical violence. Your safety is the most important consideration.

- **Move closer to someone in uniform.** Most people unconsciously associate uniforms with authority or power. If there is anyone in your area in any type of uniform, such as a security guard, doctor, police officer, or bus driver, try to stand or sit near them. Then leave the situation as soon as you can.

- **Start talking to someone else.** Harassment can be easier to ignore if you are in a group or talking to someone else. If you are alone, look for someone around you to talk to. Many people around you in public places will be willing to call 911 for you if you feel unsafe.

- **Call someone on your phone.** Pretend to talk on your phone even if the person does not answer. Tell the person on the phone where you are, for example, "I am at the Pine Street stop on the number 42 line and should be there soon." This may discourage a harasser from continuing the harassment if they think you can tell others about it.

- **Report them.** If the harassers are in a car, write down their license plate number and call the police. If the harassers are wearing a shirt or driving a vehicle that identifies their company, call or e-mail the company to report what the employees did. You can also report street harassment online. If you have a smartphone, record a video of the harassment and let the person being harassed know that you are doing so.

If you see someone else being harassed, and feel safe doing so, try to help. You can support the person being harassed without talking to the person doing the harassing. Ask the person being harassed if they are okay, or if you can help them move away from the situation. Offer to record the harassment with a smartphone.

Chapter 12

Sexual Coercion

Coercion can make you think you owe sex to someone. It might be from someone who has power over you, such as a teacher, landlord, or a boss. No person is ever required to have sex with someone else.

What Is Sexual Coercion?

Sexual coercion is unwanted sexual activity that happens after being pressured in nonphysical ways that include:

- Being worn down by someone who repeatedly asks for sex

- Being lied to or being promised things that were not true to trick you into having sex

- Having someone threaten to end a relationship or spread rumors about you if you do not have sex with them

- Having an authority figure, such as a boss, property manager, loan officer, or professor, use their influence or authority to pressure you into having sex

In a healthy relationship, you never have to have sexual contact when you do not want to. Sexual contact without your consent is assault. Sexual coercion means feeling forced to have sexual contact with someone.

About This Chapter: This chapter includes text excerpted from "Sexual Coercion," Office on Women's Health (OWH), U.S. Department of Health and Human Services (HHS), March 14, 2019.

Who Commits Sexual Coercion

Anyone, including friends, coworkers, bosses, landlords, dates, partners, family members, and strangers, can use coercion. Sexual coercion is most likely to happen with someone you already have some type of relationship with. Sexual activity should always happen with your consent. If you are being pressured or coerced into sexual activity, that may be a type of sexual assault and it may be against the law.

Protective factors may lessen the likelihood of sexual violence victimization or perpetration. These factors can exist at individual, relational, community, and societal levels.

- Parental use of reasoning to resolve family conflict
- Emotional health and connectedness
- Academic achievement
- Empathy and concern for how one's actions affect others

(Source: "Sexual Violence—Risk and Protective Factors," Centers for Disease Control and Prevention (CDC).)

What Are Some Examples of Sexual Coercion?

Sexual coercion can be any type of nonphysical pressure used to make you participate in sexual activity that you do not agree to. See the chart below for ways someone might use sexual coercion:

Table 12.1. Examples of Sexual Coercion

Ways Someone Might Use Sexual Coercion	What She or He May Say
Wearing you down by asking for sex again and again or making you feel bad, guilty, or obligated	"If you really loved me, you would do it." "Come on; it is my birthday." "You do not know what you do to me."
Making you feel like it is too late to say no	"But you have already gotten me all worked up." "You cannot just make someone stop."
Telling you that not having sex will hurt your relationship	"Everything's perfect. Why do you have to ruin it?" "I'll break up with you if you do not have sex with me."
Lying or threatening to spread rumors about you	"Everyone thinks we already have, so you might as well." "I will just tell everyone you did it anyway."

Table 12.1. Continued

Ways Someone Might Use Sexual Coercion	What She or He May Say
Making promises to reward you for sex	"I will make it worth your while." "You know I have a lot of connections."
Threatening your children or other family members	"I will do this to your child if you do not do it with me."
Threatening your job, home, or school career	"I really respect your work here. I would hate for something to change that." "I have not decided yet who is getting bonuses this year." "Do not worry about the rent. There are other things you can do." "You work so hard; it would be a shame for you not to get an A."
Threatening to reveal your sexual orientation publicly or to family or friends	"If you do not do this, I will tell everyone you are gay."

How Can I Respond in the Moment to Sexual Coercion?

Sexual coercion is not your fault. If you are feeling pressured to do something you do not want to do, speak up or leave the situation. It is better to risk a relationship ending or hurting someone's feelings than to do something you are not willing to do.

If the person trying to coerce you is in a position of power over you (such as a boss, landlord, or teacher), it is best to leave the situation as quickly and safely as possible. It might be difficult, but if you can report the person to someone in authority, you are taking steps to stop it from happening again. Some possible verbal responses include:

- "If you really care for me, you will respect that I do not want to have sex."

- "I do not owe you an explanation or anything at all."

- "You must be mistaken. I do not want to have sex with you."

Be clear and direct with the person trying to coerce you. Tell the person how you feel and what you do not want to do. If the person is not listening to you, leave the situation. If you or your family is in physical danger, try to get away from the person as quickly as possible. Call 911 if you are in immediate danger.

How Can I Get Help after Being Sexually Coerced?

Sexual coercion can be a type of sexual violence. If you are in immediate danger, call 911. If you are in a safe place, call the National Sexual Assault Hotline at 800-656-HOPE (800-656-4673) or chat online with a trained hotline worker on the National Sexual Assault Online Hotline at any time to get help.

Some sexual coercion is against the law or violates school, rental, or workplace policies. Sexual coercion from someone at school, work, or a rental company or loan office is usually called "sexual harassment." If you are younger than 18 years, tell a trusted adult about what happened. If you are an adult, consider talking to someone about getting help and reporting the person to the local authorities. You could talk to a counselor, the human-resources department, or the local police.

You can also file a sexual-harassment complaint with a federal agency. For workplace sexual harassment complaints, contact the Equal Employment Opportunity Commission (EEOC). For school sexual-harassment complaints, contact the U.S. Department of Education (ED). For housing sexual-harassment complaints, contact the U.S. Department of Housing and Urban Development (HUD) or the U.S. Department of Justice (DOJ) at 844-380-6178 or fairhousing@usdoj.gov.

Chapter 13

Incest

One of the least discussed issues related to child abuse is incest. The victims of incest often do not want to talk about it, because of the powerful societal taboo attached to the act. According to the U.S. Bureau of Justice Statistics (BJS), about 44 percent of sexual-assault victims are under the age of 18. The data also show that many perpetrators are known to the victims, and one-third are members of the victims' own families. And although it is commonly believed that only men initiate incest, in fact, women can be the perpetrators of such abuse. But since this takes place at a much lower rate than incest by men, and since so many of such cases are not reported, it often goes unnoticed.

Considering the gravity of the issue, it is vital to understand what incest is and what can be done about it. This chapter aims to define incest, identify the causes of incest, elucidate the reasons behind the difficulty in sharing information about sexual abuse by a family member, and suggest ways to find help and support for the victim.

Defining Incest

"Incest" is defined as sexual contact, including intercourse, between close relatives. In most cultures, incest is considered immoral, and in virtually all parts of the United States and many other countries it is also illegal. An adult engaging in incest with a child, however, is considered child abuse under the law, and while legislation pertaining to sexual assault varies, incest with a minor is illegal in all U.S. jurisdictions. The trauma experienced by a young victim of incest can be severe, and the incident can have a serious impact upon the life of the survivor.

About This Chapter: "Incest," © 2016 Omnigraphics. Reviewed August 2019.

Although incest can take place between consenting adults, when it occurs between adults and children some common forms include:

- Incest between a parent and a child

- Incest between an older and younger sibling

- Incest between another older relative (for example, an uncle or aunt) and a child

---

Childhelp National Child Abuse Hotline

Call or text 800-4-A-CHILD (800-422-4453). Professional crisis counselors are available 24 hours a day, 7 days a week, in over 170 languages. All calls are confidential. The hotline offers crisis intervention, information, and referrals to thousands of emergency, social service, and support resources.

(Source: "How to Report Suspected Child Maltreatment," Child Welfare Information Gateway, U.S. Department of Health and Human Services (HHS).)

Signs and Symptoms of Abuse

To identify whether a child has been a victim of incest, both physical and psychological symptoms must be considered. The physical symptoms include vaginal or rectal pain, vaginal discharge, bleeding, painful urination, bed-wetting, and constipation. The psychological signs include self-harm, nightmares, eating disorders, sleep disorders, aggressive behavior, withdrawal from social interactions, posttraumatic stress disorder (PTSD), lack of concentration, poor performance at school, depression, phobias, and precocious sexual behavior.

Characteristics of Incest Offenders

Learning to identify offenders is very important in order to protect children from becoming victims of incest. There are certain characteristics, conditions, and behaviors that are often evident in abusive incest situations. Some examples:

- Adolescent perpetrators often seek victims who are quite young. They tend to abuse the victims for a considerably long period of time. And they may behave more violently than adult perpetrators.

- The absence or unavailability of parents may present the opportunity for incest by siblings or other relatives.

- Dominant or abusive siblings often tend to use incest as a way of expressing their power over the other(s).

- Incest is not always between an adult and a child. Studies have revealed that sibling incest is the most prevalent form of incest.

Difficulty in Sharing Information on Sexual Abuse with a Family Member

The very thought of sexual abuse can be disturbing, and talking about it can often be very traumatic. It can become even more difficult to share such incidents if the survivor and the perpetrator are part of the same family.

Some struggles that a victim might face while sharing such information with another family member include:

- Concern about the abuser's future

- Response or reaction by the family towards the incident, perpetrator, and also the survivor

- Negligence or downplaying the issue by the family

- Being told that such things are normal in most families

- Inability of the family to recognize the incest as a type of abuse

- The victim being unaware of available help or difficulty in finding a trustworthy person

- Fear of being harassed by the perpetrator

Helping the Victims of Incest

Victims of incest may feel hopeless and can thus be hesitant to seek help. If you observe any symptoms of this type of abuse, some ways to help include:

- **Have a talk.** By talking to a child who has experienced abuse, you can provide them with comfort and try to ease their pain.

- **Show faith.** When a victim of abuse reveals their traumatic experience, lend a patient ear. Assure them that you are absolutely serious about what they are saying, and let them know that you are on their side. Then seek the assistance of child protective services.

- **Child Protective Services.** Reporting to child protective services is an option whether the victim is a minor or a vulnerable adult (that is, one who is susceptible to harm due to mental illness, age, or other factors). Contacting the U.S. Department of Health and Human Services (HHS) or the police are other options available to help get assistance for the victim.

References

1. "Incest," Rape, Abuse & Incest National Network (RAINN), July 2, 2015.

2. Willacy, Hayley, Dr. "Incest," *Patient*, February 21, 2013.

Chapter 14

Sexual Violence against Women

What Is Sexual Violence?

Sexual violence is sexual activity when consent is not obtained or not freely given. It is a serious public-health problem in the United States. Sexual violence impacts every community and affects people of all genders, sexual orientations, and ages—anyone can experience or perpetrate sexual violence. The perpetrator of sexual violence is usually someone known to the victim, such as a friend, current or former intimate partner, coworker, neighbor, or family member.

Sexual violence is associated with several risk and protective factors. It is connected to other forms of violence and causes serious health and economic consequences. By using a public-health approach that addresses risk and protective factors for multiple types of violence, sexual violence, and other forms of violence can be prevented.

How Big Is the Problem?

Sexual violence affects millions of people each year in the United States. Researchers know that the numbers underestimate this significant problem as many cases go unreported. Victims may be ashamed, embarrassed, or afraid to tell the police, friends, or family about the violence. Victims may also keep quiet because they have been threatened with further harm if they tell anyone or do not think that anyone will help them.

About This Chapter: This chapter includes text excerpted from "Preventing Sexual Violence," Centers for Disease Control and Prevention (CDC), March 12, 2019.

Still, we do have data that show:

- **Sexual violence is common.** 1 in 3 women and 1 in 4 men experienced sexual violence involving physical contact during their lifetimes. Nearly 1 in 5 women and 1 in 38 men have experienced completed or attempted rape and 1 in 14 men was made to penetrate someone (completed or attempted) during his lifetime.

- **Sexual violence starts early.** 1 in 3 female rape victims experienced it for the first time between 11 to 17 years old and 1 in 8 reported that it occurred before age 10. Nearly 1 in 4 male rape victims experienced it for the first time between 11 to 17 years old and about 1 in 4 reported that it occurred before age 10.

- **Sexual violence is costly.** Recent estimates put the cost of rape at $122,461 per victim, including medical costs, lost productivity, criminal-justice activities, and other costs.

What Are the Consequences?

The consequences of sexual violence are physical, like bruising and genital injuries, and psychological, such as depression, anxiety, and suicidal thoughts.

The consequences may also be chronic. Victims may suffer from posttraumatic stress disorder (PTSD) and experience recurring gynecological, gastrointestinal, cardiovascular, and sexual-health problems.

Sexual violence is also linked to negative health behaviors. For example, victims are more likely to smoke, abuse alcohol, use drugs, and engage in risky sexual activity.

The trauma resulting from sexual violence can have an impact on a survivor's employment in terms of time off from work, diminished performance, job loss, or being unable to work. These disrupt earning power and have a long-term effect on the economic well-being of survivors and their families. Readjustment after victimization can be challenging: victims may have difficulty in their personal relationships, in returning to work or school, and in regaining a sense of normalcy.

In addition, sexual violence is connected to other forms of violence. For example, girls who have been sexually abused are more likely to experience other forms of violence and additional sexual violence, and be a victim of intimate-partner violence in adulthood. Perpetrating bullying in early middle school is associated with sexual-harassment perpetration in adolescence.

> ## Sexual Violence Is Preventable
>
> Sexual violence impacts health in many ways and can lead to short and long-term physical and mental-health problems. Victims may experience chronic pain, headaches, and sexually transmitted diseases. They are often fearful or anxious and may have problems trusting others. Promoting healthy and respectful relationships can help reduce sexual violence.
>
> If you are or someone you know is a victim of sexual violence:
>
> - Contact the Rape, Abuse & Incest National Network (RAINN) hotline at 800-656-HOPE (800-656-4673). Help is free, confidential, and available 24/7.
> - Contact your local emergency services at 911.
>
> *(Source: "Preventing Sexual Violence," Centers for Disease Control and Prevention (CDC).)*

Risk and Protective Factors

Risk factors are linked to a greater likelihood of sexual violence (SV) perpetration. They are contributing factors and might not be direct causes. Not everyone who is identified as at risk becomes a perpetrator of violence. A combination of individual, relational, community, and societal factors contribute to the risk of becoming a perpetrator of SV. Understanding these factors can help identify various opportunities for prevention.

Risk Factors for Perpetration
Individual Risk Factors

- Alcohol and drug use

- Delinquency

- Lack of empathy

- General aggressiveness and acceptance of violence

- Early sexual initiation

- Coercive sexual fantasies

- Preference for impersonal sex and sexual risk-taking

- Exposure to sexually explicit media

- Hostility towards women
- Adherence to traditional gender role norms
- Hypermasculinity
- Suicidal behavior
- Prior sexual victimization or perpetration

Relationship Factors

- Family environment characterized by physical violence and conflict
- Childhood history of physical, sexual, or emotional abuse
- Emotionally unsupportive family environment
- Poor parent–child relationships, particularly with fathers
- Association with sexually aggressive, hypermasculine, and delinquent peers
- Involvement in a violent or abusive intimate relationship

Community Factors

- Poverty
- Lack of employment opportunities
- Lack of institutional support from police and judicial system
- General tolerance of SV within the community
- Weak community sanctions against SV perpetrators

Societal Factors

- Societal norms that support sexual violence
- Societal norms that support male superiority and sexual entitlement
- Societal norms that maintain women's inferiority and sexual submissiveness
- Weak laws and policies related to SV and gender equity
- High levels of crime and other forms of violence

Protective Factors for Perpetration

Protective factors may lessen the likelihood of SV victimization or perpetration. These factors can exist at individual, relational, community, and societal levels.

- Parental use of reasoning to resolve family conflict

- Emotional health and connectedness

- Academic achievement

- Empathy and concern for how one's actions affect others

Chapter 15

Sexual Assault of Men

What Is Sexual Assault?

"Sexual assault" is any type of sexual activity or contact that happens without your consent. Sexual assault can include noncontact activities, such as someone "flashing" you (exposing themselves to you) or forcing you to look at sexual images.

Sexual assault is also called "sexual violence" or "abuse." Legal definitions of sexual assault and other crimes of sexual violence can vary slightly from state to state. If you have been assaulted, it is never your fault.

Sexual Assault: Males

At least 1 out of every 10 (or 10%) of men in our country has suffered from trauma as a result of sexual assault. Like women, men who experience sexual assault may suffer from depression, posttraumatic stress disorder (PTSD), and other emotional problems as a result. However, because women and men have different life experiences due to their different gender roles, emotional symptoms following trauma can look different in men than they do in women.

About This Chapter: Text under the heading "What Is Sexual Assault?" is excerpted from "Sexual Assault," Office on Women's Health (OWH), U.S. Department of Health and Human Services (HHS), March 14, 2019; Text beginning with the heading "Sexual Assault: Males" is excerpted from "Sexual Assault: Males," National Center for Posttraumatic Stress Disorder (NCPTSD), U.S. Department of Veterans Affairs (VA), September 24, 2018.

Intimate Partner Violence

- About 1 in 3 men experienced contact sexual violence, physical violence, and/or stalking by an intimate partner during their lifetime.
- Nearly 56 percent of men who were victims of contact sexual violence, physical violence, and/or stalking by an intimate partner first experienced these or other forms of violence by that partner before age 25.

Sexual Violence

- Nearly 1 in 4 men in the United States experienced some form of contact sexual violence in their lifetime.
- About 1 in 14 men in the United States were made to penetrate someone during their lifetime.
- More than 1 in 38 men in the United States experienced completed or attempted rape victimization in their lifetime.
- Among male victims of completed or attempted rape, about 71 percent first experienced such victimization prior to age 25.

Stalking

- About 1 in 17 men in the United States were victims of stalking at some point in their lifetime.
- Nearly 41 percent of male victims first experienced stalking before age 25.

(Source: "Intimate Partner Violence, Sexual Violence, and Stalking among Men," Centers for Disease Control and Prevention (CDC).)

Who Are the Perpetrators of Male Sexual Assault?

- Those who sexually assault men or boys differ in a number of ways from those who assault only females.

- Boys are more likely than girls to be sexually abused by strangers or by authority figures in organizations, such as schools, the church, or athletics programs.

- Those who sexually assault males usually choose young men and male adolescents (the average age is 17 years old) as their victims and are more likely to assault many victims, compared to those who sexually assault females.

- Perpetrators often assault young males in isolated areas where help is not readily available. For instance, a perpetrator who assaults males may pick up a teenage hitchhiker on a remote road or find some other way to isolate his intended victim.

- As is true about those who assault and sexually abuse women and girls, most perpetrators of males are men. Specifically, men are perpetrators in about 86 out of every 100 (or 86%) of male victimization cases.

- Despite popular belief that only gay men would sexually assault men or boys, most male perpetrators identify themselves as heterosexuals and often have consensual sexual relationships with women.

What Are Some Symptoms Related to Sexual Trauma in Boys and Men?

Particularly when the assailant is a woman, the impact of sexual assault upon men may be downplayed by professionals and the public. However, men who have early sexual experiences with adults report problems in various areas, at a much higher rate than those who do not, such as:

- **Emotional disorders.** Men and boys who have been sexually assaulted are more likely to suffer from PTSD, anxiety disorders, and depression than those who have never been abused sexually.

- **Substance abuse.** Men who have been sexually assaulted have a high incidence of alcohol and drug use. For example, the probability for alcohol problems in adulthood is about 80 out of every 100 (or 80%) for men who have experienced sexual abuse, as compared to 11 out of every 100 (or 11%) for men who have never been sexually abused.

- **Risk-taking behavior.** Exposure to sexual trauma can lead to risk-taking behavior during adolescence, such as running away and other delinquent behaviors. Having been sexually assaulted also makes boys more likely to engage in behaviors that put them at risk for contracting human immunodeficiency virus (HIV) (such as having sex without using condoms).

- **Help for men who have been sexually assaulted.** Men who have been assaulted often feel stigmatized, which can be the most damaging aspect of the assault. It is important for men to discuss the assault with a caring and unbiased support person, whether that person is a friend, clergyman, or clinician. However, it is vital that this person be knowledgeable about sexual assault and men.

A local rape crisis center may be able to refer men to mental-health practitioners who are well-informed about the needs of male sexual assault victims. If you are a man who has been assaulted and you suffer from any of these difficulties, please seek help from a mental-health professional who has expertise working with men who have been sexually assaulted.

Chapter 16

Child Pornography

Child pornography is a form of child sexual exploitation. Federal law defines child pornography as any visual depiction of sexually explicit conduct involving a minor (persons less than 18 years old). Images of child pornography are also referred to as child sexual abuse images.

Federal law prohibits the production, distribution, importation, reception, or possession of any image of child pornography. A violation of federal child pornography laws is a serious crime, and convicted offenders face fines and severe statutory penalties.

Child Pornography Online

The term "child pornography" is used in federal statutes, and hence, it is also commonly used by lawmakers, prosecutors, investigators, and the public to describe sexual exploitation of children. However, this term fails to describe the true horror that is faced by countless children every year. The production of child pornography creates a permanent record of a child's sexual abuse. When these images are placed on the Internet and disseminated online, the victimization of the children continues in perpetuity. Experts and victims agree that victims depicted in child pornography often suffer a lifetime of revictimization by knowing the images of their sexual abuse are on the Internet forever. The children exploited in these images must live with the permanency, longevity, and circulation of such a record of their sexual victimization. This often creates lasting psychological damage to the child, including disruptions in sexual development, self-image, and developing trusting relationships with others in the future.

About This Chapter: This chapter includes text excerpted from "Child Pornography," U.S. Department of Justice (DOJ), July 25, 2017.

The expansion of the Internet and advanced digital technology lies parallel to the explosion of the child pornography market. Child pornography images are readily available through virtually every Internet technology, including social networking websites, file-sharing sites, photo-sharing sites, gaming devices, and even mobile apps. Child pornography offenders can also connect on Internet forums and networks to share their interests, desires, and experiences abusing children, in addition to selling, sharing, and trading images.

These online communities have promoted communication and collaboration between child pornography offenders, thereby fostering a larger relationship premised on a shared sexual interest in children. This has the effect of eroding the shame that typically would accompany this behavior, as well as desensitizing those involved to the physical and psychological damage caused to the child victims. For this reason, online communities attract and encourage new individuals to join them in the sexual exploitation of children.

The methods many offenders use to evade law enforcement detection have also become increasingly sophisticated. Purveyors of child pornography continue to use various encryption techniques and anonymous networks on "The Dark Internet," attempting to hide their amassed collections of illicit child abuse images. Several sophisticated online criminal organizations have even written security manuals to ensure that their members follow preferred security protocols and encryption techniques in an attempt to evade law enforcement and facilitate the sexual abuse of children.

Unfortunately, no area of the United States or the country in the world is immune from individuals who seek to sexually exploit children through child pornography. The continuous production and distribution of child pornography increases the demand for new and more egregious images, perpetuating the continued molestation of child victims, as well as the abuse of new children.

Federal law prohibits the production, distribution, reception, and possession of an image of child pornography using or affecting any means or facility of interstate or foreign commerce (See 18 U.S.C. § 2251; 18 U.S.C. § 2252; 18 U.S.C. § 2252A). Specifically, Section 2251 makes it illegal to persuade, induce, entice, or coerce a minor to engage in sexually explicit conduct for purposes of producing visual depictions of that conduct. Any individual who attempts or conspires to commit a child pornography offense is also subject to prosecution under federal law.

(Source: "Citizen's Guide to U.S. Federal Law on Child Pornography," U.S. Department of Justice (DOJ).)

Victims of Child Pornography

It is important to distinguish child pornography from the more conventional understanding of the term "pornography." Child pornography is a form of child sexual exploitation, and each image graphically memorializes the sexual abuse of that child. Each child involved in the production of an image is a victim of sexual abuse.

While some child sexual abuse images depict children in great distress and the sexual abuse is self-evident, other images may depict children that appear complacent. However, just because a child appears complacent does not mean that sexual abuse did not occur. In most child pornography cases, the abuse is not a one-time event, but rather an ongoing victimization that progresses over months or years. It is common for producers of child pornography to groom victims, or cultivate a relationship with a child and gradually sexualize the contact over time. The grooming process fosters a false sense of trust and authority over a child in order to desensitize or break down a child's resistance to sexual abuse. Therefore, even if a child appears complacent in a particular image, it is important to remember that the abuse may have started years before that image was created.

Furthermore, victims of child pornography suffer not just from the sexual abuse inflicted upon them to produce child pornography, but also from knowing that their images can be traded and viewed by others worldwide. Once an image is on the Internet, it is irretrievable and can continue to circulate forever. The permanent record of a child´s sexual abuse can alter her or his life forever. Many victims of child pornography suffer from feelings of helplessness, fear, humiliation, and lack of control given that their images are available for others to view in perpetuity.

Unfortunately, emerging trends reveal an increase in the number of images depicting sadistic and violent child sexual abuse, and an increase in the number of images depicting very young children, including toddlers and infants.

Chapter 17

Commercial Child Sexual Exploitation

"Commercial Sexual Exploitation of Children" (CSEC)—this term refers to a range of crimes and activities involving the sexual abuse or exploitation of a child for the financial benefit of any person or in exchange for anything of value (including monetary and nonmonetary benefits) given or received by any person. Examples of crimes and acts that constitute CSEC include:

- Child sex trafficking/the prostitution of children

- Child sex tourism involving commercial sexual activity

- The commercial production of child pornography

- The online transmission of live video of a child engaged in sexual activity in exchange for anything of value

CSEC also includes situations where a child, whether or not at the direction of any other person, engages in sexual activity in exchange for anything of value, which includes nonmonetary things, such as food, shelter, drugs, or protection from any person.

Depending on the specific circumstances, CSEC may also occur in the context of Internet-based marriage brokering, early marriage, and children performing in sexual venues.

About This Chapter: Text in this chapter begins with excerpts from "Commercial Sexual Exploitation of Children," Office of Juvenile Justice and Delinquency Prevention (OJJDP), U.S. Department of Justice (DOJ), June 21, 2016. Reviewed August 2019; Text beginning with the heading "Child Sex Trafficking" is excerpted from "Child Sex Trafficking," U.S. Department of Justice (DOJ), July 25, 2017; Text beginning with the heading "Risk and Impact" is excerpted from "Sex Trafficking," Centers for Disease Control and Prevention (CDC), February 13, 2019.

Child Sex Trafficking

Some of our most vulnerable children also face the threat of being victimized by commercial sexual exploitation. Runaways, throwaways, sexual assault victims, and neglected children can be recruited into a violent life of forced prostitution.—Deputy Attorney General James Cole speaks at the National Strategy Conference on Combating Child Exploitation in San Jose, California, May 17, 2011

"Child sex trafficking" refers to the recruitment, harboring, transportation, provision, obtaining, patronizing, or soliciting of a minor for the purpose of a commercial sex act. Offenders of this crime who are commonly referred to as "traffickers," or "pimps," target vulnerable children and gain control over them using a variety of manipulative methods. Victims frequently fall prey to traffickers who lure them in with an offer of food, clothes, attention, friendship, love, and a seemingly safe place to sleep. After cultivating a relationship with the child and engendering a false sense of trust, the trafficker will begin engaging the child in prostitution, and use physical, emotional, and psychological abuse to keep the child trapped in a life of prostitution. It is common for traffickers to isolate victims by moving them far away from friends and family, altering their physical appearances, or continuously moving them to new locations. Victims are heavily conditioned to remain loyal to the trafficker and to distrust law enforcement. No child is immune to becoming a victim of child sex trafficking, regardless of the child's race, age, socioeconomic status, or location, and every child involved in this form of commercial sexual exploitation is a victim.

Technological advances, particularly the Internet and mobile devices, have facilitated the sex trafficking of children by providing a convenient worldwide marketing channel. Individuals can now use websites and social media to advertise, schedule, and purchase sexual encounters with minors. The Internet and mobile devices also allow pimps and traffickers to reach a larger clientele base than in the past, which may expose victims to greater risks and dangers.

Child sex trafficking investigations present unique challenges to law enforcement and require a robust multijurisdictional response, with multiple agencies playing a critical role in ensuring the protection of victims and effective prosecution of offenders. The method by which most traffickers identify, recruit, market, and maintain their victims results in a unique combination of sustained violent criminal behavior with reluctant victims and witnesses. Although interviews of sex-trafficking victims frequently identify traffickers and other accomplices, some child victims may resist identifying their traffickers because of fear or other means of manipulation that the pimp has exercised over them. Furthermore, the victim may only know their traffickers' street name and cannot fully identify their traffickers.

Child sex trafficking victims are often not recognized as victims and may be arrested and jailed. The dangers faced by these children—from the traffickers, their associates, and from customers—are severe. These children become hardened by the treacherous environment in which they must learn to survive. As such, they do not always outwardly present as sympathetic victims. They also frequently suffer from short- and long-term psychological effects, such as depression, self-hatred, and feelings of hopelessness. These child victims also need specialized services that are not widely available given they often have illnesses, drug addictions, physical and sexual trauma, lack of viable family and community ties, and total dependence—physical and psychological—on their abusers.

Sex trafficking is a type of human trafficking and is a form of modern-day slavery. It is a serious public-health problem that negatively affects the well-being of individuals, families, and communities. Human trafficking occurs when a trafficker exploits an individual with force, fraud, or coercion to make them perform commercial sex or work. It involves the use of force, fraud, or coercion to make an adult engage in commercial sex acts, but any commercial sexual activity with a minor, even without force, fraud, or coercion, is considered trafficking. This type of violence exploits women, men, and children across the United States and around the world. Sex trafficking is preventable. Understanding the shared risk and protective factors for violence can help prevent trafficking from happening in the first place.

(Source: "Sex Trafficking," Centers for Disease Control and Prevention (CDC).)

International Sex Trafficking of Minors

One form of sex trafficking involves the cross-border transportation of children. In these situations, traffickers recruit and transfer children across international borders in order to sexually exploit them in another country. The traffickers can be individuals working alone, organized crime groups, enterprises, or networks of criminals working together to traffic children into prostitution across country lines.

This form of sex trafficking is a problem in the United States, and recovered victims originate from all over the world, including less-developed areas such as South and Southeast Asia, Central America, and South America, to more developed areas, such as Western Europe. Once in the United States, a child may be trafficked to any or multiple states within the country. These victims are often trafficked far from home, and thrown into unfamiliar locations and culture. They may be given a false passport or other documentation to conceal their age and true identity. They may also struggle with the English language. All these factors make it extremely difficult for these children to come forward to law enforcement.

In addition, many foreign victims originate from nations that suffer from poverty, turbulent politics, and unstable economies. Children from these countries are seen as easy targets by traffickers because they face problems of illiteracy, limited employment opportunities, and bleak financial circumstances in their home country. It is not uncommon for a foreign victim to be coerced by a trafficker under false pretenses. The child is told that a better life or job opportunity awaits them in the United States. However, once in the United States they are introduced into a life of prostitution controlled by traffickers.

Domestic Sex Trafficking of Minors

The United States not only faces a problem of foreign victims trafficked into the country, but there is also a homegrown problem of American children being recruited and exploited for commercial sex. Under federal law, a child does not need to cross international or even state borders to be considered a victim of commercial sexual exploitation, and unfortunately, American children are falling victim to this crime within the United States.

Pimps and traffickers sexually exploit children through street prostitution, and in adult night clubs, illegal brothels, sex parties, motel rooms, hotel rooms, and other locations throughout the United States. Many recovered American victims are street children, a population of runaway or throwaway youth who often come from low-income families, and may suffer from physical abuse, sexual abuse, and family abandonment issues. This population is seen as an easy target by pimps because the children are generally vulnerable, without dependable guardians, and suffer from low self-esteem. Victims of the prostitution of children, however, come from all backgrounds in terms of class, race, and geography (i.e., urban, suburban, and rural settings).

Often in domestic sex-trafficking situations, pimps will make the child victim feel dependent on prostitution for life necessities and survival. For example, a pimp will lure a child with food, clothes, attention, friendship, love, and a seemingly safe place to stay. After cultivating a relationship with a child and engendering a false sense of trust, the pimp will begin engaging the child in prostitution. It is also common for pimps to isolate victims by moving them far away from friends and family, altering their physical appearances, or continuously moving victims to new locations. In many cases, victims become so hardened by the environment in which they must learn to survive that they are incapable of leaving the situation on their own.

Child Victims of Prostitution

The term "prostitution" can delude or confuse one's understanding of this form of child sexual exploitation. It is important to emphasize that the children involved are victims. Pimps and traffickers manipulate children by using physical, emotional, and psychological abuse to keep them trapped in a life of prostitution. It is not uncommon for traffickers to beat, rape, or torture their victims. Some traffickers also use drugs and alcohol to control them.

Technological advances, in particular the Internet, have facilitated the commercial sexual exploitation of children by providing a convenient worldwide marketing channel. Individuals can now use websites to advertise, schedule, and purchase sexual encounters with minors. The Internet and web-enabled cell phones also allow pimps and traffickers to reach a larger clientele base than in the past, which may expose victims to greater risks and dangers.

In addition, many child victims suffer from physical ailments, including tuberculosis, infections, drug addiction, malnutrition, and physical injuries resulting from violence inflicted upon them. Venereal diseases also run rampant. Children may also suffer from short- and long-term psychological effects, such as depression, low self-esteem, and feelings of hopelessness.

Risk and Impact

Trafficking victimization and perpetration share risks and consequences associated with child abuse and neglect, intimate-partner violence, sexual violence, and gang violence.

Victims can come from all backgrounds and become trapped in different locations and situations.

- Many victims are women and girls, though men and boys are also impacted.

- Victims include all races, ethnicities, sexual orientations, gender identities, citizens, noncitizens, and income levels.

- Victims are trapped and controlled through assault, threats, false promises, perceived sense of protection, isolation, shaming, and debt.

- Victims do not have to be physically transported between locations to be victimized.

Perpetrators of human trafficking often target people who are poor, vulnerable, living in an unsafe situation, or searching for a better life. For example, youth with a history of abuse and neglect or who are homeless are more likely to be exploited.

Consequences of sexual violence, including sex trafficking, can be immediate and long term, including physical and relationship problems, psychological concerns, and chronic health outcomes.

What States and Communities Need to Know

Efforts have focused on increasing community awareness of human trafficking and addressing exploitation after it occurs. Fewer programs and policies have been implemented and evaluated to reduce upstream risks that may prevent trafficking before it occurs. Strategies based on the best available evidence exist to prevent related forms of violence, and they may also reduce sex trafficking. States and communities can implement and evaluate comprehensive efforts that:

- Encourage healthy behaviors in relationships
- Foster safe homes and neighborhoods
- Identify and address vulnerabilities during healthcare visits
- Reduce demand for commercial sex
- End business profits from trafficking-related transactions

The Centers for Disease Control and Prevention's (CDC) suite of technical packages can help states and communities take advantage of the best available evidence to prevent violence. Each package is intended as a resource to guide and informs prevention decision-making in communities and states.

Chapter 18

Online Sextortion

Online sextortion occurs when an adult, through threat or manipulation, coerces a minor into producing a sexually explicit image and sending it over the Internet.

Why Would Any Child or Teen Agree to Do Such a Thing?

Individuals carrying out this crime are skilled and ruthless in coercing minors and have honed their techniques and approaches to maximize their chances at success. The entry point to a young person can be any number of mobile or online sites, applications, or games. The approach may come as compliments or flattery or in the pretense of beginning a romantic relationship.

Another entry point is to offer the child something they value in exchange for taking a quick picture. This could be a possibility of a modeling contract, online game credits or codes, or money, cryptocurrency, and gift cards.

The third common point of entry is to go right to threats by either claiming they already have an image of the young person that they will distribute or threatening to harm the child or other people or things the child cares about.

Once the perpetrator has the first image, they use the threat of exposure or other harm to keep the child producing more and more explicit material.

About This Chapter: This chapter includes text excerpted from "Dangerous Connections—Youth Face a Risk of Sextortion Online," Federal Bureau of Investigation (FBI), May 30, 2019.

The New Version of "Do Not Talk to Strangers"

- When you are online, has anyone you do not know ever tried to contact or talk to you?
- What did you do or what would you do if that happened?
- Why do you think someone would want to reach a kid online?
- You know, it is easy to pretend to be someone you are not online and not every person is a good person. Make sure you block or ignore anything that comes in from someone you do not know in real life.

How Do I Protect the Young People I Know?

Information-sharing and open lines of communication are the best defense. Young people need to know this crime is happening and understand where the risks are hiding. Explain to the children and teens in your life that people can pretend to be anyone or anything online. A stranger reaching out to them online may be doing so with bad intent, and no matter what the platform or application claims, nothing "disappears" online. If they take a photo or video, it always has the potential to become public.

You may choose to place certain limits on your children's Internet use or spot check their phones and other devices to see what applications they are using and with whom they are communicating. This can be part of an open and ongoing conversation about what is and is not appropriate online. It also may be worth considering a rule against devices in bedrooms overnight or shutting off Wi-Fi access at night. Caregivers may also want to review the settings on a young person's social media accounts with them. Keeping accounts private can prevent predators from gathering their personal information.

The other crucial element is to keep the door open to your children, so that they know they can come to you and ask for help. Let them know that your first move will be to help—always. These predators are powerful, and because of fear, the victims suffer ever more negative consequences as the crime carries on over days, weeks, and months.

If you are the adult a child trusts with this information, comfort them, help them understand they have been the victim of a crime, and help them report it to law enforcement.

Part Two
Violence and the Teen Experience

Chapter 19

Teen Exposure to Violence, Crime, and Abuse

Exposure to violence is a national crisis that affects approximately two out of every three of our children. U.S. Surgeon General Julius B. Richmond declared violence a public-health crisis of the highest priority. Whether the violence occurs in children's homes, neighborhoods, schools, playgrounds, or playing fields, locker rooms, places of worship, shelters, streets, or in juvenile-detention centers, the exposure of children to violence is a uniquely traumatic experience that has the potential to profoundly derail the child's security, health, happiness, and ability to grow and learn—with effects lasting well into adulthood.

Approximately 3 in 5 children (57.7%) experienced at least one exposure to physical assault, sexual victimization, maltreatment, property victimization, and witness violence.

Rates of lifetime exposure to violence continued to be high, especially for the oldest youth (ages 14 to 17), showing how exposure to violence accumulates as a child grows.

More than 54.5 percent of youth report being assaulted in their lifetime as recorded by the second National Survey of Children's Exposure to Violence (NatSCEV II).

(Source: "Children's Exposure to Violence, Crime, and Abuse: An Update," Office of Juvenile Justice and Delinquency Prevention (OJJDP), U.S. Department of Justice (DOJ).)

Exposure to violence in any form harms children, and different forms of violence have different negative impacts:

- **Sexual abuse** places children at high risk for serious and chronic health problems, including posttraumatic stress disorder (PTSD), depression, suicidality, eating disorders,

About This Chapter: This chapter includes text excerpted from "Report of the Attorney General's National Task Force on Children Exposed to Violence," U.S. Department of Justice (DOJ), December 12, 2012. Reviewed August 2019.

sleep disorders, substance abuse, and deviant sexual behavior. Sexually abused children often become hypervigilant about the possibility of future sexual violation and experience feelings of betrayal by the adults who failed to care for and protect them.

- **Physical abuse** puts children at high risk for lifelong problems with medical illness, PTSD, suicidality, eating disorders, substance abuse, and deviant sexual behavior. Physically abused children are at heightened risk for cognitive and developmental impairments, which can lead to violent behavior as a form of self-protection and control. These children often feel powerless when faced with physical intimidation, threats, or conflict and may compensate by becoming isolated (through truancy or hiding) or aggressive (by bullying or joining gangs for protection). Physically abused children are at risk for significant impairment in memory processing and problem-solving and for developing defensive behaviors that lead to consistent avoidance of intimacy.

- **Intimate partner violence** within families puts children at high risk for severe and potentially lifelong problems with physical health, mental health, and school and peer relationships, as well as for disruptive behavior. Witnessing or living with domestic or intimate-partner violence often burdens children with a sense of loss or profound guilt and shame because of their mistaken assumption that they should have intervened or prevented the violence or, tragically, that they caused the violence. They frequently castigate themselves for having failed in what they assume to be their duty to protect a parent or sibling(s) from being harmed, for not having taken the place of their horribly injured or killed family member, or for having caused the offender to be violent.

Children exposed to intimate-partner violence often experience a sense of terror and dread that they will lose an essential caregiver through permanent injury or death. They also fear losing their relationship with the offending parent, who may be removed from the home, incarcerated, or even executed. Children will mistakenly blame themselves for having caused the batterer to be violent. If no one identifies these children and helps them heal and recover, they may bring this uncertainty, fear, grief, anger, shame, and sense of betrayal into all of their important relationships for the rest of their lives.

- **Community violence** in neighborhoods can result in children witnessing assaults and even killings of family members, peers, trusted adults, innocent bystanders, and perpetrators of violence. Violence in the community can prevent children from feeling safe in their own schools and neighborhoods. Violence and ensuing psychological trauma can lead children to adopt an attitude of hypervigilance, to become experts at detecting threat or perceived threat—never able to let down their guard in order to be ready for the next outbreak of violence. They may come to believe that violence is "normal," that violence is "here to stay," and that relationships are too fragile to trust because one never knows when violence will take the life of a friend or loved one. They may turn to gangs or criminal activities to prevent others from viewing them as weak and to counteract feelings of despair and powerlessness, perpetuating the cycle of violence and increasing their risk of incarceration. They are also at risk for becoming victims of intimate-partner violence in adolescence and in adulthood.

The picture becomes even more complex when children are "polyvictims" (exposed to multiple types of violence). As many as 1 in 10 children in this country are polyvictims, according to the U.S. Department of Justice and the Centers for Disease Control and Prevention's groundbreaking National Survey of Children's Exposure to Violence (NatSCEV). The toxic combination of exposure to intimate-partner violence, physical abuse, sexual abuse, and/or exposure to community violence increases the risk and severity of posttraumatic injuries and mental-health disorders by at least twofold and up to as much as tenfold. Polyvictimized children are at very high risk for losing the fundamental capacities necessary for normal development, successful learning, and a productive adulthood.

The financial costs of children's exposure to violence are astronomical. The financial burden on other public systems, including child welfare, social services, law enforcement, juvenile justice, and, in particular, education, is staggering when combined with the loss of productivity over children's lifetimes.

Chapter 20

Youth Violence: How Big Is the Problem?

What Is Youth Violence?

Youth violence is when young people aged 10 to 24 years intentionally use physical force or power to threaten or harm others.

Why Focus on Youth Violence

Opportunities for Action, a publication of the National Center for Injury Prevention and Control (NCIPC), the Centers for Disease Control and Prevention (CDC), focuses on preventing youth violence because the need for action to reduce youth violence is great and effective action is possible. Attention to all of the interrelated forms of violence that impact youth—child maltreatment, suicidal behavior, sexual assault, and teen dating violence—is beyond the scope of this resource and might require different prevention strategies.

> Youth violence is a leading cause of death for young people and results in more than 475,000 nonfatal injuries each year. Adverse childhood experiences, like youth violence, are associated with negative health and well-being outcomes across the life course. Youth violence increases the risk for behavioral and mental-health difficulties, including future violence perpetration and victimization, smoking, substance use, obesity, high-risk sexual behavior, depression, academic difficulties, school dropout, and suicide.
>
> *(Source: "Preventing Youth Violence," Centers for Disease Control and Prevention (CDC).)*

About This Chapter: This chapter includes text excerpted from "Preventing Youth Violence: Opportunities for Action," Centers for Disease Control and Prevention (CDC), June 2014. Reviewed August 2019.

Focus on Youth Violence Prevention

The term "youth violence" used by the CDC and in this resource refers to when young people aged 10 to 24 years intentionally use physical force or power to threaten or harm others. The World Health Organization (WHO) has described this behavior as "violence between individuals who are unrelated, and who may or may not know each other, generally taking place outside the home." Youth violence typically involves youth perpetrating violence against other young people. A young person can be involved with youth violence as a victim, an offender, or a witness. Youth violence can take different forms, such as fighting, bullying, threats with weapons, and gang-related violence. These different forms of youth violence can vary in where and how often they occur and who is impacted. They can also vary in the harm that results and can include physical harm, such as injuries or death, as well as psychological harm. However, the different forms of youth violence can be prevented. The evidence-based actions in this resource are appropriate for preventing all forms of youth violence.

Preventing Youth Violence: Opportunities for Action focuses on youth violence because there is an enormous breadth and depth of knowledge about youth violence and how to effectively guide community action to prevent it. For youth violence, research has provided a strong understanding about the burden and trends, the factors that influence the likelihood it will occur, and a variety of effective prevention strategies. However, this same level of understanding is not yet available for other forms of violence that youth may experience, such as dating violence, sexual violence, and suicide. Research demonstrates that the causes of youth violence and other forms of violence often are similar, but knowledge is limited about whether the evidence-based youth violence prevention strategies and action steps discussed in this resource also lower the risk for other forms of violence. Other forms of violence might require unique preventive action, and a full discussion of the research that is the foundation for these different prevention approaches is beyond the scope of this resource.

Youth Violence: A Leading Cause of Death and Physical Injury for Young People

Youth homicide in the United States is a significant public-health issue. In 2011, 4,708 (7.3 per 100,000) youth aged 10 to 24 years were victims of homicide. Homicide is the third leading cause of death among young people aged 10 to 24 years, responsible for more deaths in this age group than the next seven leading causes of death combined (see Figure 20.1). For each young homicide victim, we lose an entire lifetime of contributions to families, potential employers, and communities. The number of youth who are physically harmed but do not die as the result of youth violence is significantly higher. In 2011, we saw that for every young homicide victim, there were approximately 142 youth with nonfatal physical assault-related injuries treated in U.S. emergency departments. A total of 599,336 youth aged 10 to 24 years (928 per 100,000) were treated in U.S. emergency departments for nonfatal physical assault-related injuries in 2012. This means that each day approximately 13 young people are victims of homicide and an additional 1,642 are treated in emergency departments for physical assault-related injuries.

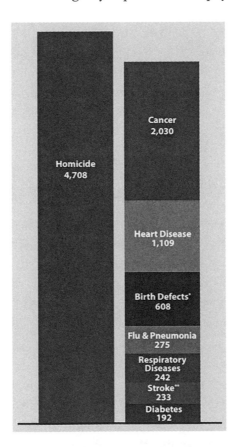

Figure 20.1. More Youth Aged 10 to 24 Die from Homicide than from the Next Seven Leading Causes of Death Combined *(Source: 2011 Fatalities; Web-Based Injury Statistics Query and Reporting System (WISQARS).)*
*Congenital Anomalies
**Cerebrovascular Diseases

Violence-Related Behaviors Reported by Youth

Official data from death certificates and emergency departments are critical to helping understand and address youth violence, but they only tell part of the story. The full extent of the violence that youth perpetrate and experience as victims goes far beyond these data sources. The Youth Risk Behavior Survey (YRBS) conducted by the CDC in 2013 indicates that 24.7 percent of high-school students reported having been in at least one physical fight in the year before the survey. Nearly 18 percent of high-school students reported they carried a weapon (e.g., gun, knife, or club), and 5.5 percent reported they carried a gun at least 1 day in the month prior to being surveyed.

Youth violence also occurs in schools and negatively impacts students' ability to attend and to participate fully. In 2013, nearly 20 percent of high-school students reported being bullied at school, and 6.9 percent said they had been threatened or injured with a weapon on school property in the past year. Furthermore, 7.1 percent of high-school students reported missing at least 1 day of school in the past 30 days because they felt unsafe either at school or on their way to or from school.

Youth Violence Remains a Critical Problem

Although the prevalence of several forms of youth violence has declined since the early 1990s, the declines are inconsistent and the public-health burden is still too high. For instance, examination of youth homicide trends show rates have declined over time, but these declines are stalling. The overall homicide rate among youth aged 10 to 24 years reached a peak in 1993 at 15.9 per 100,000, and then from 1994 to 1999 declined 41 percent (15.2 per 100,000 in 1994 to 8.9 in 1999). This promising decline has slowed over the last decade. Between 2000 and 2010, youth homicide rates have declined approximately 1 percent per year. As illustrated in Figure 20.2, the youth homicide rate has remained between 7.3 and 9 homicides per 100,000 youth each year from 2000 to 2011 and has been substantially and consistently higher than the overall homicide rate for all ages. Additionally, the youth homicide rate in the United States is higher than the rate for other high-income countries. For example, international research on adolescent and young adult males aged 15 to 24 has shown that the homicide rate in the United States is between 3 and 40 times higher than the homicide rate in other high-income countries.

Trends in other forms of youth violence also show declines over time. For instance, Figure 20.3 illustrates significant declines in high-school students' reports of being in a physical fight over the last decade. However, even with these declines, the levels of violence remain unacceptably high. The most recent data indicate that 1 in 4 high-school students reported being in at least 1 physical fight, and 1 in 12 high-school students reported fighting at least once on school property within the past year.

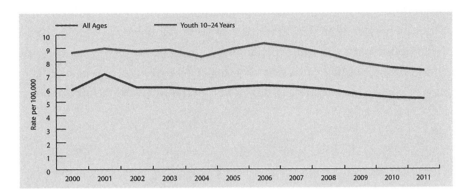

Figure 20.2. Trends in Homicide Rates in the United States, 2000 to 2011* *(Source: Web-based Injury Statistics Query and Reporting System (WISQARS).)*
Homicide rates for all ages are age-adjusted to the standard 2000 population; rates for those ages 10 to 24 years are age-specific.

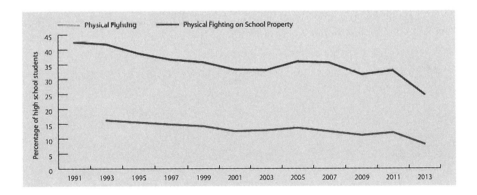

Figure 20.3. Prevalence of Physical Fighting among High-School Students in the United States, 1991 to 2013* *(Source: Youth Online: High-School Youth Risk Behavior Survey (YRBS).)*
Percentage of high-school students fighting on school property not available for 1991.

The variability of the prevalence of youth violence over time is similar to shifts in violent crime rates. Although the causes for these patterns are uncertain, previous research suggests that changes in youth homicide and violent crime rates in the mid-1980s to early 1990s were related in part to the emergence of crack cocaine and the associated growth in drug use and drug-related crime, increased weapon carrying, and weak economic conditions. When youth violence started to decline in the mid-1990s, there were various community changes occurring, such as an increased emphasis on violence as a public-health problem and the need to use evidence-based prevention approaches.

National trends suggest that the prevention of youth violence is possible. But, even with promising reductions, youth are still experiencing high levels of violence and youth violence persists as an important public health issue. Strategic, data-driven steps can be taken to reenergize declines in youth violence rates and to assure that downward trends are not reversed.

Chapter 21

Physical Fighting among Teens

Violence among young people is a serious problem. Different types of violence among youth include:

- Hitting, pinching, punching, or kicking

- Robbery

- Using a weapon

- Sexual assault and rape

- Bullying

Effects of Youth Violence

Every year, thousands of young people in the United States die from violence. Violence causes physical injuries, including cuts, bruises, and broken bones. Violence also causes emotional issues, such as being very afraid, nervous, or depressed. Even just seeing violence can lead to serious problems.

How Can I Stay Safe from Violence?

Here are a few tips to help you stay safe from violence among youth:

- **Choose your friends carefully.** Stay away from people who are involved in violence. Also, try to avoid people who have a hard time controlling how they act when angry.

About This Chapter: This chapter includes text excerpted from "Violence," girlshealth.gov, Office on Women's Health (OWH), September 16, 2015. Reviewed August 2019.

- **Stick near safe adults.** Hang out where teachers or other responsible adults are around. For after school, consider joining a club, sports, or volunteer activity.

- **Try to stay away from weapons.**

  - If a classmate brings a gun, knife, or other weapon to school, tell a teacher or other adult right away.

  - If you are out after school and someone is carrying a weapon, leave right away.

  - If you have been carrying a weapon to feel safe, talk to an adult about other ways to cope with fear.

- **Learn about safe places.** Try to find out about local places you can go when you feel in danger. These include police stations, firehouses, and libraries. In some places, you can join a special program to help kids in danger. They post a yellow "Safe Place" sign. To find one of these, text your current location to 69866. You can also call 800-786-2929 for help.

- **Practice "safety in numbers."** Try to walk in groups. If you feel in danger while walking alone, go to a place where there are other people as soon as you can.

Despite surveys showing encouraging data that high-school students are making better health choices such as "not fighting" and "not smoking," the Centers for Disease Control and Prevention states that there are way too many young people who get involved in physical violence. Youth are the future. Youth need outreach that will help them make healthy choices to live long and lead healthy lives.

(Source: "Cigarette Smoking among U.S. High-School Students at Lowest Level in 22 Years," Centers for Disease Control and Prevention)

Ways to Help Prevent Violence

It is not okay for someone to hurt you, and it is not okay for you to hurt someone else. If you are involved in violence, talk to an adult. Here are a few tips:

- **Lead by example.** Be a model for peace your friends can follow.

- **Speak up.** When people talk about violence, let them know you think it is not okay.

- **Share info.** Suggest ways friends can avoid tough situations: staying away from drugs and alcohol and trying activities that are safe and fun, such as sports or a school club.

- **Step in.** If things are getting tense, see if you can help people calm down. If not, do not put yourself in danger. Get the help of an adult.

- **Lend a hand.** Support other people who have been physically or emotionally hurt. That way, you may help them from lashing out as well. Plus, it is just the kind of thing to do!

- **Get involved.** See if your school or community has a violence-prevention program and join the program.

Chapter 22

Electronic Aggression (Cyberbullying)

With technological innovations and increased access to technology, youth are more likely to own and use cell phones, computers, and other electronic devices than ever before. Increased access to technology has benefits, but it also increases the risk of abuse. There is growing concern about electronic aggression—or cyberbullying—defined as any type of harassment or bullying (teasing, telling lies, making fun of someone, making rude or mean comments, spreading rumors, or making threatening or aggressive comments) that occurs through e-mail, a chat room, instant messaging, a website (including blogs), text messaging, and videos or pictures posted on websites or sent through cell phones.

Mirroring the increase in youth accessing and using technology, the number of youth between ages 10 and 17 in 2005 who indicated they had been involved in cyberbullying was twice the number who had reported involvement in 1999 to 2000. Estimates of the number of youth who have been victims of electronic aggression and cyberbullying vary from 9 to 43 percent, depending on the definition of electronic aggression/cyberbullying used and the time period that youth are reporting about.

Electronic Aggression and Teen Dating Violence

The relationship between electronic aggression and teen dating violence has not been widely explored. Initial information gathered from interviews with 56 young adults (aged 18 to 21) who experienced teen dating violence suggests that technology plays an important role

---

About This Chapter: This chapter includes text excerpted from "Electronic Aggression," Youth.gov, February 7, 2012. Reviewed August 2019.

in intimate relationships, providing a new space for perpetration of a range of teen dating violence behaviors and influencing the privacy, autonomy, and safety of youth in relationships.

There are two sources of federally collected data on youth bullying:

- The 2017 School Crime Supplement (National Center for Education Statistics and Bureau of Justice) indicates that, among students ages 12 to 18 who reported being bullied at school during the school year, 15 percent were bullied online or by text.
- The 2017 Youth Risk Behavior Surveillance System (Centers for Disease Control and Prevention) indicates that an estimated 14.9 percent of high-school students were electronically bullied in the 12 months prior to the survey.

(Source: "What Is Cyberbullying?" StopBullying.gov, U.S. Department of Health and Human Services (HHS).

Sexting

In addition, a number of surveys and heightened media concern have focused on sexting. "Sexting" is defined in a number of different ways, but is "most commonly used to describe the creation and transmission of sexual images by minors" through technologies such as cell phones and the Internet. While many of the studies looking at the prevalence rates of sexting have proved inconsistent and included major flaws and limitations, two 2011 studies provide context for the rates of certain forms of youth sexting and the relationship between youth sexting and arrests.

A national survey of youth, ages 10 to 17, found that:

- A total of 9.6 percent of youth reported they had appeared in, created, or received sexually explicit or nearly nude images.

- Furthermore, 2.5 percent reported they had created or appeared in images, with 1.3 percent of those identified as sexually explicit; 7.1 percent reported only receiving images, with 5.9 percent of those images identified as sexually explicit.

- About a quarter of youth who appeared in or created images (21%) or received images (25%) reported feeling very or extremely embarrassed, afraid, or upset.

- Romance was the most commonly reported reason for being involved in sexting, though pranks and attempting to start a relationship were also reported.

- Only a small portion of youth reported that they forwarded images on that they created, appeared in, or received.

The study suggests that there is substantial variation in the rates of sexting based on how it is defined.

A second study looking at arrest rates for sexting found that in cases of youth-produced sexual images (youth 17 and under) handled by law enforcement, there are often "aggravating" circumstances (e.g., adult involvement or a minor involved in malicious, nonconsensual, or abusive behavior) beyond the creation and dissemination of sexual images. Furthermore, the study found that arrests are unlikely in sexting cases when adults are not involved.

Chapter 23

Substance Abuse and Violence: What Is the Connection?

Drugs and Violence Go Hand-In-Hand

A national survey (the National Survey on Drug Use and Health (NSDUH)) found that more than one-quarter (26.7%) of girls age 12 to 17 reported engaging in some kind of violent behavior in the last year. There is more in this age group:

- 18.6 percent got into a serious fight at school or work in the past 12 months

- 14.1 percent participated in a group-against-group fight

- 5.7 percent attacked others with the intent to hurt them seriously

The study also found that violence and drug use are linked: girls who engaged in violent behaviors were two to three times more likely to have binged on alcohol or used marijuana or other illicit drugs in the past month. Girls engaging in violent behavior were also more likely to report missing school and getting bad grades.

About This Chapter: Text under the heading "Drugs and Violence Go Hand-In-Hand" is excerpted from "Drugs and Violence Go Hand-In-Hand," National Institute on Drug Abuse (NIDA) for Teens, April 12, 2011. Reviewed August 2019; Text under the heading "Love and Drugs and Violence" is excerpted from "Love and Drugs and Violence," National Institute on Drug Abuse (NIDA) for Teens, February 16, 2016. Reviewed August 2019; Text beginning with the heading "Substance-Use Problems and Serious Delinquency Are Linked" is excerpted from "Substance Use and Delinquent Behavior among Serious Adolescent Offenders," National Criminal Justice Reference Service (NCJRS), December 2010. Reviewed August 2019.

Love and Drugs and Violence

There is a connection between people in abusive dating relationships and drugs and alcohol.

Actually, it is a two-way street. Drugs and alcohol increase the risk for dating violence, and people who are victims of dating violence are at increased risk for using drugs and alcohol.

Being drunk or drugged can make someone more likely to physically or emotionally hurt a person they are in a relationship with. Drugs and alcohol make it harder to keep your emotions in check and to make the right choices. They also make it easier to act impulsively without thinking through the consequences. And the people on the receiving end of that abuse are more likely to turn to drugs and alcohol to cope with the depression and anxiety that result from being victimized.

Substance Use and Violence among Youth

- 14 percent of high-school students reported having ever used select illicit or injection drugs (i.e., cocaine, inhalants, heroin, methamphetamines, hallucinogens, or ecstasy)

- 14 percent of students reported the nonprescription use of opioids

- Injection drug use places youth at direct risk for human immunodeficiency virus, and drug use broadly places youth at risk of overdose

- Youth opioid use is directly linked to sexual risk behaviors

- Students who report ever using prescription drugs without a doctor's prescription are more likely than other students to have been the victim of physical or sexual dating violence

- Drug use is associated with sexual risk behavior, experience of violence, and mental-health and suicide risks

(Source: "High-Risk Substance Use among Youth," Centers for Disease Control and Prevention (CDC).)

Abuse between teens in a romantic relationship is known as "teen dating violence." It happens when one person intentionally hurts the other—or when they both do it to each other. Dating violence can be emotional, physical, and/or sexual, and it also includes stalking. It can be with a current or former partner. It can happen in person or electronically. And it has real consequences for a person's health, today and in the future.

Abusive relationships do not always start out that way. Often, they start with teasing, or periods of jealousy or being controlling. But, as with many unhealthy behaviors, over time it can get worse. For nearly 10 percent of high-school students surveyed by the Centers for Disease Control and Prevention (CDC) in 2013, "worse" means that in the last year they were hit, slapped, or physically hurt by their partner.

The best way to avoid teen dating violence is by having healthy relationships. This does not mean there is not any conflict in the relationship, because that is not realistic—even for the most in-love people ever. It means both people learning how to resolve their differences respectfully. That can make all the difference.

Substance-Use Problems and Serious Delinquency Are Linked

Researchers consistently find a strong link between substance-use problems and serious delinquency, regardless of how they structure the inquiry.

Studies of youth in juvenile court demonstrate that a majority of court-involved adolescents have used illegal substances and that more serious and chronic adolescent offenders have used more substances and are more likely to qualify for a diagnosis of a substance-use disorder (SUD).

Investigators who study large samples of community youth observe a strong association between reported serious offending and substance use in these groups.

Researchers who follow adolescent offenders over time find that substance use at one age is one of the most consistent indicators of continued serious offending at a later age.

The issue of when and how individuals develop these co-occurring patterns of substance use and illegal activity is less clear. Some of the same factors that put an individual at risk for involvement in criminality also put that individual at risk for substance-use problems. Parental SUDs, poor parenting, conflictual family environments, and dispositional factors, such as sensation-seeking and behavioral disinhibition place an adolescent at higher risk of using drugs and alcohol and/or engaging in illegal acts.

In addition, adolescents with poor affect regulation, high levels of environmental stress, or depression may use drugs and alcohol to medicate themselves as a coping mechanism. However, these relations are less consistently found—especially once "externalizing behaviors" (e.g., substance use and criminal offending) are considered—and often appear in complex interactions. The relation between negative mood and alcohol use has been reported to be stronger among adolescents with fewer conduct problems.

Substance Use and Offending Fluctuate in Similar Patterns over Time

It is clear that these two behaviors are associated over time, although there does not seem to be a clear progression from one to the other. Several investigators report evidence that behavior problems and aggression at a younger age predict later adolescent illicit substance use, escalations in use over time, and later diagnoses of substance abuse and dependence. In addition, studies suggest that early substance use predicts subsequent criminal behavior in adolescents.

The advances in statistical methods (e.g., joint trajectory analyses) have produced other insights into this temporal relationship. Joint trajectory analyses allow the researcher to examine the comparability of the patterns of these two behaviors as they progress over the same time period. Research using this technique has demonstrated that criminal behavior and substance use follow parallel courses over time, suggesting a reciprocal relationship between the two behaviors. Whether the relationship is sequential or reciprocal can be debated; it may be that the relationship follows different patterns in different groups of youth. It is clear, however, that delinquent behavior and substance-use problems go hand in hand in adolescence.

Multiple Mechanisms May Link the Behaviors

Substance use and delinquency can interrelate in several ways over the course of adolescence to promote dual involvement and set the stage for a difficult entry into young adulthood.

Substance use in and of itself is certainly not the primary cause of involvement in illegal activity. Substance use, however, may initiate or heighten the risk of offending either independently or in conjunction with other risk factors. There are several ideas about the ways that substance use might exert this effect, as illustrated in figure 23.1.

Substance use and offending might have a simple reciprocal relationship. "Being high" can lower inhibitions against involvement in criminal acts (a psychopharmacological explanation), and/or committing crime might be a way to obtain funds to support substance use (an instrumental explanation). According to this formulation, one behavior indicates that the other behavior is more likely to occur.

As described earlier, substance use and offending might also be linked because they are both driven by common causes such as parental SUDs, disrupted and conflictual family environments, or shared dispositional risk factors. For example, Young and colleagues found a single spectrum that linked novelty seeking, conduct disorder, substance experimentation, and attention deficit hyperactivity disorder (ADHD) in a sample of adolescent twins. One explanation is that a common tendency toward novelty-seeking and difficulty with behavioral regulation leads to a variety of externalizing behaviors, including substance use and criminal offending. Alternatively, adolescents dealing with a particularly difficult or pervasive set of problems, like difficulties learning in school and violent home life, might find escape in either substance use or illegal activity or both.

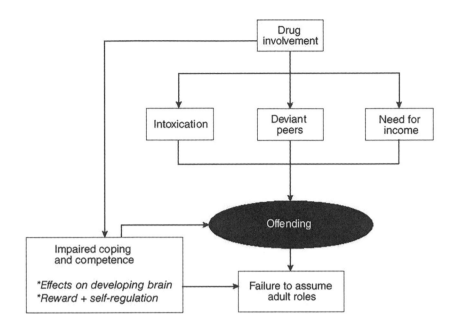

Figure 23.1. Factors That May Link Substance Use and Offending in Adolescents

However, the common links are not necessarily limited to the individual adolescent. The influence of the peer group and/or neighborhood (social context) might determine the co-occurrence of substance use and offending. A large proportion of serious delinquent acts in mid- and late-adolescence are committed in groups, and substance use might be a particularly potent component of the group process. Alternatively, regular substance use may place adolescents in group situations where crime (particularly violence) is more likely. Continued gang involvement, which increases the risk for crime and substance use during late adolescence, is an extreme case of this dynamic. Similarly, youth who live in high-crime neighborhoods might be introduced to drug use or recruited for criminal activities at a disproportionate rate compared with youth who live in more stable neighborhoods.

Finally, criminal offending and substance use may both be part of a process of delayed development. In the years following adolescence, an individual's continued drug or alcohol use may reduce her or his chances of a successful transition to developmentally appropriate adult roles such as employee, spouse, and parent. Adolescent substance use can produce a false sense of reality and autonomy that interferes with the development of emerging social competencies and coping skills. Some data support this idea: Adolescents' illegal drug use predicts a lower level of autonomy and less competence in young adulthood, and adolescents in the juvenile-justice system have a lower level of decisionmaking ability than do adolescents in the community who are of similar age and ethnic background. However, the interplay among maturity, attainment of developmental competencies, drug use, and delinquency is largely unexplored terrain.

Substance Use and Offending Decrease in Late Adolescence

Another intriguing question about these behaviors, aside from how they fuel each other during adolescence, is how and why they both usually cease in early adulthood. Many studies show that both substance-use problems and delinquency start during mid-adolescence and then stop or sharply decrease for many individuals in their 20s and 30s. Criminologists agree on the existence of an age–crime curve, which shows that the likelihood of both official and self-reported criminal activity decreases during late adolescence and early adulthood, with less than half of serious adolescent offenders continuing their criminal career into adulthood. Notably, similar age curves are observed for alcohol and drug use, substance-use problems, and substance-use diagnoses. One or more processes during late adolescence and early adulthood cause some individuals who engaged in these activities when they were younger—even very serious offenders or heavy substance users—to stop altogether or slow down their rate of offending and/or substance use if they remain active.

It is also clear that this dropoff does not follow the same pattern for everyone. Numerous analyses of data on longitudinal criminal offending and substance use indicate that this change follows several different patterns over time. Some subgroups continue at a high rate, others stop quickly and completely, and still others drop off at different rates of decline or at later ages. Although differences in sampling strategies, outcome measures, and analytic approaches affect the number of groups and the shapes of the "dropoff" curves obtained, studies consistently find different pathways of desistance from both substance-use problems and criminal involvement in the period from late adolescence to early adulthood. A better understanding of life events or interventions that affect these pathways would have important implications for developing interventions to enhance the desistance process.

Use the Substance Abuse and Mental Health Services Administration (SAMHSA) Treatment Locator to find substance use or other mental-health services in your area. If you are in an emergency situation, this toll-free, 24-hour hotline can help you get through this difficult time: call 800-273-TALK (800-273-8255), or visit the Suicide Prevention Lifeline (suicidepreventionlifeline.org).

(Source: "Hazing and Alcohol: Time to Break with 'Tradition,'" National Institute on Drug Abuse (NIDA) for Teens)

Little Is Known about What Promotes Desistance

Several general mechanisms may promote desistance from substance use and/or criminal activity. One possibility is that normal developmental change in late adolescence and early adulthood makes criminal behavior and/or substance use less attractive or acceptable. As individuals become more mature socially, emotionally, and intellectually, changes in their moral reasoning, considerations regarding the future, impulse control, or susceptibility to peer influence may steer them away from antisocial, risky, and dangerous behavior and toward more socially desirable and safer activities. Immediate thrills and impressing friends hold less sway in the now-larger picture of the world. In addition, individuals may acquire new skills (either personal or vocational) that lead to new opportunities and offer alternative forms of validation. A different, but related, possibility is that the transition into adult roles (employment, family, and citizenship) promotes new behavioral patterns and demands that make involvement in antisocial activity less acceptable and rewarding.

Criminologists have long discussed the notion that increased involvement in "routine activities" should curb criminal involvement because working at a job, engaging in more serious romantic relationships, starting a family, and fulfilling community roles should result in reduced exposure to settings where antisocial activities are the norm. In concrete terms, individuals who spend their daytime hours in a supervised workplace, their evening hours with their spouse and children, and their nighttime hours sleeping to rest for the next workday have little opportunity to engage in serious antisocial behaviors.

Evidence on substance abuse shows that adult role transitions are related to decreases in alcohol and drug use, and it is likely that regular fulfillment of activities related to adult roles also moves individuals out of the circles where criminal involvement is more prevalent and accepted. A significant corollary of the general developmental view adds the dimension of social investment as a potentially important factor in this process. According to this view, it is not simply social roles that are important. Rather, the strength of individuals' attachment and commitment to these new roles and opportunities plays a large part in determining whether they will continue their antisocial activities. If these new roles and opportunities create valued experiences (e.g., a loving relationship, respect as part of a workgroup) that are important to the individual offender, the individual increases her or his "social capital" and may reach a point where the new lifestyle becomes a reality that is worth protecting.

Once individuals form a commitment to work and family, they have something to lose and, therefore, something to guard. Many contend that positive change then occurs as an internal psychological realignment of self-conceptions takes hold; that is, an individual takes a proactive role in creating new opportunities for positive social involvement and integrates experiences and opportunities in light of a newfound, "reformed" self. In short, many substance-abusing juvenile offenders will desist from one or both of these behaviors in early adulthood, but very little is known about how these processes of desistance operate or what factors influence them. Without longitudinal information about the interaction of these two antisocial behaviors over time, it is difficult to guide the design of effective programs and policies for these adolescents.

Chapter 24

Teen Dating Violence

Teen dating violence (TDV) is a type of intimate partner-violence. It occurs between two people in a close relationship. It includes four types of behavior:

- **Physical violence** is when a person hurts or tries to hurt a partner by hitting, kicking, or using another type of physical force.

- **Sexual violence** is forcing or attempting to force a partner to take part in a sex act, sexual touching, or a nonphysical sexual event (e.g., sexting) when the partner does not or cannot consent.

- **Psychological aggression** is the use of verbal and nonverbal communication with the intent to harm another person mentally or emotionally and/or exert control over another person.

- **Stalking** is a pattern of repeated, unwanted attention and contact by a partner that causes fear or concern for one's own safety or the safety of someone close to the victim.

Dating violence can take place in person or electronically, such as repeated texting or posting sexual pictures of a partner online without consent. Unhealthy relationships can start early and last a lifetime. Teens often think some behaviors, such as teasing and name-calling, are a "normal" part of a relationship—but these behaviors can become abusive and develop into serious forms of violence. However, many teens do not report unhealthy behaviors because they are afraid to tell family and friends.

About This Chapter: This chapter includes text excerpted from "Preventing Teen Dating Violence," Centers for Disease Control and Prevention (CDC), March 12, 2019.

117

In 2017, 6.9 percent of high-school students (among 68.3 percent of students who dated or went out with someone in the past year) had experienced sexual dating violence, defined as being forced to do sexual things, including such things as kissing, touching, or being physically forced to have sexual intercourse, they did not want to do by someone they were dating or going out with.

(Source: "Youth Risk Behavior Survey—Data Summary and Trends Report 2007 to 2017," Centers for Disease Control and Prevention (CDC).)

How Big Is the Problem?

Teen dating violence is common. It affects millions of teens in the United States each year. Data from the Centers for Disease Prevention and Control's (CDC) Youth Risk Behavior Survey and the National Intimate Partner and Sexual Violence Survey indicate that:

- Nearly 1 in 11 female and approximately 1 in 15 male high-school students report having experienced physical dating violence in the last year.

- About 1 in 9 female and 1 in 36 male high-school students report having experienced sexual dating violence in the last year.

- 26 percent of women and 15 percent of men who were victims of contact sexual violence, physical violence, and/or stalking by an intimate partner in their lifetime first experienced these or other forms of violence by that partner before age 18.

- The burden of TDV is not shared equally across all groups—sexual minority groups are disproportionately affected by all forms of violence, and some racial/ethnic minority groups are disproportionately affected by many types of violence.

What Are the Consequences?

Unhealthy, abusive, or violent relationships can have severe consequences and short- and long-term negative effects on a developing teen. For instance, youth who are victims of TDV are more likely to:

- Experience symptoms of depression and anxiety

- Engage in unhealthy behaviors, such as using tobacco, drugs, and alcohol

- Exhibit antisocial behaviors, such as lying, theft, bullying, or hitting

- Think about suicide

Violence in an adolescent relationship sets the stage for problems in future relationships, including intimate-partner violence and sexual-violence perpetration and/or victimization throughout life. For instance, youth who are victims of dating violence in high school are at higher risk for victimization during college.

How Can We Stop Teen Dating Violence before It Starts?

Supporting the development of healthy, respectful, and nonviolent relationships has the potential to reduce the occurrence of TDV and prevent its harmful and long-lasting effects on individuals, their families, and the communities where they live. During the preteen and teen years, it is critical for youth to begin to learn the skills needed—such as effectively managing feelings and using healthy communication—to create and foster healthy relationships.

The CDC developed Dating Matters®: Strategies to Promote Healthy Teen Relationships to stop teen dating violence before it starts. It focuses on 11- to 14-year-olds and includes multiple prevention components for individuals, peers, families, schools, and neighborhoods. All of the components work together to reinforce healthy relationship messages and reduce behaviors that increase the risk of dating violence.

Steps to Prevent Teen Dating Violence

- Teach safe and healthy relationship skills

  - Socioemotional learning programs for youth

  - Healthy relationship programs for couples

- Engage influential adults and peers

  - Men and boys as allies in prevention

  - Bystander empowerment and education

  - Family-based programs

- Disrupt the developmental pathways toward partner violence

- Early childhood home visitation
- Preschool enrichment with family engagement
- Parenting skills and family relationship programs
- Treatment for at-risk children, youth, and families
- Create protective environments
  - Improve school climate and safety
  - Improve organizational policies and workplace climate
  - Modify the physical and social environments of neighborhoods
- Strengthen economic supports for families
  - Strengthen household financial security
  - Strengthen work–family support
- Support survivors to increase safety and lessen harms
  - Victim-centered services
  - Housing programs
  - First responder and civil legal protections
  - Patient-centered approaches
  - Treatment and support for survivors of intimate-partner violence, including teen dating violence

Chapter 25

Bullying

What Is Bullying?

Bullying is unwanted, aggressive behavior among school-aged children that involves a real or perceived power imbalance. The behavior is repeated, or has the potential to be repeated, over time. Both kids who are bullied and who bully others may have serious, lasting problems.

In order to be considered bullying, the behavior must be aggressive and include:

- **An imbalance of power:** Kids who bully use their power—such as physical strength, access to embarrassing information, or popularity—to control or harm others. Power imbalances can change over time and in different situations, even if they involve the same people.

- **Repetition:** Bullying behaviors happen more than once or have the potential to happen more than once.

Bullying includes actions, such as making threats, spreading rumors, attacking someone physically or verbally, and excluding someone from a group on purpose.

Types of Bullying

There are three types of bullying:

- **Verbal bullying** is saying or writing mean things. Verbal bullying includes:
  - Teasing

About This Chapter: This chapter includes text excerpted from "What Is Bullying," StopBullying.gov, U.S. Department of Health and Human Services (HHS), May 30, 2019.

- Name-calling

- Inappropriate sexual comments

- Taunting

- Threatening to cause harm

- **Social bullying,** sometimes referred to as "relational bullying," involves hurting someone's reputation or relationships. Social bullying includes:

  - Leaving someone out on purpose

  - Telling other children not to be friends with someone

  - Spreading rumors about someone

  - Embarrassing someone in public

- **Physical bullying** involves hurting a person's body or possessions. Physical bullying includes:

  - Hitting, kicking, punching

  - Spitting

  - Tripping, pushing

  - Taking or breaking someone's things

  - Making mean or rude hand gestures

Where and When Bullying Happens

Bullying can occur during or after school hours. While most reported bullying happens in the school building, a significant percentage also happens in places such as on the playground or the bus. It can also happen traveling to or from school, in the youth's neighborhood, or on the Internet.

Frequency of Bullying

There are two sources of federally collected data on youth bullying:

- The 2017 School Crime Supplement (National Center for Education Statistics (NCES) and Bureau of Justice) indicates that, nationwide, about 20 percent of students between the ages of 12 and 18 experienced bullying.

- The 2017 Youth Risk Behavior Surveillance System (YRBSS) (Centers for Disease Control and Prevention (CDC)) indicates that, nationwide, 19 percent of students in grades 9 to 12 report being bullied on school property in the 12 months preceding the survey.

Effects of Bullying

Bullying can affect everyone—those who are bullied, those who bully, and those who witness bullying. Bullying is linked to many negative outcomes including impacts on mental health, substance use, and suicide.

Teens who are bullied can experience negative physical, school, and mental-health issues. They are more likely to experience:

- Depression and anxiety, increased feelings of sadness and loneliness, changes in sleep and eating patterns, and loss of interest in activities they used to enjoy. These issues may persist into adulthood.

- Health complaints

- Decreased academic achievement—Grade Point Average (GPA) and standardized test scores—and school participation. They are more likely to miss, skip, or drop out of school.

A very small number of bullied youth might retaliate through extremely violent measures. In 12 of 15 school-shooting cases in the 1990s, the shooters had a history of being bullied.

Teens who bully others can also engage in violent and other risky behaviors into adulthood. They are more likely to:

- Abuse alcohol and other drugs as adults

- Get into fights, vandalize property, and drop out of school

- Engage in early sexual activity

- Have criminal convictions and traffic citations as adults

- Be abusive toward their romantic partners, spouses, or children as adults

Bystanders

Youth who witness bullying are more likely to:

- Have increased use of tobacco, alcohol, or other drugs

- Have increased mental-health problems, including depression and anxiety

- Miss or skip school

Relationship between Bullying and Suicide

Media reports often link bullying with suicide. However, most youth who are bullied do not have thoughts of suicide or engage in suicidal behaviors.

Although youth who are bullied are at risk of suicide, bullying alone is not the cause. Many issues contribute to suicide risk, including depression, problems at home, and trauma history. Additionally, specific groups have an increased risk of suicide, including American Indian and Alaskan Native, Asian American, and lesbian, gay, bisexual, and transgender youth. This risk can be increased further when these youth are not supported by parents, peers, and schools. Bullying can make an unsupportive situation worse.

Support Kids Who are Bullied

- Listen and focus on the child
- Learn what has been going on and show you want to help
- Assure the child that bullying is not her or his fault
- Know that kids who are bullied may struggle with talking about it
- Consider referring the kids to a counselor or other mental-health service
- Follow up and show a commitment to making bullying stop

(Source: "Support the Kids Involved," StopBullying.gov, U.S. Department of Health and Human Services (HHS).)

Bullying and Youth with Disabilities and Special Health Needs

Children with disabilities—such as physical, developmental, intellectual, emotional, and sensory disabilities—are at an increased risk of being bullied. Any number of factors—physical vulnerability, social-skill challenges, or intolerant environments—may increase the risk. Research suggests that some children with disabilities may bully others as well.

Kids with special health needs, such as epilepsy or food allergies, also may be at higher risk of being bullied. Bullying can include making fun of kids because of their allergies or exposing them to the things they are allergic to. In these cases, bullying is not just serious, it can mean life or death.

Creating a Safe Environment for Youth with Disabilities

Special considerations are needed when addressing bullying in youth with disabilities. There are resources to help kids with disabilities who are bullied or who bully others. Youth with disabilities often have Individualized Education Programs (IEPs) or Section 504 plans that can be useful in crafting specialized approaches for preventing and responding to bullying. These plans can provide additional services that may be necessary. Additionally, civil-rights laws protect students with disabilities against harassment.

Creating a Safe Environment for Youth with Special Health Needs

Youth with special health needs—such as diabetes requiring insulin regulation, food allergies, or youth with epilepsy—may require accommodations at school. In these cases, they do not require an IEP or Section 504 plan. However, schools can protect students with special health needs from bullying and related dangers. If a child with special health needs has a medical reaction, teachers should address the medical situation first before responding to the bullying. Educating kids and teachers about students' special health needs and the dangers associated with certain actions and exposures can help keep kids safe.

Federal Civil-Rights Laws and Youth with Disabilities

When bullying is directed at a child because of her or his established disability and it creates a hostile environment at school, bullying behavior may cross the line and become "disability harassment." Under Section 504 of the Rehabilitation Act of 1973 and Title II of the Americans with Disabilities Act (ADA) of 1990, the school must address the harassment.

Bullying Prevention for Children with Special Healthcare Needs

Having special healthcare needs due to neurological, developmental, physical, and mental-health conditions can add to the challenges children and teens face as they learn to navigate social situations in school and in life. While bullying and cyberbullying is an unfortunate reality for many young people, children with special healthcare needs are at greater risk for being targeted by their peers.

One reason children and young adults with special healthcare needs might be at higher risk for bullying is lack of peer support. Having friends who are respected by peers can prevent and protect against bullying. Ninety-five percent of 6- to 21-year-old students with disabilities were served in public schools in 2013. However, children with special healthcare needs may have difficulty getting around the school, trouble communicating and navigating social interactions, or may show signs of vulnerability and emotional distress. These challenges can make them be perceived as different, and increase their risk of aggression from peers.

Young people with special needs may benefit from, both individualized and class-wide approaches to address the specific effects of their condition and prevent them from becoming the target or perpetrator of bullying. Teachers, school staff, and other students need to understand the specific impairments of a child's health condition, so that they can develop strategies and supports to help them participate and succeed in class and with their peers.

Potential Perceived Differences

Children and youth with special needs are impacted by their conditions in a variety of ways. Every child is unique, and so are the ways that their health condition affects them. Some impairments, such as brain injuries or neurological conditions, can impact a child's understanding of social interactions and they may not even know when they are being bullied. Here are a few ways that disabilities may affect children:

- Children and youth with cerebral palsy (CP), spina bifida, or other neurological or physical conditions can struggle with physical coordination and speech.

- Brain injuries can impair speech, movement, comprehension, and cognitive abilities or any combination of these. A child or youth with a brain injury may have trouble with body movements, or speaking in a way that others can understand. It could take them longer to understand what is being said or to respond.

- Children and young people with autism spectrum disorder (ASD), attention deficit hyperactivity disorder (ADHD), and Tourette syndrome (TS) may have difficulties with social interactions, sensitivities, impulsivity, and self-regulating their behavior or effectively communicating.

- A child or young person who experiences anxiety or depression or who has a mental-health condition may be withdrawn, quiet, fearful, anxious, or vulnerable. They may exhibit intense social awkwardness or have difficulty speaking.

- Children who have epilepsy or behavioral disorders may exhibit erratic or unusual behavior that makes them stand out among their peers.

Supporting Special Needs and Preventing Bullying at School

Strategies to address a student's special needs at school can also help to prevent bullying and have positive outcomes for all students, especially tactics that use a team approach, foster peer relationships, and help students develop empathy. Some strategies include:

- Engaging students in developing high-interest activities in which everyone has a role to play in designing, executing, or participating in the activity

- Providing general upfront information to peers about the kinds of support children with special needs require, and have adults facilitate peer support

- Creating a buddy system for children with special needs

- Involving students in adaptive strategies in the classroom so that they participate in assisting and understanding the needs of others

- Conducting team-based learning activities and rotate student groupings

- Implementing socioemotional learning activities

- Rewarding positive, helpful, inclusive behavior

Peer Support Makes a Difference

Here are a few examples of innovative strategies used by schools to promote peer-to-peer learning, foster relationships, and prevent bullying:

- One high school created a weekly lunch program where students with and without special healthcare needs sat and ate lunch together. Several senior students led the group and invited their friends to join. All kinds of students participated. The students got to know each other through question-and-answer periods and discussions over lunch. They discovered things they had in common and formed friendships. A group of them went to the prom together.

- Youth at one school held a wheelchair soccer night. Students with special healthcare needs that used wheelchairs coached their peers in how to use and navigate the wheelchairs to play. The students helped another peer who used a wheelchair who was interested in photography by mounting a digital camera on her chair so she could be the game photographer.

- Another school created a club rule that required clubs to rotate leadership responsibilities in club meetings so that every member had a chance to run the group. This allowed students with special healthcare needs to take on leadership roles.

Peer support is an important protective factor against bullying. By working together, teachers, parents, and students can develop peer education, team-building, and leadership activities that foster friendships, build empathy, and prevent bullying to make schools safer and more inclusive for all students, including children with special healthcare needs.

Chapter 26

Hazing

Hazing is when a person who wants to join a group is expected to do things that are very embarrassing, dangerous, or illegal. The group might be a club, sorority, fraternity, or team, for example. People sometimes think hazing is just a harmless part of joining a group. But, hazing can really hurt someone physically and emotionally.

Hazing can take many forms. Examples of hazing can include the following:

- Making someone stay awake for many hours

- Yelling, swearing, or insulting someone

- Forcing someone to wear very embarrassing clothes

- Telling someone they have to eat disgusting things

- Physical beatings

- Pressuring someone to drink a lot of alcohol

- Making someone get a tattoo

What Are the Warning Signs of Hazing?

Here are some possible signs of hazing:

- You have heard from friends about a group using hazing.

About This Chapter: Text in this chapter begins with excerpts from "Hazing versus Bullying," girlshealth.gov, Office on Women's Health (OWH), April 15, 2014. Reviewed August 2019; Text beginning with the heading "Hazed Become the Hazers—Time to Break the Tradition" is excerpted from "Hazing and Alcohol: Time to Break with 'Tradition,'" National Institute on Drug Abuse (NIDA) for Teens, April 10, 2015. Reviewed August 2019.

- You feel a knot in your stomach.

- You have been warned by teachers or other adults that the group is dangerous.

- You have seen the group push others to do things that you believe are wrong or dangerous.

- You feel afraid to break away from the group.

- The group leaders are very mean.

- The group leaders do things that do not seem right and then make you promise not to tell anyone.

What Can I Do to Stay Safe from Hazing?

If you are concerned about hazing, try to find out if a group is known for having mean rituals. If you think you are going to a place where you might be hazed, have a plan to stay safe. Stick together with friends you trust, and make sure you have a way to get home safely.

If you are being hazed, tell an adult. Some states have laws against hazing. Remember, no one has a right to hurt you or pressure you to do something that feels wrong!

Hazed Become the Hazers—Time to Break the Tradition

We all want to belong. Whether it is to the chess club or the football team or a sorority or fraternity, belonging to a group of people who are bonded together gives us the feeling that we are not alone. In high school, and especially in college, when people leave their hometowns and are trying to fit into a new environment, these clubs can feel like a lifeline. And for many people, these groups become like family—you can be a "Sorority Sister" and "Fraternity Brother."

But, what is the cost of joining? All too often, it is going through an embarrassing and potentially dangerous initiation ritual—known as "hazing."

Hazing can often be confidentially reported to school officials. There is also a national, toll-free, antihazing hotline at 888-NOT-HAZE (888-668-4293). Not sure if it is hazing? Call anyway. Ask yourself whether you would tell a potential member about the activity before they joined.

Basically, hazing is when an organized group participates in activities that involve harassment, humiliation, and/or physical and emotional abuse as a way of letting someone join their club, team, organization, etc. Hazing can be violent and it can cause serious physical harm, including death in extreme cases. Some typical forms of hazing include:

- Drinking games (which often involve having people drink a lot of alcohol very quickly)

- Sleep deprivation, kidnapping, beating a person up, or sexual abuse

- Enduring harsh weather without proper clothing

- Branding, tattooing, or piercing

- Walking a "gauntlet" of people who have battering sticks and weapons

More than 50 percent of college students and 47 percent of high-school students involved in clubs, teams, and organizations experience hazing. It is passed down from class to class. The hazed become the hazers and the cycle of bad behavior continues.

Since 1970, at least one college student dies in the United States each year because of an initiation gone wrong. Studies have found that, in college, making people drink too much alcohol is the most common form of hazing. Alcohol also makes it easier to haze. Being drunk helps those who are doing the hazing feel less bad about abusing the new pledges.

Stand Up against Hazing

There is no shame in saying "no" or standing up for yourself—but it is usually easier to do before the hazing begins. Learn as much as you can about the pledging process for the group you want to join. Know that not every club, group, or house is going to ask you to do the same things. While it is true that most people survive the pledging or initiation process, it is equally true that, for some people, the beatings or binge drinking have led to deaths.

Ideally, you will find a group whose initiation is not about humiliation. After all, do you really want to be part of a group that purposely hurts new members? Or tries to make them physically sick? Or that has racist chants? Or sexist websites?

Team-building and other bonding exercises do not have to be negative. Lots of groups organize other activities that people have to do to join the group—but it does not cost them their dignity or risk their health or well-being. These include:

- Doing community service

- Going out for group events

- Playing recreational games/sports

- Organizing a fundraising event

- Completing a ropes course, leadership courses, or other similar activities

- Tutoring or mentoring

This list goes on and on—because there are always better alternatives to bullying, or hazing, or any form of abuse. And maybe it has been a "tradition" to be hurtful and hateful—but we are not alone in thinking that it is time to break these traditions.

How to Help Someone Who Has Passed Out

Check four "PUBS" signs to determine if the situation is an emergency:

- Puking (while passed out)

- Unresponsive to stimulation (pinch or shake)

- Breathing (slow, shallow, or no breathing)

- Skin (blue, cold, or clammy)

If even one of these signs is present, call 911. Do not wait—call 911.

And never leave someone alone to "sleep it off." If someone has passed out, they have had a dangerous amount of alcohol and they should be monitored to make sure none of the symptoms mentioned occur.

Alcohol is also one of the ways people die from hazing. It is what killed 18-year-old college freshman Lynn Gordon Bailey ("Gordie"). He participated in a hazing ritual that involved drinking too much alcohol, and three weeks into his first year at college, he died from that ritual. Gordie was not a small guy—he was an athlete. Probably no one would have thought when they looked at him that he would die from drinking too much. But, no matter how fit you are, if you drink too much alcohol too quickly for your body to process, your vital organs can shut down, and you can die. Hearing Gordie's story may help people to think about what could have been done differently.

Chapter 27

Youth Gangs

What Is a Gang?

There is no universally agreed-upon definition of a "gang" in the United States. "Gang," "youth gang," and "street gang" are terms widely and often interchangeably used in mainstream coverage. Reference to gangs often implies youth gangs. In some cases, youth gangs are distinguished from other types of gangs; how youth is defined may vary as well.

Motorcycle gangs, prison gangs, hate groups, adult organized-crime groups, terrorist organizations, and other types of security-threat groups are frequently but not always treated separately from gangs in both practice and research.

Gangs and Gang Crime

Gang members engage in a higher level of serious and violent crime than their nongang-involved peers. Research about gangs is often intertwined with research about gun violence and drug crime. It is clear that gangs, guns, drugs, and violence are interconnected.

When communities assess their gun-violence problem, they often uncover a gang-violence problem. Communities that recognize the unique challenges associated with reducing gangs and related crime problems, such as gun violence, become safer and healthier, and maybe more resilient to future crime threats.

About This Chapter: Text under the heading "What Is a Gang?" is excerpted from "What Is a Gang? Definitions," National Institute of Justice (NIJ), U.S. Department of Justice (DOJ), October 27, 2011. Reviewed August 2019; Text under the heading "Gangs and Gang Crime" is excerpted from "Overview of Gangs and Gang Crime," National Institute of Justice (NIJ), U.S. Department of Justice (DOJ), October 27, 2011; Text under the heading "Adverse Effects" is excerpted from "Adverse Effects," Youth.gov, March 6, 2013. Reviewed August 2019.

National Institute of Justice (NIJ)-funded research and initiatives focus on building knowledge about promising practices in preventing gang membership and gang violence.

Programs and other efforts to prevent and reduce gang violence build on what we have learned from past evaluations of similar programs; evaluations can guide the development of better programs for the future.

Evaluations of gang-prevention programs have identified key factors in designing and implementing positive interventions. These factors include:

- Working with the local community

- Engaging city leaders

- Partnering with social service agencies

- Involving community members who have the respect of local gang leaders and members

- Addressing gang-related issues at multiple levels

Interagency collaboration, especially at the local level and across several levels of government, gives civic leaders a multidisciplinary perspective on issues related to preventing gang joining and gang-related crime.

> Violence is a rare occurrence in proportion to all gang activities. It should be noted that violent behavior is not the only behavior in which gang members partake. For the most part, gang members "hang out" and are involved in other normal adolescent social activities, but drinking, drug use, and drug trafficking are also common.
>
> *(Source: "Youth Gangs and Violence," Office of Juvenile Justice and Delinquency Prevention (OJJDP), U.S. Department of Justice (DOJ).)*

Adverse Effects

Youth gang involvement impacts the health and welfare of the individual, as well as that of her or his family, peers, and community.

Youth Involved in Gangs

The numerous consequences stemming from gang involvement can have varying degrees of short- and long-term negative outcomes. Youth who become involved in gangs face the increased risk of:

- Dropping out of school

- Teen parenthood

- Unemployment

- Victimization

- Drug and alcohol abuse

- Committing petty and violent crimes

- Juvenile conviction and incarceration

Further, a youth's involvement with a gang (or gangs) also leads to an increased likelihood of economic hardship and family problems in adulthood, which in turn, contribute to involvement in street crime and/or arrest in adulthood. Research has suggested that the longer an adolescent stays in a gang the more disruption she or he will experience while transitioning into adulthood and in adulthood itself.

Impact on Communities

Large communities, those with a population over 50,000, are at the greatest risk of significant gang activity, and community members face heightened fear that they, their families, schools, or businesses, will become victims of theft and/or violence. Further, communities with gang activity are disproportionately affected by theft, negative economic impact, vandalism, assault, gun violence, illegal drug trade, and homicide.

Impact on Society

On the societal level, youth gang involvement costs local, state, and federal governments a substantial amount of money in prevention, response, incarceration, and rehabilitation efforts. It has been estimated that overall crime in the United States costs taxpayers $655 billion annually with a substantial amount of this crime attributed to gang activity.

Chapter 28

Hate Crimes

What Is a Hate Crime?

Figure 28.1. Hate Crime

In the simplest terms, a hate crime must include both "hate" and a "crime."

Hate

The term "hate" can be misleading. When used in a hate-crime law, the word "hate" does not mean rage or anger or general dislike. It means bias against persons with specific characteristics that are defined by the relevant law.

Most hate-crime laws cover crimes committed because of race, color, and religion. Many also prohibit crimes committed on the basis of perceived or actual disability, gender, gender identity, and sexual orientation.

About This Chapter: Text beginning with the heading "What Is a Hate Crime?" is excerpted from "Learn about Hate Crimes," U.S. Department of Justice (DOJ), October 28, 2018; Text under the heading "Hate Crime Statistics" is excerpted from "Hate Crime Statistics," U.S. Department of Justice (DOJ), November 28, 2018.

Crime

The "crime" in hate crime is often a violent crime, such as assault, murder, arson, vandalism, or threats to commit such crimes. It may also cover conspiring or asking another person to commit such crimes, even if the crime was never carried out.

Under the First Amendment of the U.S. Constitution, people cannot be prosecuted simply for their beliefs. Many people may be very offended or upset about beliefs that are untrue or based upon false stereotypes. However, it is not a crime to express offensive beliefs or to join with others who share such views. On the other hand, the First Amendment does not permit anyone to commit a crime, just because that conduct is rooted in philosophical beliefs.

Why Do We Have Hate-Crime Laws?

Hate crimes have a broader effect than most other kinds of violent crime. A hate crime victimizes not only the immediate target but also impacts every member of the group that the direct victim represents. Hate crimes affect families, communities, and sometimes the entire nation.

On average, U.S. residents experienced an estimated 250,000 hate-crime victimizations each year between 2004 and 2015. Most of these were not reported to law enforcement.

Hate-Crime Statistics

The Federal Bureau of Investigation's (FBI) Uniform Crime Reporting (UCR) Program serves as the national repository for crime data collected by law enforcement. Its primary objective is to generate reliable information for use in law-enforcement administration, operation, and management. Reported yearly, the 2017 data, submitted by 16,149 law-enforcement agencies (up 5.9 percent from 15,254 agencies in 2016), provide information about the offenses, victims, offenders, and locations of hate crimes. Of these agencies, 2,040 reported 7,175 hate-crime incidents involving 8,437 offenses.

Victims of Hate Crime Incidents

- 7,106 single-bias incidents involved 8,493 victims
- The 69 multiple-bias incidents involved 335 victims

Offenses by Crime Category

Among the 8,437 hate crime offenses reported:

- Crimes against persons: 60.3 percent
- Crimes against property: 36.9 percent
- Crimes against society: 2.8 percent

Known Offenders

Of the 6,370 known offenders:

- 50.7 percent were White
- 21.3 percent were Black or African American
- 19.1 percent race unknown

Other races accounted for the remaining known offenders.

Of the 5,131 known offenders for whom ethnicity was reported:

- 25.0 percent were not Hispanic or Latino
- 8.8 percent were Hispanic or Latino
- 1.6 percent were in a group of multiple ethnicities
- 64.5 ethnicity unknown

Of the 4,895 known offenders for whom ages were known:

- 83.0 percent were 18 years of age or older

Location Type

Law-enforcement agencies may specify the location of an offense within a hate-crime incident as 1 of 46 location designations.

- Most hate crime incidents, 27.5 percent, occurred in or near residences/homes
- 17.9 percent occurred on highways/roads/alleys/streets/sidewalks
- 10.5 percent occurred at schools/colleges
- 5.8 percent happened in parking/drop lots/garages
- 4.1 percent took place in churches/synagogues/templates/mosques
- The location was reported as other/unknown of 11.5 percent of hate-crime incidents

The remaining 23.7 percent of hate-crime incidents took place at other or multiple locations.

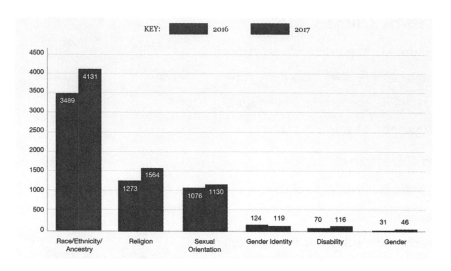

Figure 28.2. Single-Bias Incident, Bias Motivation by Category

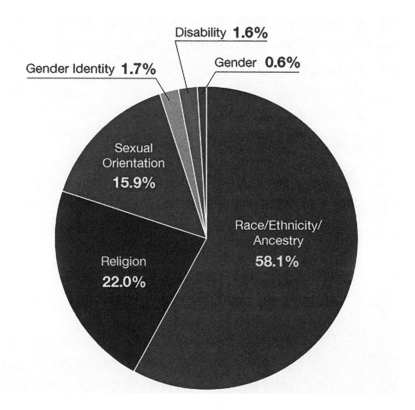

Figure 28.3. Bias-Motivation Categories for Single-Bias Incidents in 2017

Chapter 29

School Violence and Effects of School-Violence Exposure

School violence is youth violence that occurs on school property, on the way to or from school or school-sponsored events, or during a school-sponsored event. A young person can be a victim, a perpetrator of, or a witness to school violence. School violence may also involve or impact adults. Youth violence includes various behaviors. Some violent acts—such as bullying, pushing, and shoving—can cause more emotional harm than physical harm. Other forms of violence, such as gang violence and assault (with or without weapons), can lead to serious injury or even death.

Why Is School Violence a Public-Health Problem?

School associated violent deaths are rare.

- 31 homicides of school-age youth, ages 5 to 18 years, occurred at school during the 2012 to 2013 school year.

- Of all youth homicides, less than 2.6 percent occur at school, and this percentage has been relatively stable for the past decade.

In 2014, there were about 486,400 nonfatal violent victimizations at school among students 12 to 18 years of age.

About This Chapter: Text in this chapter begins with excerpts from "Understanding School Violence," Centers for Disease Control and Prevention (CDC), 2016. Reviewed August 2019; Text beginning with the heading "What Are the Short- and Long-Term Health Effects?" is excerpted from "School Violence Fact Sheet," Education Resources Information Center (ERIC), U.S. Department of Education (ED), 2008. Reviewed August 2019.

Approximately nine percent of teachers report that they have been threatened with injury by a student from their school; five percent of schoolteachers reported that they had been physically attacked by a student from their school.

In 2013, 12 percent of students ages 12 to 18 reported that gangs were present at their school during the school year.

In a 2015 nationally representative sample of youth in grades 9 to 12:

- 7.8 percent reported being in a physical fight on school property in the 12 months before the survey.

- 5.6 percent reported that they did not go to school on one or more days in the 30 days before the survey because they felt unsafe at school or on their way to or from school.

- 4.1 percent reported carrying a weapon (gun, knife or club) on school property on one or more days in the 30 days before the survey.

- 6.0 percent reported being threatened or injured with a weapon on school property one or more times in the 12 months before the survey.

- 20.2 percent reported being bullied on school property and 15.5 percent reported being bullied electronically during the 12 months before the survey.

How Does School Violence Affect Health?

Deaths resulting from school violence are only part of the problem. Many young people experience nonfatal injuries. Some of these injuries are relatively minor and include cuts, bruises, and broken bones. Other injuries, like gunshot wounds and head trauma, are more serious and can lead to permanent disability.

Not all injuries are visible. Exposure to youth violence and school violence can lead to a wide array of negative health behaviors and outcomes, including alcohol and drug use and suicide. Depression, anxiety, and many other psychological problems, including fear, can result from school violence.

Who Is at Risk for School Violence?

A number of factors can increase the risk of a youth engaging in violence at school. However, the presence of these factors does not always mean that a young person will become an offender.

Risk factors for school and youth violence include:

- Prior history of violence

- Drug, alcohol, or tobacco use

- Association with delinquent peers

- Poor family functioning

- Poor grades in school

- Poverty in the community

How Can We Prevent School Violence?

The goal is to stop school violence from happening in the first place. Several prevention strategies have been identified.

- Universal, school-based prevention programs can significantly lower rates of aggression and violent behavior. These programs are delivered to all students in a school or grade level. They teach about various topics and develop skills, such as emotional self-awareness and control, positive social skills, problem solving, conflict resolution, and teamwork.

Funding Provisions: Community-Oriented Policing Services (COPS)

The School Violence Prevention Program (SVPP) provides funding directly to states, units of local government, Indian tribes, and public agencies (school districts, police departments, sheriff's departments, etc.) to be used to improve security at schools and on school grounds in the grantees' jurisdictions through evidence-based school-safety programs that may include one or more of the following:

- Coordination with local law enforcement

- Training for local law-enforcement officers to prevent school violence against others and self

- Placement and use of metal detectors, locks, lighting, and other deterrent measures

- Acquisition and installation of technology for expedited notification of local law-enforcement during an emergency

- Any other measure that, in the determination of the director of the COPS Office, may provide a significant improvement in security

(Source: "2019 COPS Office STOP School Violence: School Violence Prevention Program," Office of Community Oriented Policing Services (COPS), U.S. Department of Justice (DOJ).)

- Parent- and family-based programs can improve family relations and lower the risk for violence by children, especially when the programs are started early. These programs provide parents with education about child development and teach skills to communicate and solve problems in nonviolent ways.

- Street outreach programs can significantly reduce youth violence. These programs connect trained staff with at-risk youth to conduct conflict mediation, make service referrals, and change beliefs about the acceptability of violence.

How Does the Centers for Disease Control and Prevention Approach Prevention?

The Centers for Disease Control and Prevention (CDC) uses a four-step approach to address public-health problems like school violence:

Step 1: Define the Problem

Before we can prevent school violence, we need to know how big the problem is, where it is, and who it affects. The CDC learns about a problem by gathering and studying data. These data are critical because they help know where prevention is most needed.

Step 2: Identify Risk and Protective Factors

It is not enough to know that school violence affects certain students in certain areas. We also need to know why. The CDC conducts and supports research to answer this question. We can then develop programs to reduce or get rid of risk factors and to increase protective factors.

Step 3: Develop and Test Prevention Strategies

Using information gathered in research, the CDC develops and evaluates strategies to prevent school violence.

Step 4: Ensure Widespread Adoption

In this final step, the CDC shares the best prevention strategies. The CDC may also provide funding or technical help so communities can adopt these strategies.

What Does the Centers for Disease Control and Prevention Do to Prevent School Violence?

The CDC leads many activities that help to understand and effectively prevent school violence. Some of these activities include:

- **Youth Risk Behavior Surveillance System (YRBSS).** The YRBSS monitors health-risk behaviors among youth, including physical fighting, bullying, weapon carrying, and suicide. Data are collected every 2 years and provide nationally representative information about youth in grades 9 to 12.
  www.cdc.gov/healthyyouth/data/yrbs/index.htm

- **Understanding School Violence School-Associated Violent Death Study.** The CDC leads a collaboration with the U.S. Department of Education (ED) and the U.S. Department of Justice (DOJ) to monitor school-associated violent deaths at the national level.
  www.cdc.gov/ViolencePrevention/youthviolence/schoolviolence/SAVD.html

- **School Health Policies and Practices Study (SHPPS).** The SHPPS is a national survey that assesses policies and practices at the state, district, school, and classroom levels. Eight elements of school health are assessed, including approaches to keep a school environment safe and to prevent violence.
  www.cdc.gov/healthyyouth/shpps

- **Health Curriculum Analysis Tool (HECAT).** The HECAT contains guidance, appraisal tools, and resources to help schools conduct an analysis of health education curricula based on the National Health Education Standards (NHES) and CDC's Characteristics of an Effective Health Education Curriculum. The results can help schools select or develop curricula to address a number of topics, including violence prevention.
  www.cdc.gov/healthyyouth/hecat

- **School Health Index (SHI).** The SHI is a self-assessment and planning tool that schools can use to improve their health and safety policies and programs. Five topics are covered, including violence.
  www.cdc.gov/healthyschools/shi/index.htm

- **National Centers for Excellence on Youth Violence Prevention (YVPCs).** Through collaborations between researchers and local organizations (including the local health

department), the YVPCs work with high-risk communities to carry out and evaluate a multifaceted, science-based approach for reducing youth violence.
www.cdc.gov/violenceprevention/ace

- **Guide to Community Preventive Services.** The Community Guide is a resource for systematic reviews of research and recommendations about what works to improve public health. Examination of youth violence-prevention strategies have included firearm laws, therapeutic foster care, universal school-based violence-prevention programs, and transfer of juveniles to adult courts.
www.thecommunityguide.org

- **Striving To Reduce Youth Violence Everywhere (STRYVE).** The CDC's national STRYVE initiative provides information, training, and tools to help increase public-health leadership in preventing youth violence, promote the widespread use of evidence-based prevention strategies, and reduce national rates of youth violence.
www.cdc.gov/violenceprevention/stryve

School Violence Prevention Program

- The Office of Community-Oriented Policing Services (COPS Office) has long demonstrated a commitment to school safety and to ensuring students' success in supportive, safe environments.

- The COPS Office STOP School Violence: School Violence-Prevention Program (SVPP) is a competitive award program designed to provide funding to improve security at schools and on school grounds in the grantees' jurisdictions through evidence-based school-safety programs.

- For FY 2018, the COPS Office awarded more than $24 million in SVPP funds to 91 agencies benefiting more than 5,000 schools and 3 million students.

- For information about programs and resources, call the COPS Office Response Center at 800-421-6770 or visit the COPS Office website at www.cops.usdoj.gov.

(Source: "2019 COPS Office STOP School Violence: School Violence Prevention Program," Office of Community Oriented Policing Services (COPS), U.S. Department of Justice (DOJ).)

What Are the Short- and Long-Term Health Effects?

School-associated violent deaths are only part of the problem. A number of students seek medical care for nonfatal, violence-related injuries. Some of these injuries are relatively minor and include cuts, bruises, and broken bones. Other injuries, such as gunshot wounds and head trauma, are more serious and can lead to permanent disability.

Not all injuries are visible. Depression, anxiety, and many other psychological problems, including fear, can result from school violence. In 2005, 6 percent of high-school students participating in a nationwide survey reported that they did not go to school on one or more of the previous 30 days because they feared for their safety. Student fears about safety increased between 1993 and 2005, but have not changed significantly since 2005. Another study found that as many as 160,000 students go home early on any given day because they are afraid of being bullied.

What Are the Risk Factors for Perpetrating Youth Violence?

Research on youth violence has increased understanding of the factors that make some populations more likely to commit violent acts. Having such risk factors increases the likelihood that a young person will become violent, but these factors are not necessarily the direct causes of youth or school violence. Such risk factors include:

Individual Risk Factors

- History of violent victimization
- Attention deficits, hyperactivity, or learning disorders (ADHD)
- History of early aggressive behavior
- Association with delinquent peers
- Involvement in gangs
- Involvement with drugs, alcohol, or tobacco
- Low intelligence quotient (IQ)
- Poor academic performance
- Low commitment to school or school failure
- Poor behavioral control
- Deficits in social, cognitive, or information-processing abilities
- High emotional distress

- Antisocial beliefs and attitudes

- Social rejection by peers

- Exposure to violence and conflict in the family

- Lack of involvement in conventional activities

Relationship Risk Factors

- Harsh, lax, or inconsistent disciplinary practices

- Low parental involvement

- Low emotional attachment to parents or caregivers

- Low parental education and income

- Parental substance abuse or criminality

- Poor family functioning (e.g., communication)

- Poor monitoring and supervision of children

Community/Societal Risk Factors

- Diminished economic opportunities

- High concentrations of poor residents

- High level of transiency

- High level of family disruption

- Low levels of community participation

- Socially disorganized neighborhoods

Chapter 30

Teen Firearm Violence

Gun Violence and Youth

Youths in the United States can be involved with violence as perpetrators, victims, or witnesses/bystanders. Violence is the "intentional use of physical force or power, threatened or actual, against oneself, another person, or against a group or community, that either results in or has a high likelihood of resulting in injury, death, psychological harm, maldevelopment, or deprivation." Applying this definition to the scope of this literature review, youth gun violence is when a gun or firearm is present in the process of youth (ages 10 to 24) intentionally using force or power to threaten or harm others. A youth is a victim of gun violence when she or he is injured or killed as a consequence of someone (a youth or an adult) intentionally using a gun to threaten or harm someone (whether the youth victim was the intended target or not). This chapter focuses on intentional gun violence involving youths ages 10 to 24, which includes homicides (victimization and perpetration), nonfatal injuries, suicides, community violence, and school violence/school shootings. Unintentional gun violence (including accidental injuries or deaths from guns) will not be explored.

Scope of the Problem

The scope of the problem of youth gun violence in the United States is reflected by the incidence and prevalence of gun-related homicides, suicides, and nonfatal injuries of youths. There are as many as 33,000 gun-related deaths every year in the United States, and youths

About This Chapter: This chapter includes text excerpted from "Gun Violence and Youth," Office of Juvenile Justice and Delinquency Prevention (OJJDP), U.S. Department of Justice (DOJ), December 2016. Reviewed August 2019.

24 and younger represent about 20 percent of that number. Even youths who are not hurt or killed by guns but who witness gun violence are likely to experience adverse outcomes later in life. While mass shootings tend to be the focus of national news stories, they account for less than half of 1 percent of gun deaths each year.

Youth Gun Homicide

Homicide was the third-leading cause of death among youths 10 to 24 years old in 2014. This reflects a decline from 1999, when homicide was the second-leading cause of death among youth. Between 1993 and 2010, the firearm homicide rate declined by 51 percent for 18- to 24-year-olds and by 65 percent for 12- to 17-year-olds. Similarly, between 1994 and 2010, serious violent crime against 12- to 17-year-olds involving a firearm declined by 95 percent.

Youth Victims of Gun Homicide

Firearms were the murder weapon in 86 percent of youth homicides in 2014. The following information, using a variety of data sources, provides greater detail on youth homicides attributable to firearms:

- During 2014, homicides with a firearm accounted for 3,702 homicides committed against youths ages 10 to 24.

- Of the 3,702 firearm homicides committed against youth, 68 percent were carried out against African Americans, 19 percent against Hispanics, 12 percent against Whites, and 1 percent against American Indians/Alaskan Natives or Asians/Pacific Islanders.

- Youth firearm-homicide victims are more likely to be male, with 89 percent of homicides against youths ages 10 to 24 in 2014 committed against males.

- Youths ages 15 to 24 experienced a higher rate of homicides with a firearm than any other age group, at about 8.2 per 100,000 people.

- During 2009 to 2010, 70 percent of all firearm homicides of 10- to 19-year-olds were committed in the most populous metropolitan statistical areas in the country.

Overall, these trends reflect that youth homicide victims ages 15 to 24 are more likely to be male and African American or Hispanic and to live in highly populous/urban areas of the country.

Youths Who Commit Gun Homicides

Based on the Uniform Crime Report (UCR) Supplementary Homicide Reports (SHRs), there were an estimated 3,374 homicides with a firearm committed by known 12- to 24-year-olds in 2014.

- Of the estimated 3,374 homicides committed by known youths, 70 percent of the cases involved an African American individual, 27 percent of cases involved a White individual, and 1 percent were American Indians, Alaskan Natives, Asians, or Pacific Islanders. The UCR SHR demographic data cannot be broken down by ethnicity (Hispanic versus non-Hispanic).

- Males accounted for more than 90 percent of the known 12- to 24-year-olds who committed homicide with a firearm in 2014.

- The estimated number of firearm-related homicides committed by known juvenile offenders (ages 12 to 17) more than quadrupled between 1984 and 1994, from 543 to 2,271. However, between 1994 and 2001 the rate of firearm-related homicides committed by juveniles declined. Firearm-related homicides by juveniles increased by 50 percent from 2001 to 2007, but decreased from 2007 to 2014 by 39 percent.

Overall, these trends reflect that the majority of firearm-related homicides involving known youths are perpetrated by males and African Americans.

Nonfatal Gun Violence

There is conflicting information about whether the trend in nonfatal firearm-related violence has been increasing or decreasing over time. Data from the Centers for Disease Control and Prevention (CDC)—which is primarily based on reports from U.S. emergency departments—indicate that nonfatal gunshot injuries (specifically rates of assaults and self-harm) are increasing. However, data from the Bureau of Justice Statistics' (BJS) National Crime Victimization Survey (NCVS) suggest there has been a decline in the rates of nonfatal firearm victimizations of youths, which includes victimization reports in which the offender had shown or used a firearm. Using available data from these sources, the following trends emerge when the scope is limited to those ages 12 to 17 and 18 to 24:

- According to CDC (2016) estimates, there was a roughly 7 percent increase in the rate of nonfatal firearm gunshot injuries for youths ages 12 to 17 from 2001 to 2014 (from 21.1 to 22.6 per 100,000) and a 20 percent increase for youths ages 18 to 24 (from 59.5 to 71.2 per 100,000).

- In contrast, the NCVS reported that the rate for nonfatal firearm victimizations against youths 12 to 17 declined by about 36 percent between 2001 and 2011 (from 2.2 to 1.4 per 1,000). Further, the rate declined by about 24 percent for 18- to 24-year-olds during the same period (from 6.8 to 5.2 per 1,000).

Disparities between these two data sources could explain the differences between the reported trends. Planty and Truman acknowledge the differences in NCVS and CDC trend data. Their report notes that NCVS is a residential household survey and does not include hidden populations such as those who are homeless or institutionalized (e.g., jails or mental-health facilities). Further, some of the CDC estimates used to calculate injury trends may be based on small sample sizes and should be interpreted with caution.

Youth Gun Suicide

According to the CDC's National Vital Statistics System (NVSS), suicide was the 10th leading cause of death in the United States in 2014; however, it was the second-leading cause of death in youths 10 to 24 years old. This is in contrast to suicide's rank as the third-leading cause of death among youths 10 to 24 in 1999, showing that, while homicides may be decreasing for youths, suicides are increasing.

- Of the 5,504 youths ages 10 to 24 who died by suicide in 2014, almost half (2,444) were carried out with a firearm.

- Of the 2,444 suicides with a firearm by youths 10 to 24 years old in 2014, 76 percent were White, 10 percent were African American, 10 percent were Hispanic, and 4 percent were by American Indians, Alaskan Natives, Asians, and Pacific Islanders.

- Males ages 10 to 24 years old (88%) were more likely than their female counterparts to kill themselves with a firearm (12%).

Overall, the numbers suggest that the majority of suicides committed by 10- to 24-year-olds are male and White.

Community Gun Violence

While youths can be directly exposed to gun violence—through victimization or perpetration—they can also be indirectly exposed, by witnessing gun violence in their communities. Youths who witness gun violence experience similar negative psychological and physical harm as youths who have had direct exposure.

There are various forms of violence that youths may witness in their lifetimes, including assaults, physical abuse, thefts, and shootings. According to the National Survey of Children's Exposure to Violence (NatSCEV) (conducted in 2014), about 38 percent of children age 17 and younger have witnessed violence in the family or the community in their lifetimes. With regard to specific exposure to gun violence:

- About 8 percent of children reported being exposed to a shooting (including hearing gunshots or seeing someone shot) in their lifetimes, with children 14 to 17 years reporting the highest levels of exposure to a shooting (13%). Additionally, boys were more likely than girls to report exposure to shootings.

- Youth exposure to shootings has decreased between 2008 and 2014, although this change has been minimal.

- Youths are more likely to witness assault in their communities in their lifetimes than to be exposed to a shooting (28% compared with 8%, respectively).

- Although the national level of youth exposure to shootings is low, violent crimes in urban areas are more likely to involve guns than those in suburban or rural areas.

Overall, although exposure to gun violence is not as prevalent as other forms of community violence, it is still a potentially traumatic event that many youths will experience in their lifetimes.

School Gun Violence

During the school year of 2011 to 12, school-related homicides accounted for less than 2 percent of all homicides. While school shootings are rare, most homicides against youth at school were committed with a firearm.

- During the 2009 to 2010 school year, there were 1,749 reports of firearm-possession incidents at schools (a rate of 3.5 per 100,000 people). During the 2013 to 2014 school year, this number decreased to 1,501 (a rate of 3.0 per 100,000).

- About 4 percent of students in grades 9 to 12 reported carrying a weapon at least 1 day during the previous 30 days in 2015, a decline from about 12 percent in 1993.

- In 2013, 3.7 percent of students ages 12 to 18 reported having access to a loaded gun without adult permission, either at school or away from school, which is a decrease from 6.7 percent in 2007.

- White male students were more likely to have carried a gun than any other demographic.

School Shootings

According to Stanford's Mass Shootings in America database, there have been an estimated 220 victims in school-related mass shootings, 140 of which were fatalities, from the Columbine High School shooting in 1999 through the Umpqua Community College shooting in 2015.

Bushman and colleagues examined the differences between and similarities of school shooters and street shooters. Overall, they noted that school shooters generally were White, male adolescents from stable, low-crime towns or suburbs, and they generally did not know the people they killed personally. Conversely, street shooters tend to live in densely populated areas with high crime levels and poverty rates, and they tend to aim to hurt or kill individuals they know. In addition, using data from the 2004 Survey of Inmates in State Correctional Facilities (the most recent data available), the report authors found that nearly half of all street shooters under age 18 obtain their weapons from street or black-market sources, 37 percent receive them from a friend or family member, and 13 percent steal them. In contrast, findings from other data sources have shown that more than half of school shooters obtain their weapons from home or a relative.

Youth Risk Behavior Survey Report

- In 2017, 6 percent of students were threatened or injured with a weapon at school.

- 9.4 percent of lesbian, gay, or bisexual students and 11.1 percent students not sure of their sexual identity were threatened or injured with a weapon at school.

- 7.6 percent of students who had sexual contact with only the opposite sex and 12.1 percent of students who had sexual contact with only the same sex or with both sexes were threatened or injured with a weapon at school.

(Source: "Youth Risk Behavior Survey—Data Summary and Trends Report 2007 to 2017," Centers for Disease Control and Prevention (CDC).)

International Comparisons of Youth Gun Violence

In 2012, firearms were involved in nearly 50 percent of all homicides committed worldwide. In addition, according to a World Health Organization (WHO) global status report on violence prevention, 43 percent of annual homicides worldwide involve youths ages 10 to 29 years. Youths are disproportionately affected by homicide regardless of country-level of income; however, the youth homicide rate in the United States is higher than other high-income countries (e.g., Australia, Canada, United Kingdom). For example, in 2003, the firearm homicide rate among U.S. youths ages 15 to 24 was 42 times as high as the rate for youths in similar high-income nations.

Gun Prevalence Compared with Other Weapons

From 2004 through 2013, most violent victimizations committed by adolescents ages 12 to 17 were simple assaults that did not involve a weapon. However, among homicides with a weapon committed by youth, firearms were the weapon of choice.

- According to the SHRs, of the 4,743 reported homicides committed by youths ages 12 to 24 with a weapon in 2014, 71 percent were carried out by firearm. In contrast, about 12 percent were committed with a knife, 6 percent were committed with a personal weapon (e.g., hands, fists, feet), 8 percent were committed with another type (e.g., poison) or unknown weapon, and only 3 percent were committed with a blunt object.

Risk Factors for Youth Gun Violence

A significant body of research suggests that youth engagement in the most serious forms of violence is strongly linked to the convergence and interaction of individual, family, peer, school, and community risk factors. Risk factors are categorized as having the ability to increase the likelihood of youth violence. There is no single risk factor or a specific combination of risk factors that can predict who is more likely to engage in violent behavior. However, the more individual, family, peer, school, and community risk factors present in a youth's life, the greater the probability of youth violence.

Among the known risk factors for youth violence, emotional distress, violence exposure, alcohol use, and peer delinquency have been directly linked to youth gun violence. Of these risk factors, the strongest and most consistent predictor of youth gun violence is the exposure to or a history of violence. In addition, the access to and availability of firearms increase the likelihood of weapon-related violence among youth.

Exposure to Violence

Research suggests there is a cumulative effect of risk factors across individual, family, peer, school, and community domains that increases the probability of youth gun violence. The events and circumstances characteristic of the environment (home, community, and school) have an influence on the development of individual risk factors for gun violence. For example, "Sixty percent of all U.S. youths report exposure to some form of violence in a given year." Exposure to violence refers to direct exposure (personal victimization) or indirect exposure (witnessing or hearing about the victimization of a family member, friend, or neighbor). Studies suggest a significant relationship between exposure to guns and shootings and psychological trauma.

Violence exposure is linked to emotional distress, anxiety, depression, and posttraumatic stress disorder (PTSD). The psychological injuries connected to the exposure to violence are often ignored, but this is problematic since the most significant predictor of future violent behavior for both male and female youths is a history of violence.

Access and Availability to Firearms

Violence exposure and violence commission predict each other over time. Thus, what differentiates youth gun violence from other serious forms of violence is the presence of a firearm. The access and availability of firearms is a facilitating factor in youth gun violence. Youths who have witnessed violence in their environments are more likely to carry weapons and become involved in assaultive behavior. In these instances, violent behavior progresses from physical fighting to more deadly forms, such as gun violence. Part of what enables youths to progress to more deadly forms of violence is related to their access to and the availability of firearms in their homes and communities. Youths who live in homes where firearms are present but not safely stored are more likely to be involved in some form of gun violence. Weapons have become a significant element in the homicide and suicide deaths among teens. Community violence has led to a prevailing fear, among youth, of being shot and of weapon-carrying in self-defense. Consequently, of all risk factors associated with youth violence, exposure to violence and availability of firearms most increase the likelihood of engaging in youth gun violence.

Notably, however, there is significant variation in the impact of risk factors on youths. Certain psychological and biological characteristics—including hyperactivity and antisocial behavior—link male youths to more serious forms of violent behavior than female youths. Female youths who are exposed to violence are more likely to internalize their symptoms and are less likely than male youths to cope in positive manners, leading to other individual risk factors. Whites and Asians tend to witness crime less often than African American and Hispanic youths do. Yet, even when compared with Hispanic youths, Black youths were more vulnerable to violent behavior in that they tended to live in neighborhoods with higher levels of violent crime and were more likely to engage in violent crime themselves. Male youths from all racial and ethnic backgrounds have a greater likelihood of dying from a gunshot wound, compared with all other natural causes combined. Consequently, research suggests that there may be gender, racial, and ethnic differences in the factors that lead to youth gun violence.

Protective Factors against Youth Gun Violence

Resiliency theory indicates that some youths exposed to such risk factors do not develop negative, violent behaviors because of the influence of protective factors. Protective factors are the events, opportunities, and experiences in the lives of youth that lessen or buffer against the probability of violence. Protective factors help youths overcome the negative effects of risk factors and are essential in helping them compensate for or protect against the effects of risk on healthy development.

Parent and School Connectedness

Of these protective factors for serious forms of youth violence, there are two that have been shown to make a slight impact on youth gun violence. Research suggests that parent and school connectedness counterbalance the risk of exposure to, and committing, violence. Parental presence and proper supervision can assist in controlling where and with whom youths spend their time, thus reducing the likelihood of violence exposure. However, parental connectedness may be a significant buffer against violence only for Latinos and not Whites and African Americans. High education aspirations and the physical interventions often found in schools, such as the use of weapon detectors, allow for the development of a safe connection to the school environment. However, high educational aspirations are a protective factor only for Latinos and African Americans, and the effects of school connectedness on exposure to weapon violence may not extend beyond the building walls. Given the racial and ethnic disparities for these protective factors, caution should be taken to avoid generalizing their ability to protect and buffer against youth gun violence for all youth.

Overall, given the paucity of research on risk and protective factors that directly affect youth gun violence, more attention should be paid to this area of research. Knowing what factors increase or decrease the risk for all forms of youth violence is necessary to the process of designing empirically based gun prevention strategies. Concentrated prevention efforts to enhance protective factors, such as parental and school connectedness, may help youth overcome the debilitating effects of risks, such as exposure to violence and the access to and the availability of firearms and ultimately make a significant impact on youth gun violence.

Chapter 31

Terrorism

What Is International Terrorism?

International terrorism is perpetrated by individuals and/or groups inspired by or associated with designated foreign terrorist organizations or nations (state-sponsored), for example, the December 2, 2015, shooting in San Bernardino, CA, that killed 14 people and wounded 22, which involved a married couple who radicalized for some time prior to the attack and were inspired by multiple extremist ideologies and foreign terrorist organizations.

What Is Domestic Terrorism?

Domestic terrorism is perpetrated by individuals and/or groups inspired by or associated with primarily U.S.-based movements that espouse extremist ideologies of a political, religious, social, racial, or environmental nature, for example, the June 8, 2014, Las Vegas shooting, during which two police officers inside a restaurant were killed in an ambush-style attack, which was committed by a married couple who held antigovernment views and who intended to use the shooting to start a revolution.

The Current Threat

The Federal Bureau of Investigation (FBI) is committed to remaining agile in its approach to the terrorism threat, which has continued to evolve significantly since the September 11,

About This Chapter: This chapter includes text excerpted from "Terrorism," Federal Bureau of Investigation (FBI), October 24, 2017.

2001, terror attacks on U.S. soil. The threat landscape has expanded considerably, even though it is important to note that the more traditional threat posed by al Qaeda and its affiliates is still present and active. The threat of domestic terrorism also remains persistent overall, with actors crossing the line from First Amendment protected rights to committing crimes to further their political agenda.

Evolution of the Terrorism-Threat Landscape

The three factors that have contributed to the evolution of the terrorism-threat landscape are:

- **The Internet:** International and domestic actors have developed an extensive presence on the Internet through messaging platforms and online images, videos, and publications, which facilitate the groups' ability to radicalize and recruit individuals receptive to extremist messaging. Such messaging is constantly available to people participating in social networks dedicated to various causes, particularly younger people comfortable with communicating in the social-media environment.

- **Use of Social Media:** In addition to using the Internet, social media has allowed both international and domestic terrorists to gain unprecedented, virtual access to people living in the United States in an effort to enable homeland attacks. The Islamic State of Iraq and Syria (ISIS), in particular, encourages sympathizers to carry out simple attacks where they are located against targets—in particular, soft targets—or to travel to ISIS-held territory in Iraq and Syria and join its ranks as foreign fighters. This message has resonated with supporters in the United States and abroad, and several recent attackers have claimed to be acting on ISIS' behalf.

- **Homegrown Violent Extremists (HVEs):** The FBI, however, cannot focus solely on the terrorist threat emanating from overseas—but also must identify those sympathizers who have radicalized and become HVEs within the United States and aspire to attack our nation from within. HVEs are defined by the Bureau as global jihad-inspired individuals who are based in the United States, have been radicalized primarily in the United States, and are not directly collaborating with a foreign terrorist organization. The FBI is investigating suspected HVEs in every state.

How Citizens Can Protect Themselves and Report Suspicious Activity

It is important for people to protect themselves both online and in-person, and to report any suspicious activity they encounter.

The simplest way to accomplish this is to:

- Remain aware of your surroundings

- Refrain from oversharing personal information

- Say something if you see something

Additional information regarding how to report suspicious activity and protect the community is available via the resources below.

- **Nationwide SAR Initiative (NSI):** The Nationwide Suspicious Activity Reporting (SAR) Initiative is a joint collaborative effort by the U.S. Department of Homeland Security (DHS); the Federal Bureau of Investigation; and state, local, tribal, and territorial law-enforcement partners. This initiative provides law enforcement with another tool to help prevent terrorism and other related criminal activity by establishing a national capacity for gathering, documenting, processing, analyzing, and sharing SAR information.

Reporting Threats and Crime

Members of the public can report violations of U.S. federal law or suspected terrorism or criminal activity as follows:

Contact online

- Use the online tips and public leads form to report information on criminal activity and suspected terrorist threats
- Report cyber crimes by filing a complaint with the Internet Crime Complaint Center (IC3)

Contact via telephone or mail

- Contact your local FBI office or closest international office 24 hours a day, 7 days a week
- Call 800-CALL-FBI (800-225-5324) for the Major Case Contact Center
- Call 866-720-5721 to report fraud, waste, and abuse involving disaster relief to the National Center for Disaster Fraud (NCDF) or write to NCDF, Baton Rouge, LA 70821-4909

- **Community Preparedness Tools:** Businesses are encouraged to connect, plan, train, and report. Applying these four steps prior to an incident or attack can help better prepare businesses and their employees to proactively think about the role they play in the safety and security of their businesses and communities.

If someone is in imminent danger, call 911 or your local police immediately.

Chapter 32

Hurting Yourself

Self-Harm: An Overview

"Self-harm" refers to a person's harming their own body on purpose. About 1 in 100 people hurts themself in this way. More females hurt themselves than males. A person who self-harms usually does not mean to kill themselves. But, they are at higher risk of attempting suicide if they do not get help.

Self-harm tends to begin in the teen or early-adult years. Some people may engage in self-harm a few times and then stop. Others engage in it more often and have trouble stopping.

Many people cut themselves because it gives them a sense of relief. Some people use cutting as a means to cope with a problem. Some teens say that when they hurt themselves, they are trying to stop feeling lonely, angry, or hopeless.

It is possible to overcome the urge to hurt yourself. There are other ways to find relief and cope with your emotions. Counseling may help.

Self-Harm and Cutting

Self-harm, sometimes called "self-injury," is when a person purposely hurts their own body. There are many types of self-injury, and cutting is one type that you may have heard about. If you are hurting yourself, you can learn to stop. Make sure you talk to an adult you trust, and keep reading to learn more.

About This Chapter: Text under the heading "Self-Harm: An Overview" is excerpted from "Self-Harm," MentalHealth.gov, U.S. Department of Health and Human Services (HHS), August 22, 2017; Text under the heading "Self-Harm and Cutting" is excerpted from "Cutting and Self-Harm," girlshealth.gov, Office on Women's Health (OWH), January 7, 2015. Reviewed August 2019.

What Are the Ways People Hurt Themselves?

Some types of injury leave permanent scars or cause serious health problems, sometimes even death. These are some forms of self-injury:

- Cutting yourself (such as using a razor blade, knife, or other sharp object)
- Punching yourself or punching things (like a wall)
- Burning yourself with cigarettes, matches, or candles
- Pulling out your hair
- Poking objects into body openings
- Breaking your bones or bruising yourself
- Poisoning yourself

The Dangers of Self-Injury

Some teens think self-injury is not a big deal, but it is. Self-injury comes with many risks. For example, cutting can lead to infections, scars, and even death. Sharing tools for cutting puts a person at risk of diseases such as human immunodeficiency virus (HIV) and hepatitis. Also, once you start self-injuring, it may be hard to stop. And teens who keep hurting themselves are less likely to learn how to deal with their feelings in healthy ways.

Who Hurts Themselves?

People from all different kinds of backgrounds hurt themselves. Among teens, girls may be more likely to do this than boys.

People of all ages hurt themselves, too, but self-injury most often starts in the teen years.

People who hurt themselves sometimes have other problems, such as depression, eating disorders, drug or alcohol abuse, or repressed memories of abuse.

Why Do Some Teens Hurt Themselves?

Some teens who hurt themselves keep their feelings bottled up inside. The physical pain then offers a sense of relief, like the feelings are getting out. Some people who hold back strong emotions begin to feel like they have no emotions, and the injury helps them to at least feel something.

Some teens say that, when they hurt themselves, they are trying to stop feeling painful emotions such as rage, loneliness, or hopelessness. They may injure to distract themselves from the emotional pain. Or they may be trying to feel some sense of control over what they feel.

If you are depressed, angry, or having a hard time coping, talk with an adult you trust. You also can contact a helpline. Remember, you have a right to be safe and happy!

If you are hurting yourself, please get help. It is possible to get past the urge to hurt yourself. There are other ways to deal with your feelings. You can talk to your parents, your doctor, or another trusted adult, like a teacher or religious leader. Therapy can help you find healthy ways to handle problems.

What Are Signs of Self-Injury in Others?

- Having cuts, bruises, or scars

- Wearing long sleeves or pants even in hot weather

- Making excuses about injuries

- Having sharp objects around for no clear reason

How Can I Help a Friend Who Is Self-Injuring?

If you think a friend may be hurting themself, try to get your friend to talk to a trusted adult. Your friend may need professional help. A therapist can suggest ways to cope with problems without turning to self-injury. If your friend would not get help, you should talk to an adult. This is too much for you to handle alone.

What If Someone Pressures Me to Hurt Myself?

If someone pressures you to hurt yourself, think about whether you really want a friend who tries to cause you pain. Try to hang out with other people who do not treat you this way. Try to hang out with people who make you feel good about yourself.

Chapter 33

Teen Suicide

It is a sad truth that teens sometimes think about ending their lives. If you are feeling awful, you may think that suicide is the only answer—but it is not! Do not let suicide be the ending of your story. People want to help, and you can feel better.

Why Do Some Teens Think about Suicide?

Some teens feel so terrible and overwhelmed that they think life will never get better. Some things that may cause these feelings include:

- The death of someone close

- Having depression or other mental-health issues, such as an eating disorder, attention deficit hyperactivity disorder (ADHD), or anxiety

- Having alcohol or drug problems

- Parents getting divorced

- Seeing a lot of anger and violence at home

- Having a hard time in school

- Being bullied

About This Chapter: Text in this chapter begins with excerpts from "Feeling Suicidal," girlshealth.gov, Office on Women's Health (OWH), January 7, 2015. Reviewed August 2019; Text under the heading "Talking to Your Teenager after a Suicide Attempt in Your Family" is excerpted from "How to Talk to a Teenager about a Suicide Attempt in Your Family," Mental Illness Research, Education and Clinical Centers (MIRECC), U.S. Department of Veterans Affairs (VA), April 19, 2015. Reviewed August 2019.

- Having problems with friends

- Experiencing a trauma like being raped or abused

- Being angry or heartbroken over a relationship breakup

- Feeling like you do not belong, either in your family or with friends

- Feeling rejected because of something about you, such as being gay

- Having an ongoing illness or disability

- Feeling alone

- Feeling guilty or like a burden to other people

Also, teens sometimes may feel very bad for no one clear reason.

If you are suffering, know that things definitely can get better. You can learn ways to handle your feelings. You can work toward a much brighter future.

Turning to others can help you through tough times. If you do not feel a strong connection to relatives or friends, try talking to a school counselor, teacher, doctor, or another adult you trust.

Every teen feels anxiety, sadness, and confusion at some point. The important thing to remember is that life can get much better. There is always help out there for you or a friend.

How Can I Help a Friend Who Has Suicidal Thoughts?

If you think a friend is in immediate danger of suicide, call 911 and do not leave your friend alone.

If you think a friend is considering suicide but you are not sure, you can look for some signs. These include:

- Talking about not wanting to live

- Talking about looking for ways to die, like trying to get pills or a gun

- Talking about feeling hopeless or having no purpose

- Talking about feeling trapped or being in horrible pain

- Talking about being a burden to others

- Abusing drugs or alcohol
- Acting very nervous or on edge
- Doing dangerous things
- Sleeping a lot more than before or very little
- Not wanting to be around other people
- Changing quickly from one strong mood to another
- Doing some type of self-injury, like cutting
- Acting full of rage or talking about getting revenge
- Giving away favorite things

If a friend seems suicidal, ask the person to talk to you about what is going on. Listening shows you care. Remember, though, that you cannot help the person on your own. Encourage your friend to contact a suicide hotline. Suggest that your friend talk to an adult, and possibly offer to go with them.

Even if your friend does not want to talk with an adult, you need to tell one as quickly as possible. This can be a relative, school nurse, counselor, teacher, or coach, for example. If you

Know the Suicide Warning Signs

- Feeling like a burden
- Being isolated
- Increased anxiety
- Feeling trapped or in unbearable pain
- Increased substance use
- Looking for a way to access lethal means
- Increased anger or rage
- Extreme mood swings
- Expressing hopelessness
- Sleeping too little or too much
- Talking or posting about wanting to die
- Making plans for suicide

(Source: "Suicide Rising across the U.S.," Centers for Disease Control and Prevention (CDC).)

are worried that your friend will be mad, remember that you are doing the right thing. You could save your friend's life.

If a friend posts suicidal thoughts online, you can report the post and help the person get support.

What If I Am Thinking about Suicide?

If you are thinking about suicide, get help right away. You can contact the Lifeline helpline by chat, or call 800-273-TALK (800-273-8255). The people there can talk to you about your problems and help you make a plan to stay safe. They also can give you information about ways to get help in person.

If you are in immediate danger of hurting yourself, call 911. You also can go to the nearest hospital emergency department.

Right now, your pain may feel too overwhelming to handle. Suicide may feel like the only way to get relief when you are suffering. But, people get past suicidal thoughts, and things can get better.

You can find ways to feel better. Writing is one way to lower your pain. You might list things that you love or your hopes for the future. You also can hang up photos, messages, and other things that remind you that life is worth living. Also, reach out to people who care about you.

Do not try using drugs or alcohol to feel better. These things will not solve your problems. They will only create more problems.

What If Someone I Know Attempts or Dies by Suicide?

If someone you know attempts or dies by suicide, you may feel like it is your fault in some way. That is not true! You also may feel many different emotions, including anger, grief, or even emotional numbness. All of your feelings are okay. There is no one right or wrong way to feel.

If you are having trouble dealing with your feelings, talk to a trusted adult. You have suffered a terrible loss, but life can feel okay again. Reach out to people who care about you. Connecting is so important at this tough time.

Talking to Your Teenager after a Suicide Attempt in Your Family

It is important to talk to your teenager about the suicide attempt to help them understand what has happened. Without the support of family and friends, they may try to make sense of this confusing situation themself. Sometimes teenagers blame themselves for something they may or may not have done. Teenagers may not want to talk directly about their worries or feelings. Instead, they may show them in other ways. They may isolate, or not talk to their friends out of shame, uneasiness, or fear of being misunderstood or rejected. It is helpful to share a hopeful outlook and, when appropriate, involve your teen in activities that may help make a positive difference.

To Consider If You Should Speak with Your Teenager

- If your teenager was exposed to the crisis and traumatized, they will need some basic understanding of what happened.

- Even if they were not exposed to the suicide attempt, you should share the basics of the attempt with them, including any obvious injuries, and let their questions guide you from there. Help them make sense of what happened in the context of mental illness (and/or substance abuse), and include the support of a mental-health professional in this conversation if you are not familiar with mental illness.

- If marriage or family problems contributed to a suicide attempt, avoid details that would put the teenager in the middle, between parents or other family members.

- If the family member is in the hospital, talk to your teenager as soon as possible.

- The goal is to answer their questions in a calm, nonjudgmental way, so they will not be afraid to ask more questions.

How Should You Talk to Your Teenager?

- Pick a place that is private, where your teenager will feel free to express themselves. Try to provide multiple opportunities to talk, even when a teen seems unresponsive or reluctant.

- Provide a safe space for your teen to express even uncomfortable feelings, including anger. Ask them questions that will help them open up to you.

- Be aware of your own feelings and how you are coming across. Your teenager may be more likely to listen if you appear calm and approachable.

- Keep checking in with your teenager. This will send the message that you are open to answering questions over time. Be honest.

- Offer extra support, affection, and attention during this time (family meals, time together).

- Be prepared to discuss concerns about whether your teenager is at risk for similar behaviors.

Other Ways to Support Your Teenager

- For younger teens, help them keep a healthy structure in their daily routines, such as homework time, dinnertime, and bedtime routines.

- For older teenagers, who are more independent and more likely to structure the majority of their own time, you can talk to and encourage them to practice self-care. "Dad is in the hospital now, but we both would like to see you keep on doing such a good job with your schoolwork. You said it helps you to sleep if you work out after school. Would you like to invite Paul to go with you to the gym this week?"

- While providing stability, also remain flexible to a teenager's needs during a disruptive time.

- Get other support people involved (family, friends or clergy). This will benefit you and, in turn, benefit your teen.

- Although it is normal for many teenagers to avoid parent's affection, do not be surprised if they need more physical comfort during a stressful time.

- Teenagers can regress when stressed and may act like they did during younger stages of development.

- As the parent/relative who has been hospitalized becomes more stable, visiting them in the hospital and attending a family-therapy session with a mental-health professional could be quite helpful and reassuring.

- Show appreciation for your teenager taking on additional tasks while you attend to the relative's needs.

- Teenagers may benefit from discussing boundaries about disclosing information with friends, classmates, and on social-media outlets.

What Do I Say to My Teenager?

- Start with your teen's level of awareness and understanding of the situation. "Last night your brother was having a difficult time. What do you remember?"

- Use your teen's level of understanding and questions about the event as a guide when describing what happened. "As you have noticed, Mom has been feeling depressed lately and drinking alcohol to cope. She felt so down last night that she had some suicidal thoughts and feelings."

- Inform your teenager about emotional struggles and healthy problem-solving and coping strategies. "Grandpa has been very depressed. Sometimes when people feel that way, they can also feel hopeless about the future and they are not able to think of healthy ways to deal with problems. Have you experienced those feelings? How do you cope?"

- Address guilt, blame, shame, and responsibility. "I want you to know that this is not your fault or anyone's fault."

- Assure your teenager that the family member is getting treatment and care. "Dad is getting treatment at the hospital to help him deal with depression, and to connect him with other people who understand his situation and support him as he gets well."

- Let your teen know that their daily routine will stay the same. "Even though it is different that Mom is not here, you will still go to school tomorrow."

- Encourage your teen to express their feelings, and let them know that their reactions are expected and normal. Invite them to ask any questions, and share their thoughts about the situation. "How are you feeling with everything that is going on? Sometimes it can feel like there was something we could or should have done when something like this happens. Have you felt this way? What do you do when that happens?"

- Help create a connection between the teenager and family members. Tell them when they can expect to see the family member again. "Would you like to go with me to visit your sister? She is going to stay in the hospital for a few days. Would you like to e-mail her or send her a card?"

- Allow your teen not to talk if desired, and to choose who they talk to. Discuss how your teen can share information with family and friends. "If you do not want to talk about it now, I understand. Maybe you will feel ready to talk about things in a few days. Your friend Jane has supported you before; do you think it might help to talk with her?"

- Let your teen know you are getting support, and encourage them to find ways to build and rely on their own support system. "I have been talking with Grandma about this, and have also decided to talk to a Psychologist. You can come with me if you like. There are also support groups in town you can join. You could also talk about this with your guidance counselor or your teacher."

- Help your teen prepare for the family member's return if they have spent time in the hospital following a suicide attempt. "Your sister will be ready to leave the hospital on Thursday. Is there anything you would like to talk about or ask me before she comes home?"

> The National Suicide Prevention Lifeline is a 24-hour, toll-free, confidential suicide prevention hotline available to anyone in suicidal crisis or emotional distress. When you call 800-273-TALK (800-273-8255), you are connected to the nearest crisis center in a national network of more than 150 that provide crisis counseling and mental-health referrals day and night. The Lifeline also provides informational materials, such as brochures, wallet cards, posters, and booklets. Translators speaking approximately 150 languages are available.
>
> *(Source: "Preventing Youth Suicide," Youth.gov)*

Chapter 34

Lesbian, Gay, Bisexual, and Transgender Youth and Violence

Most lesbian, gay, and bisexual (LGB) youth are happy and thrive during their adolescent years. Having a school that creates a safe and supportive learning environment for all students and having caring and accepting parents are especially important. Positive environments can help all youth achieve good grades and maintain good mental and physical health. However, some LGB youth are more likely than their heterosexual peers to experience negative health and life outcomes. For youth to thrive in schools and communities, they need to feel socially, emotionally, and physically safe and supported. A positive school climate has been associated with decreased depression, suicidal feelings, substance use, and unexcused school absences among LGB students.

Lesbian, Gay, and Bisexual Youth Experiences with Violence

Compared with other students, negative attitudes toward LGB persons may put these youth at increased risk for experiences with violence. "Violence" can include behaviors, such as bullying, teasing, harassment, and physical assault. (Note, less data is available for transgender youth in this area.)

According to data from the 2015 national Youth Risk Behavior Survey (YRBS), the Youth Risk Behavior Surveillance System (YRBSS) monitors six categories of health-related behaviors that contribute to the leading causes of death and disability among youth and adults:

- Behaviors that contribute to unintentional injuries and violence

About This Chapter: This chapter includes text excerpted from "LGBT Youth," Centers for Disease Control and Prevention (CDC), June 21, 2017.

- Sexual behaviors related to unintended pregnancy and sexually transmitted diseases, including human immunodeficiency virus (HIV) infection

- Alcohol and other drug use

- Tobacco use

- Unhealthy dietary behaviors

- Inadequate physical activity

The YRBSS also measures the prevalence of obesity and asthma and other health-related behaviors plus sexual identity and sex of sexual contacts.

The YRBSS includes a national school-based survey conducted by the Centers for Disease Control and Prevention (CDC) and state, territorial, tribal, and local surveys conducted by state, territorial, and local education and health agencies and tribal governments. Data from the YRBSS of LGB students report findings such as:

- 10 percent were threatened or injured with a weapon on school property

- 34 percent were bullied on school property

- 28 percent were bullied electronically

- 23 percent of LGB students who had dated or gone out with someone during the 12 months before the survey had experienced sexual dating violence in the prior year

- 18 percent of LGB students had experienced physical dating violence

- 18 percent of LGB students had been forced to have sexual intercourse at some point in their lives

Effects on Education and Mental Health

Exposure to violence can have negative effects on the education and health of any young person and may account for some of the health-related disparities between LGB and heterosexual youth. According to the 2015 YRBS, LGB students were 140 percent (12% versus 5%) more likely to not go to school at least one day during the 30 days prior to the survey because of safety concerns, compared with heterosexual students. While not a direct measure of school performance, absenteeism has been linked to low graduation rates, which can have lifelong consequences.

A complex combination of factors can impact youth health outcomes. LGB youth are at greater risk for depression, suicide, substance use, and sexual behaviors that can place them at increased risk for HIV and other sexually transmitted diseases (STDs). Nearly one-third

(29%) of LGB youth had attempted suicide at least once in the prior year compared to 6 percent of heterosexual youth. In 2014, young gay and bisexual men accounted for 8 out of 10 HIV diagnoses among youth.

Understanding and Responding to Lesbian, Gay, Bisexual, Transgender, and Questioning Adolescents

What Schools Can Do

Schools can implement evidence-based policies, procedures, and activities designed to promote a healthy environment for all youth, including LGBTQ+ students. For example, research has shown that in schools with LGBTQ+ support groups (such as gay–straight alliances),

A positive school climate has been associated with decreased depression, suicidal feelings, substance use, and unexcused school absences among LGB students.

To help promote health and safety among LGB youth, schools can implement the following policies and practices:

- Encourage respect for all students and prohibit bullying, harassment, and violence against all students

- Identify "safe spaces," such as counselors' offices or designated classrooms, where LGB youth can receive support from administrators, teachers, or other school staff

- Encourage student-led and student-organized school clubs that promote a safe, welcoming, and accepting school environment (e.g., gay–straight alliances or gender and sexuality alliances, which are school clubs open to youth of all sexual orientations and genders)

- Ensure that health curricula or educational materials include HIV, other sexually transmitted disease (STD), and pregnancy prevention information that is relevant to LGB youth (such as ensuring that curricula or materials use inclusive language and terminology).

- Provide trainings to school staff on how to create safe and supportive school environments for all students, regardless of sexual orientation or gender identity, and encourage staff to attend these trainings

- Facilitate access to community-based providers who have experience providing health services, including HIV/STD testing and counseling, social, and psychological services to lesbian, gay, bisexual, transgender, and questioning (LGBTQ+) youth

LGB students were less likely to experience threats of violence, miss school because they felt unsafe, or attempt suicide than those students in schools without LGB support groups. A study found that LGB students had fewer suicidal thoughts and attempts when schools had gay–straight alliances and policies prohibiting expression of homophobia in place for three or more years.

What Parents Can Do

Positive parenting practices, such as having honest and open conversations, can help reduce teen health-risk behaviors. How parents engage with their LGBTQ+ teen can have a tremendous impact on their adolescent's current and future mental and physical health. Supportive and accepting parents can help youth cope with the challenges of being an LGBTQ+ teen. On the other hand, unsupportive parents who react negatively to learning that their teen is LGBTQ+ can make it harder for their teen to thrive. Parental rejection has been linked to depression, use of drugs and alcohol, and risky sexual behavior among teens.

To be supportive, parents should talk openly and supportively with their teen about any problems or concerns. It is also important for parents to watch for behaviors that might indicate their teen is a victim of bullying or violence, or that their teen may be victimizing others. If bullying, violence, or depression is suspected, parents should take immediate action, working with school personnel and other adults in the community.

Part Three
Recognizing and Treating the Consequences of Abuse and Violence

Chapter 35

What to Do after a Sexual Assault

What Is Sexual Assault?

Sexual assault is any type of sexual activity or contact, including rape, that happens without your consent. Sexual assault can include noncontact activities, such as someone "flashing" you (exposing themselves to you) or forcing you to look at sexual images.

Sexual assault is also called "sexual violence" or "abuse." Legal definitions of sexual assault and other crimes of sexual violence can vary slightly from state to state. If you have been assaulted, it is never your fault.

What Do I Do If I Have Been Sexually Assaulted?

If you are in danger or need medical care, call 911. If you can, get away from the person who assaulted you and get to a safe place as fast as you can. You can call the National Sexual Assault Hotline at 800-656-HOPE (800-656-4673) to connect with a sexual-assault service provider in your area who can direct you to local resources.

How Can I Get Help after a Sexual Assault?

After a sexual assault, you may feel fear, shame, guilt, or shock. All of these feelings are normal, and each survivor can feel a different range of emotions at different times in the recovery

About This Chapter: Text beginning with the heading "What Is Sexual Assault?" is excerpted from "Sexual Assault," Office on Women's Health (OWH), U.S. Department of Health and Human Services (HHS), March 14, 2019; Text under the heading "Evaluating and Treating Sexual Assault Survivors for Sexually Transmitted Diseases" is excerpted from "Sexual Assault and Abuse and STDs," Centers for Disease Control and Prevention (CDC), June 4, 2015. Reviewed August 2019.

process. Sexual assault is never your fault. It may be frightening to think about talking about the assault, but it is important to get help. You can call these organizations any time, day or night. The calls are free and confidential.

- National Sexual Assault Hotline: 800-656-HOPE (800-656-4673)

- National Domestic Violence Hotline: 800-799-SAFE (800-799-7233)

Each state and territory has organizations and hotlines to help people who have been sexually assaulted. These numbers can show up on your phone bill or history, so try to use a public phone or a friend's cellphone.

What Do I Do If I Have Been Raped?

- **Get to a safe place.** Call 911 if you can. The most important thing after rape is your safety.

- **Do not wash or clean your body.** If you shower, bathe, or wash after an assault, you might wash away important evidence. Do not brush, comb, or clean any part of your body, including your teeth. Do not change clothes, if possible. Do not touch or change anything at the scene of the assault. That way, the local police will have physical evidence from the person who assaulted you.

- **Get medical care.** Call 911 or go to your nearest hospital emergency room. You need to be examined and treated for injuries. The doctor or nurse may give you medicine to prevent human immunodeficiency virus (HIV) and some other sexually transmitted infections (STIs) and emergency contraception to prevent pregnancy. The National Sexual-Assault Hotline at 800-656-HOPE (800-656-4673) can help you find a hospital with staff members who are trained to collect evidence of the sexual assault. Ask for a sexual-assault forensic examiner (SAFE) or a sexual-assault nurse examiner (SANE). A doctor or nurse will use a rape kit to collect evidence. This might be fibers, hairs, saliva, semen, or clothing left behind by the attacker. You do not have to decide whether to press charges while at the hospital. You do not need to press charges in order to have evidence collected with a rape kit.

- **If you think you were drugged, talk to the hospital staff** about testing for date-rape drugs, such as Rohypnol and GHB (gamma-hydroxybutyric acid). Date-rape drugs pass through the body quickly and may not be detectable by the time you get tested.

- **Reach out for help.** The hospital staff can connect you with the local rape crisis center. The staff there can help you make choices about reporting the sexual assault and getting help through counseling and support groups. You can also call a friend or family member you trust to call a crisis center or hotline for you. Crisis centers and hotlines have trained volunteers and other professionals (such as mental-health professionals) who can help you find support and resources near you. One hotline is the National Sexual Assault Hotline at 800-656-HOPE (800-656-4673). If you are in the military, you may also call the U.S. Department of Defense (DoD) Safe Helpline at 877-995-5247.

- **Report the sexual assault to the police.** If you want to report the assault to the police, hospital workers can help you contact the local police. If you are in immediate danger, call 911. If you want to report sexual assault that happened in the past, call your local police nonemergency number or make a report in person at the police station.

- **Talk to someone about reporting the assault to the police.** If you want to talk to someone first about reporting the assault, you can call the National Sexual Assault Hotline at 800-656-HOPE (800-656-4673). An advocate or counselor can help you understand how to report the crime. Even though these calls are free, they may appear on your phone bill. If you think that the person who sexually assaulted you may check your phone bill, try to call from a friend's phone or a public phone.

- **If the person who assaulted you was a stranger, write down as many details as you can remember** about the person and what happened. This will help you make a clear statement to police and medical providers about the sexual assault. With good information, they will be better able to help you and find the person who assaulted you.

Evaluating and Treating Sexual-Assault Survivors for Sexually Transmitted Diseases
Initial Examination

Decisions to perform these tests should be made on an individual basis. An initial examination might include the following procedures:

- Nucleic acid amplification tests (NAATs) for *Chlamydia trachomatis* (*C. trachomatis*) and *Neisseria gonorrhoeae* (*N. gonorrhoeae*) at the sites of penetration or attempted penetration. These tests are preferred for the diagnostic evaluation of adolescent or adult sexual-assault survivors.

- Nucleic acid amplification tests from a urine or vaginal specimen or point-of-care testing (POCT) (i.e., deoxyribonucleic acid (DNA) probes) from a vaginal specimen for *Trichomonas vaginalis* (*T. vaginalis*). Point-of-care testing and/or wet mount with measurement of vaginal pH and KOH application for the whiff test from vaginal secretions should be done for evidence of bacterial vaginosis (BV) and candidiasis, especially if vaginal discharge, malodor, or itching is present.

- A serum sample for evaluation of HIV, hepatitis B, and syphilis infections.

Treatment

Compliance with follow-up visits is poor among survivors of sexual assault. As a result, the following routine presumptive treatment after a sexual assault is recommended:

- An empiric antimicrobial regimen for chlamydia, gonorrhea, and trichomonas

- Emergency contraception. This measure should be considered when the assault could result in pregnancy in the survivor.

- Postexposure hepatitis B vaccination (without hepatitis B immunoglobulin (HBIG)) if the hepatitis status of the assailant is unknown and the survivor has not been previously vaccinated. If the assailant is known to be hepatitis B surface antigen (HBsAg)-positive, unvaccinated survivors should receive both the hepatitis B vaccine and HBIG. The vaccine and HBIG, if indicated, should be administered to sexual-assault survivors at the time of the initial examination, and follow-up doses of the vaccine should be administered one to two and four to six months after the first dose. Survivors who were previously vaccinated but did not receive postvaccination testing should receive a single vaccine booster dose.

- Human papillomavirus (HPV) vaccination is recommended for female survivors aged 9 to 26 years and male survivors aged 9 to 21 years. For men who have sex with men (MSM) with who have not received the HPV vaccine or who have been incompletely vaccinated, the vaccine can be administered through age 26 years. The vaccine should be administered to sexual-assault survivors at the time of the initial examination, and a follow-up dose administered at 1 to 2 months and 6 months after the first dose.

- Recommendations for HIV post-exposure prophylaxis (PEP) are individualized according to risk.

If alcohol has been recently ingested or emergency contraception is provided, metronidazole or tinidazole can be taken by the sexual-assault survivor at home rather than as directly observed therapy to minimize potential side effects and drug interactions. Clinicians should counsel persons regarding the possible benefits and toxicities associated with these treatment regimens; gastrointestinal side effects can occur with this combination. The efficacy of these regimens in preventing infections after a sexual assault has not been evaluated. For those requiring alternative treatments, refer to the specific sections relevant to the specific organism.

Chapter 36

Neglect of Children's Healthcare

Defining Neglected Health

Neglect of children's health is difficult to define in a precise way because this type of neglect can take many forms. Many different factors are considered when identifying neglect, including actual harm, the potential for harm, short- and long-term consequences, physical and mental consequences, and availability of medical care. Healthcare neglect also covers the full spectrum of a child's condition, including physical, dental, and mental health.

One simple definition states that healthcare neglect occurs when a child's basic needs are not met, and when those unmet needs present substantial or life-threatening risk to the child. Under this definition, the determination of substantial risk is somewhat subjective and depends upon the opinion of an authority figure, such as a healthcare provider or social worker. Another definition of child-health neglect goes a step further and includes the probability that meeting the child's needs would result in a greatly improved quality of life and/or possibly saving the child's life. There is also a legal definition of neglect which requires evidence that parents failed to seek medical attention for their child.

Child-healthcare neglect is also defined by severity. For example, lack of medical care for a bump or bruise might not be seen as neglect, but failure to seek medical attention for a broken or most likely broken bone would be seen as neglect. The frequency of potentially neglectful episodes is considered when defining child health neglect. Repeated or persistent absence of medical attention, when needed, is much more likely to be cited as neglect than a missed appointment or two.

About This Chapter: "Neglect of Children's Healthcare," © 2016 Omnigraphics. Reviewed August 2019.

Harm Caused by Neglect of Medical Health

Children can experience harm due to healthcare neglect in a variety of ways. Physical, mental, and behavioral problems can all arise from neglected healthcare, and children may suffer from problems in more than one area. Babies and toddlers without adequate healthcare can develop a low-weight condition known as "failure to thrive." Lack of adequate healthcare in toddlers and young children can cause brain disorders, learning disabilities, and other developmental delays. Children can suffer from emotional problems, such as depression and anxiety. In the absence of professional medical care, older children may turn to self-medicating behaviors for untreated physical or mental conditions. Self-medication often includes substance abuse, drug use, overeating, smoking, or other high-risk activities. These attempts to self-medicate can result in new health problems including cancer, addiction, or sexually transmitted diseases.

How Can Healthcare Professionals Assist Child Welfare Professionals?

Pediatric professionals, family-practice providers, hospital nurses, school nurses, urgent-care clinicians, mental-health professionals, and other healthcare professionals can support at-risk children and families, help prevent child abuse and neglect, identify and report suspected abuse or neglect, and serve as a resource for children in foster care.

- Supporting families and preventing child abuse and neglect
- Identifying and reporting suspected child abuse and neglect
- Knowing the laws about confidentiality and privacy
- Utilizing trauma-informed practices
- Being a resource for child-welfare agencies and families

(Source: "What Is Child Welfare? A Guide for Healthcare Professionals," Child Welfare Information Gateway, U.S. Department of Health and Human Services (HHS).)

Factors Determining Neglected Health

Just as there is no single definition of child-health neglect, there is also no single cause. Health neglect in children is often the result of a combination of issues at home, in the community, and in the society at large. Poverty is a major contributing factor to healthcare neglect in children, as is the environment in which a child lives. Children are much more likely to experience healthcare neglect if they live in families affected by drug or alcohol abuse, chronic unemployment, eviction or homelessness, criminal activity, chronic or serious illness, domestic violence, or social isolation. The untreated physical and mental illnesses of caregivers can also be a factor in child healthcare neglect.

The intellectual ability of caregivers often plays a role in child-healthcare neglect. In order for children to receive adequate healthcare, caregivers must be able to identify and understand the child's problem, respond appropriately to the problem, and implement recommended treatment. Other factors include a lack of understanding of the recommended treatment, perceived or actual adverse side effects of treatment, and the cost of treatment. Sometimes the child is also directly or indirectly responsible for their own healthcare neglect, such as in cases of older children refusing to comply with recommended treatment.

Incidence/Prevalence

Because healthcare neglect is difficult to define, it is difficult to measure the true extent of child-healthcare neglect. It is generally understood that neglect of children's dental care is widespread, and it is also known that millions of children in the United States live without access to adequate healthcare and health-insurance coverage.

Manifestations of Neglected Healthcare

Child-healthcare neglect manifests in several ways. The most common are not seeking medical attention when necessary, not following the recommended treatment, missed appointments, and unfilled prescriptions for medication. Some healthcare neglect occurs when caregivers are aware of the need for treatment, but refuse treatment based on religious beliefs. In these cases, lack of medical care is often not labeled as neglect. Thirty U.S. states have religious exemptions from child-abuse statutes where medical care is concerned.

Neglected healthcare can also manifest as environmental hazards. Examples include exposure to toxic materials, such as lead paint in the home, exposure to dangerous objects, such as unsecured weapons, exposure to domestic violence, failure to use a car seat or seat belt, failure to use a bicycle helmet, and prenatal drug or alcohol abuse by pregnant women.

Principles for Assessing Neglected Healthcare

When assessing child-healthcare neglect, the primary consideration is whether a child's basic needs are being met. Severity of the case is another important consideration, and is evaluated according to actual or possible harm and the degree of harm involved. The frequency of incidents is examined to identify a pattern of neglect.

Assessments often include interviews or conversations with the affected child. In these cases, interviewers may attempt to understand the situation by asking children questions, such as "Who helps you when you are sick?" or "What happens if you don't feel good?" The interviewer evaluates the child's responses to determine if the child's needs are being met. Consideration is also given to the type of possible neglect (physical, mental, etc.) and the frequency of incidents. Interviews may be conducted with caregivers as well, focusing on topics such as whether child protective services has been involved in the past, the presence or absence of support systems and other resources for caregivers, and possible interventions.

Once all relevant information has been gathered, an assessment decision can be made. Recommendations for future actions are developed, and caregivers usually receive guidance and/ or counseling to prevent further neglect of the child's health. Sometimes caregivers must first address and treat their own health problems in order to provide adequate care for the child. Depending on the issues involved, caregivers may be provided with information about child nutrition, developmental milestones, and the importance of closely monitoring the child's progress and noting any changes in the child's condition. Caregivers may also receive help in identifying informal support systems within the family, church, community, or other group.

Child Protective Services may be involved in more serious interventions, and caregivers may be referred to social services provided by the government (e.g., food stamps, Medicaid, etc.). Child-healthcare neglect often requires a long-term plan to prevent future lapses. Ongoing follow-up, support, progress reviews, and monitoring may all be required.

References

1. Dubowitz, Howard. "Neglect of Children's Healthcare," *The APSAC Handbook on Child Maltreatment, 3rd ed.* Edited by John E.B. Myers. Thousand Oaks, CA: Sage Publications, 2011.

2. "Long-Term Consequences of Child Abuse and Neglect," Child Welfare Information Gateway, U.S. Department of Health and Human Services (HHS), July 2013.

3. "Medical Neglect," *Child Welfare Manual*, May 3, 2005.

Chapter 37

Long-Term Consequences of Child Abuse and Neglect

Effects of Maltreatment on Brain Development

Just as positive experiences can assist with healthy brain development, children's experiences with child maltreatment or other forms of toxic stress, such as domestic violence or disasters, can negatively affect brain development. This includes changes to the structure and chemical activity of the brain (e.g., decreased size or connectivity in some parts of the brain) and in the emotional and behavioral functioning of the child (e.g., oversensitivity to stressful situations). For example, healthy brain development includes situations in which babies' babbles, gestures, or cries bring reliable, appropriate reactions from their caregivers. These caregiver–child interactions—sometimes referred to as "serve and return"—strengthen babies' neuronal pathways regarding social interactions and how to get their needs met, both physically and emotionally. If children live in a chaotic or threatening world, one in which their caregivers respond with abuse or chronically provide no response, their brains may become hyperalert for danger or not fully develop. These neuronal pathways that are developed and strengthened under negative conditions prepare children to cope in that negative environment, and their ability to respond to nurturing and kindness may be impaired.

The specific effects of maltreatment may depend on such factors as the age of the child at the time of the maltreatment, whether the maltreatment was a one-time incident or chronic, the identity of the abuser (e.g., parent or other adult), whether the child had a dependable

About This Chapter: This chapter includes text excerpted from "Understanding the Effects of Maltreatment on Brain Development," Child Welfare Information Gateway, U.S. Department of Health and Human Services (HHS), April 2015. Reviewed August 2019.

nurturing individual in their life, the type and severity of the maltreatment, the intervention, how long the maltreatment lasted, and other individual and environmental characteristics.

> Child maltreatment/abuse is any act or series of acts of commission or omission by a parent or other caregiver that results in harm, potential for harm, or threat of harm to a child.
>
> *(Source: "Child Maltreatment Surveillance," Centers for Disease Control and Prevention (CDC).)*

Effects of Maltreatment on Brain Structure and Activity

Toxic stress, including child maltreatment, can have a variety of negative effects on children's brains:

Hippocampus: Adults who were maltreated may have reduced volume in the hippocampus, which is central to learning and memory. Toxic stress can also reduce the capacity of the hippocampus to bring cortisol levels back to normal after a stressful event has occurred.

Corpus callosum: Maltreated children and adolescents tend to have decreased volume in the corpus callosum, which is the largest white matter structure in the brain and is responsible for interhemispheric communication and other processes (e.g., arousal, emotion, higher cognitive abilities).

Cerebellum: Maltreated children and adolescents tend to have decreased volume in the cerebellum, which helps coordinate motor behavior and executive functioning.

Prefrontal cortex: Some studies on adolescents and adults who were severely neglected as children indicate they have a smaller prefrontal cortex, which is critical to behavior, cognition, and emotion regulation, but other studies show no differences. Physically abused children also may have reduced volume in the orbitofrontal cortex, a part of the prefrontal cortex that is central to emotion and social regulation.

Amygdala: Although most studies have found that amygdala volume is not affected by maltreatment, abuse and neglect can cause overactivity in that area of the brain, which helps determine whether a stimulus is threatening and trigger emotional responses.

Cortisol levels: Many maltreated children, both in institutional and family settings, and especially those who experienced severe neglect, tend to have lower-than-normal morning cortisol levels coupled with flatter release levels throughout the day. (Typically, children have a sharp increase in cortisol in the morning followed by a steady decrease throughout the day.) On the other hand, children in foster care who experienced severe emotional maltreatment had higher-than-normal morning cortisol levels. These results may be due to the body reacting differently to different stressors. Abnormal cortisol levels can have many negative effects. Lower cortisol levels can lead to decreased energy resources, which could affect learning and socialization; externalizing disorders; and increased vulnerability to autoimmune disorders. Higher cortisol levels could harm cognitive processes, subdue immune and inflammatory reactions, or heighten the risk for affective disorders.

Other: Children who experienced severe neglect early in life while in institutional settings often have decreased electrical activity in their brains, decreased brain metabolism, and poorer connections between areas of the brain that are key to integrating complex information. These children also may continue to have abnormal patterns of adrenaline activity years after being adopted from institutional settings. Additionally, malnutrition, a form of neglect, can impair both brain development (e.g., slowing the growth of neurons, axons, and synapses) and function (e.g., neurotransmitter syntheses, the maintenance of brain tissue).

We also know that some cases of physical abuse can cause immediate direct structural damage to a child's brain. For example, according to the National Center on Shaken Baby Syndrome (NCSBS) (n.d.), shaking a child can destroy brain tissue and tear blood vessels. In the short term, this can lead to seizures, loss of consciousness, or even death. In the long term, shaking can damage the fragile brain so that a child develops a range of sensory impairments, as well as cognitive, learning, and behavioral disabilities. Other types of head injuries caused by physical abuse can have similar effects.

Effects of Maltreatment on Behavioral, Social, and Emotional Functioning

The changes in brain structure and chemical activity caused by child maltreatment can have a wide variety of effects on children's behavioral, social, and emotional functioning.

Persistent Fear Response

Chronic stress or repeated trauma can result in a number of biological reactions, including a persistent fear state. Chronic activation of the neuronal pathways involved in the fear response can create permanent memories that shape the child's perception of and response to the environment. While this adaptation may be necessary for survival in a hostile world, it can become a way of life that is difficult to change, even if the environment improves. Children with a persistent fear response may lose their ability to differentiate between danger and safety, and they may identify a threat in a nonthreatening situation. For example, a child who has been maltreated may associate the fear caused by a specific person or place with similar people or places that pose no threat. This generalized fear response may be the foundation of future anxiety disorders, such as posttraumatic stress disorder (PTSD).

Hyperarousal

When children are exposed to chronic, traumatic stress, their brains sensitize the pathways for the fear response and create memories that automatically trigger that response without conscious thought. This is called "hyperarousal." These children may be highly sensitive to nonverbal cues, such as eye contact or a touch on the arm, and they may be more likely to mis-interpret them. Consumed with a need to monitor nonverbal cues for threats, their brains are less able to interpret and respond to verbal cues, even when they are in an environment typi-cally considered nonthreatening, such as a classroom. While these children are often labeled as learning disabled, the reality is that their brains have developed so that they are constantly on the alert and are unable to achieve the relative calm necessary for learning.

Increased Internalizing Symptoms

Child maltreatment can lead to structural and chemical changes in the areas of the brain involved in emotion and stress regulation. For example, maltreatment can affect connectivity between the amygdala and hippocampus, which can then initiate the development of anxiety and depression by late adolescence. Additionally, early emotional abuse or severe deprivation may permanently alter the brain's ability to use serotonin, a neurotransmitter that helps pro-duce feelings of well-being and emotional stability.

Diminished Executive Functioning

Executive functioning generally includes three components: working memory (being able to keep and use information over a short period of time), inhibitory control (filtering thoughts and impulses), and cognitive or mental flexibility (adjusting to changing demands, priorities, or perspectives). The structural and neurochemical damage caused by maltreatment can cre-ate deficits in all areas of executive functioning, even at an early age. Executive functioning skills help people achieve academic and career success, bolster social interactions, and assist in everyday activities. The brain alterations caused by a toxic-stress response can result in lower academic achievement, intellectual impairment, decreased intelligence quotient (IQ), and weakened ability to maintain attention.

Delayed Developmental Milestones

Although neglect often is thought of as a failure to meet a child's physical needs for food, shelter, and safety, neglect also can be a failure to meet a child's cognitive, emotional, or social needs. For children to master developmental tasks in these areas, they need opportunities and encouragement from their caregivers. If this stimulation is lacking during children's early years, the weak neuronal pathways that developed in expectation of these experiences may wither and die, and the children may not achieve the usual developmental milestones. For example, babies need to experience face-to-face baby talk and hear countless repetitions of sounds in order to build the brain circuitry that will enable them to start making sounds and eventually say words. If babies' sounds are ignored repeatedly when they begin to babble at around six months, their language may be delayed. In fact, neglected children often do not show the rapid growth that normally occurs in language development at 18 to 24 months. These types of delays may extend to all types of normal development for neglected children, including their cognitive-behavioral, socioemotional, and physical development.

Weakened Response to Positive Feedback

Children who have been maltreated may be less responsive to positive stimuli than non-maltreated children. A study of young adults who had been maltreated found that they rated monetary rewards less positively than their peers and demonstrated a weaker response to reward cues in the basal ganglia areas of the brain responsible for reward processing.

Complicated Social Interactions

Toxic stress can alter brain development in ways that make interaction with others more difficult. Children or youth with toxic stress may find it more challenging to navigate social situations and adapt to changing social contexts. They may perceive threats in safe situations more frequently and react accordingly, and they may have more difficulty interacting with others. For example, a maltreated child may misinterpret a peer's neutral facial expression as anger, which may cause the maltreated child to become aggressive or overly defensive toward the peer.

Chapter 38

Seeking Mental-Health Services

If you or someone you know has a mental illness, there are ways to get help. Use these resources to find help for you, a friend, or a family member.

Finding a Healthcare Provider or Treatment

For general information on mental health and to locate treatment services in your area, call the Substance Abuse and Mental Health Services Administration (SAMHSA) Treatment Referral Helpline at 800-662-HELP (800-662-4357). SAMHSA also has a Behavioral Health Treatment Locator on its website that can be searched by location.

National agencies and advocacy and professional organizations have information on finding a mental-health professional and sometimes practitioner locators on their websites. Examples include but are not limited to:

- Anxiety and Depression Association of America (ADAA)

- Depression and Bipolar Support Alliance (DBSA)

- Mental Health America (MHA)

- National Alliance on Mental Illness (NAMI)

University or medical school-affiliated programs may offer treatment options. Search on the website of local university health centers for their psychiatry or psychology departments. You can also go to the website of your state or county government and search for the health

About This Chapter: This chapter includes text excerpted from "Help for Mental Illnesses," National Institute of Mental Health (NIMH), September 7, 2015. Reviewed August 2019.

services department. Some federal agencies that offer resources for identifying practitioners and assistance in finding low-cost health services are:

- **Health Resources and Services Administration (HRSA):** HRSA works to improve access to healthcare. The website has information on finding affordable healthcare, including health centers that offer care on a sliding-fee scale.

- **Centers for Medicare & Medicaid Services (CMS):** CMS has information on the website about benefits and eligibility for these programs and how to enroll.

- **The National Library of Medicine's (NLM)** MedlinePlus website also has lists of directories and organizations that can help in identifying a health practitioner.

- The lists of practitioners in healthcare plans provide mental-health professionals that participate in your plan.

- **Mental Health and Addiction Insurance Help:** This website from the U.S. Department of Health and Human Services (HHS) offers resources to help answer questions about insurance coverage for mental-healthcare.

Contact National Institute of Mental Health

For all questions related to mental health, requests for copies of publications, and inquiries concerning NIMH research, policies, and priorities, please contact a health information specialist at the NIMH Information Resource Center (IRC). You could also call the following telephone numbers:

- 866-615-6464 (Toll-Free)

- 301-443-8431 (TTY)

- 866-415-8051 (Toll-Free TTY)

> If you are in crisis and need immediate support or intervention, call 800-273-8255 or go to the website of the National Suicide Prevention Lifeline. Trained crisis workers are available to talk 24 hours a day, 7 days a week. Your confidential and toll-free call goes to the nearest crisis center in the Lifeline national network. These centers provide crisis counseling and mental-health referrals. If the situation is potentially life-threatening, call 911 or go to a hospital emergency room.

Chapter 39

Impact of Abuse and Trauma on Mental Health

Abuse, whether physical, emotional, verbal, or sexual, can have long-term effects on your mental health. Trauma can affect how you feel about yourself and how you relate to others. Women who have gone through abuse or other trauma have a higher risk of developing a mental-health condition, such as depression, anxiety, or posttraumatic stress disorder (PTSD). Trauma and abuse are never your fault. You can get help to heal the physical, mental, and emotional scars of trauma and abuse.

How Are Abuse and Trauma Related to Mental Health?

Trauma can happen after you experience an event or events that hurt you physically or emotionally. Trauma can have lasting effects on your mental, physical, and emotional health. Experiencing abuse or other trauma puts people at risk of developing mental-health conditions, such as:

- Anxiety disorders
- Depression
- PTSD
- Misusing alcohol or drugs
- Borderline personality disorder (BPD)

About This Chapter: This chapter includes text excerpted from "Abuse, Trauma, and Mental Health," Office on Women's Health (OWH), U.S. Department of Health and Human Services (HHS), August 28, 2018.

Abuse may have happened during childhood or as an adult. It can be emotional, verbal, physical, or sexual. Trauma can include dangerous, frightening, or extremely stressful situations or events, such as sexual assault, war, an accident or natural disaster, the sudden or violent death of a close loved one, or a serious physical health problem.

The long-term effects of abuse or trauma can include:

- Severe anxiety, stress, or fear

- Abuse of alcohol or drugs

- Depression

- Eating disorders

- Self-injury

- Suicide

Mental health includes our emotional, psychological, and social well-being. It affects how we think, feel, and act. It also helps determine how we handle stress, relate to others, and make choices. Mental health is important at every stage of life, from childhood and adolescence through adulthood.

(Source: "What Is Mental Health?" MentalHealth.gov, U.S. Department of Health and Human Services (HHS).)

How Do I Know If My Mental Health Is Affected by Past Abuse or Trauma?

It can be difficult to tell whether or how much your mental health is affected by past abuse or trauma. Sometimes the symptoms of trauma or abuse do not start to affect your life for many months or years after the event took place. If you have any of the following symptoms, talk to your doctor or nurse or reach out for help:

- Anxiety

- Trouble sleeping

- Anger

- Depression

- Changes in mood or appetite

- Abusing drugs or alcohol

What Should I Do If I Have Been Abused or Traumatized?

The sooner you can get professional help for abuse or trauma, the sooner you can begin to get better. If you have been physically hurt, visit a hospital or doctor right away. You may also need to call the police. The doctor and the police can help document what has happened to you. This documentation may be important later if you decide to press charges against someone who attacked you.

If you are experiencing changes in how you think, feel, or behave that are interfering with your ability to work or live your life normally, reach out to a mental-health professional. Find a mental-health professional near you. A mental-health professional can help make sense of any symptoms you may be having that are related to your abuse or trauma. The professional can help you find the best kinds of treatment to help manage symptoms of the abuse or trauma.

If you are in immediate danger, call 911.

You can also call helplines to talk about what happened to you or get guidance about what to do:

- National Domestic Violence Hotline: 800-799-SAFE (800-799-7233)

- National Sexual Assault Hotline: 800-656-HOPE (800-656-4673)

- Safe Helpline (for members of the military): 877-995-5247

Abuse or trauma you have suffered is not your fault. You can get better with treatment.

How Are Abuse and Trauma Treated?

Symptoms caused by abuse or trauma can usually be treated with different types of talk therapy, medicine, or both. Therapy with a professional counselor can help you work through your feelings and learn healthy ways to cope. Medicines might include antidepressants or anti-anxiety medicine. Complementary mind and body therapies, such as mindfulness and yoga*, may be offered along with traditional treatments, such as medicines and therapy.

An ancient system of practices used to balance the mind and body through exercise, meditation (focusing thoughts), and control of breathing and emotions.

Chapter 40

Depression and College Students

Many people experience the first symptoms of depression during their college years. Unfortunately, many college students who have depression are not getting the help they need. They may not know where to go for help, or they may believe that treatment would not help. Others do not get help because they think their symptoms are just part of the typical stress of college, or they worry about being judged if they seek mental-healthcare.

In reality,

- Most colleges offer free or low-cost mental-health services to students.

- Depression is a medical illness and treatments can be very effective.

- Early diagnosis and treatment of depression can relieve depression symptoms, prevent depression from returning, and help students succeed in college and after graduation.

This chapter addresses common questions about depression and how it can affect students attending college.

What Is Depression?

Depression is a common but serious mental illness typically marked by sad or anxious feelings. Most college students occasionally feel sad or anxious, but these emotions usually pass quickly—within a couple of days. Untreated depression lasts for a long time, interferes with day-to-day activities, and is much more than just being "a little down" or "feeling blue."

About This Chapter: This chapter includes text excerpted from "Depression and College Students," National Institute of Mental Health (NIMH), 2012. Reviewed August 2019.

How Does Depression Affect College Students?

In 2011, the American College Health Association–National College Health Assessment (ACHA–NCHA)—a nationwide survey of college students at two- and four-year institutions—found that about 30 percent of college students reported feeling "so depressed that it was difficult to function" at some time in the past year.

Depression can affect your academic performance in college. Studies suggest that college students who have depression are more likely to smoke. Research suggests that students with depression do not necessarily drink alcohol more heavily than other college students. But students with depression, especially women, are more likely to drink to get drunk and experience problems related to alcohol abuse, such as engaging in unsafe sex. Depression and other mental disorders often co-occur with substance abuse, which can complicate treatment.

Depression is also a major risk factor for suicide. Better diagnosis and treatment of depression can help reduce suicide rates among college students. In the Fall 2011 ACHA–NCHA survey, more than 6 percent of college students reported seriously considering suicide, and about 1 percent reported attempting suicide in the previous year. Suicide is the third leading cause of death for teens and young adults ages 15 to 24. Students should also be aware that warning signs can be different in men than women.

Are There Different Types of Depression?

Yes. The most common depressive disorders are:

- **Major depressive disorder**—also called "major depression." The symptoms of major depression are disabling and interfere with everyday activities, such as studying, eating, and sleeping. People with this disorder may have only one episode of major depression in their lifetimes. But more often, depression comes back repeatedly.

- **Dysthymic disorder**—also called "dysthymia." Dysthymia is a mild, chronic depression. The symptoms of dysthymia last for a long time—two years or more. Dysthymia is less severe than major depression, but it can still interfere with everyday activities. People with dysthymia may also experience one or more episodes of major depression during their lifetimes.

- **Minor depression**—similar to major depression and dysthymia. Symptoms of minor depression are less severe and/or are usually shorter term. Without treatment, however, people with minor depression are at high risk for developing major depressive disorder.

Other types of depression include:

- **Psychotic depression**—severe depression accompanied by some form of psychosis, such as hallucinations and delusions

- **Seasonal affective disorder**—depression that begins during the winter months and lifts during spring and summer

---

Bipolar disorder, also called "manic-depressive illness," is not as common as major depression or dysthymia but often develops in a person's late teens or early adult years. At least half of all cases start before age 25. People with bipolar disorder may show symptoms of depression and are more likely to seek help when they are depressed than when experiencing mania or hypomania.

Bipolar disorder requires different treatment than major depression, so a careful and complete medical exam is needed to assure a person receives the right diagnosis.

What Are the Signs and Symptoms of Depression?

The symptoms of depression vary. If you are depressed, you may feel:

- Sad

- Anxious

- Empty

- Hopeless

- Guilty

- Worthless

- Helpless

- Irritable

- Restless

You may also experience one or more of the following:

- Loss of interest in activities you used to enjoy

- Lack of energy

- Problems concentrating, remembering information, or making decisions

- Problems falling asleep, staying asleep, or sleeping too much

- Loss of appetite or eating too much

- Thoughts of suicide or suicide attempts

- Aches, pains, headaches, cramps, or digestive problems that do not go away

What Causes Depression

Depression does not have a single cause. Several factors can lead to depression. Some people carry genes that increase their risk of depression. But not all people with depression have these genes, and not all people with these genes have depression. Environment—your surroundings and life experiences, such as stress, also affects your risk for depression. Stresses of college may include:

- Living away from family for the first time

- Missing family or friends

- Feeling alone or isolated

- Experiencing conflict in relationships

- Facing new and sometimes difficult school work

- Worrying about finances

How Can I Find Out If I Have Depression?

The first step is to talk with a doctor or mental-healthcare provider. Your family doctor, campus health center staff, or other trusted adult may be able to help you find appropriate care.

She or he can perform an exam to help determine if you have depression or if you have another health or mental-health problem. Some medical conditions or medications can produce symptoms similar to depression.

A doctor or mental-healthcare provider will ask you about:

- Your symptoms

- Your history of depression

- Your family's history of depression

- Your medical history

- Alcohol or drug use

- Any thoughts of death or suicide

If I Think I May Have Depression, Where Can I Get Help?

Most colleges provide mental-health services through counseling centers, student-health centers, or both. Check out your college website for information.

- **Counseling centers** offer students free or very low-cost mental-health services. Some counseling centers provide short- or long-term counseling or psychotherapy, also called "talk therapy." These centers may also refer you to mental-healthcare providers in the community for additional services.

- **Student health centers** provide basic healthcare services to students at little or no cost. A doctor or healthcare provider may be able to diagnose and treat depression or refer you to other mental-health services.

If your college does not provide all of the mental-healthcare you need, your insurance may cover additional mental-health services. Many college students have insurance through their colleges, parents, or employers. If you are insured, contact your insurance company to find out about your mental-healthcare coverage.

How Is Depression Treated?

A number of very effective treatments for depression are available. The most common treatments are antidepressants and psychotherapy. Some people find that a combination of antidepressants and psychotherapy works best. A doctor or mental-healthcare provider can help you find the treatment that is right for you.

What Are Antidepressants?

Antidepressants work on brain chemicals called "neurotransmitters," especially serotonin and norepinephrine. Other antidepressants work on the neurotransmitter dopamine. Scientists have found that these particular chemicals are involved in regulating mood, but they are unsure of the exact ways that they work.

If a Doctor Prescribes an Antidepressant, How Long Will I Have to Take It?

Always follow the directions of the doctor or healthcare provider when taking medication. You will need to take regular doses of antidepressants and the full effect of these medications may not take effect for several weeks or months. Some people need to take antidepressants for a short time. If your depression is long-lasting or comes back repeatedly, you may need to take antidepressants longer.

What Is Psychotherapy?

Psychotherapy involves talking with a mental-healthcare professional to treat mental illness. Types of psychotherapy that have been shown to be effective in treating depression include:

- **Cognitive-behavioral therapy (CBT),** which helps people change negative styles of thinking and behavior that may contribute to depression

- **Interpersonal therapy (IPT),** which helps people understand and work through troubled personal relationships that may cause or worsen depression

Depending on the type and severity of your depression, a mental-health professional may recommend short-term therapy, lasting 10 to 20 weeks, or longer-term therapy.

Chapter 41

Posttraumatic Stress Disorder

After a dangerous or scary event, it is normal to feel upset, afraid, and anxious. For most people, these feelings fade within a few weeks. But some people continue to have these feelings for months or years afterward. They may keep reliving the event and avoid items and places that might remind them of what happened. This is called "posttraumatic stress disorder" (PTSD). Women are about twice as likely as men to develop PTSD in their lifetimes.

What Is Posttraumatic Stress Disorder?

Posttraumatic stress disorder happens when people who have experienced or witnessed a traumatic event continue to experience symptoms for more than a month that make it difficult to live their lives normally. Traumatic events can include physical or sexual assault, war, natural disasters, car accidents, or any event experienced as deeply scary and upsetting. Although PTSD is often associated with military service members, PTSD may develop after any type of traumatic event.

People with PTSD may continue to experience the traumatic event through flashbacks, nightmares, or memories they cannot control. These thoughts can create serious emotional pain for the person and problems at home, work, or school, or with relationships. Most often, the traumatic event happened to the person with PTSD, but sometimes PTSD can happen to a person who witnesses someone else experiencing a trauma. People who develop PTSD

About This Chapter: Text in this chapter begins with excerpts from "Post-Traumatic Stress Disorder," Office on Women's Health (OWH), U.S. Department of Health and Human Services (HHS), August 28, 2018; Text beginning with the heading "What Events Cause Posttraumatic Stress Disorder in Children?" is excerpted from "PTSD in Children and Adolescents," National Center for Posttraumatic Stress Disorder (NCPTSD), U.S. Department of Veterans Affairs (VA), December 12, 2018.

usually experience symptoms soon after the traumatic event, but sometimes symptoms do not appear for months or years afterward.

What Events Cause Posttraumatic Stress Disorder in Children and Teens?

Any life-threatening event or event that threatens physical harm can cause PTSD. These events may include:

- Sexual abuse or violence (does not require a threat of harm)

- Physical abuse

- Violent crimes, such as kidnapping or school shootings

- Motor vehicle accidents, such as automobile and plane crashes

- Natural or human-made disasters, such as fires, hurricanes, or floods

Posttraumatic stress disorder can also occur after witnessing violence. These events may include exposure to:

- Community violence

- Domestic violence

- War

Finally, in some cases, learning about these events happening to someone close to you can cause PTSD.

How Many Children and Teens Experience Traumatic Events?

The best information on very young children comes from annual statistics from the U.S. Department of Health and Human Services (HHS) on child abuse. These rates underestimate traumatic exposure given that they address abuse only and not other types of traumatic events. Also, they underestimate abuse because not all abuse is reported.

In 2011, Child Protective Services in the United States received 3.4 million referrals, representing 6.2 million children. Of those cases referred, about 19 percent were substantiated and occurred in the following frequencies.

- More than 75 percent (78.5%) suffered neglect

- More than 15 percent (17.6%) suffered physical abuse

- Less than 10 percent (9.1%) suffered sexual abuse

In older children, there have been several national studies. The National Survey of Children's Exposure to Violence (NatSCEV) reports on 1 year and lifetime prevalence of childhood victimization in a nationally representative sample of 4549 children aged 0 to 17. More than half (60.6%) of the sample experienced or witnessed victimization in the past year. Specifically in the past year:

- Almost half (46.3%) experienced physical assault

- 1 in 10 (10.2%) experienced child maltreatment

- Fewer than 1 in 10 (6.1%) had experienced sexual victimization

- More than 1 in 4 (25.3%) had witnessed domestic or community violence

As children age there is more opportunity for exposure, thus lifetime exposure was one-third to one-half higher than past year exposure. As an example, among 14- to 17-year-old girls, 18.7 have experienced a completed or attempted sexual assault in their lifetime and more than a third had witnessed parental assault.

A second national study asked 4,023 adolescents aged 12 to 17 if they had ever experienced sexual or physical assault or witnessed violence. Almost half (47%) had experienced one of these types of traumas. Specifically in their lifetime:

- 8 percent experienced sexual assault

- 22 percent experienced physical assault

- 39 percent witnessed violence

How Many Children Develop Posttraumatic Stress Disorder?

The National Comorbidity Survey Replication–Adolescent Supplement (NCS–A) is a national representative sample of over 10,000 adolescents aged 13 to 18. Results indicate that 5 percent of adolescents have met criteria for PTSD in their lifetime. Prevalence is higher for girls than boys (8.0% versus 2.3%) and increases with age. Current rates are 3.9 percent overall. There are no definitive studies on prevalence rates of PTSD in younger children in the general population.

What Are the Risk Factors for Posttraumatic Stress Disorder?

Both the type of event and the intensity of exposure impact the degree to which an event results in PTSD. For example, in one study of a fatal sniper attack that occurred at an elementary school, proximity to the shooting was directly related to the percentage of children who developed PTSD. Of those children who directly witnessed the shooting on the playground, 77 percent had moderate-to-severe PTSD symptoms, whereas 67 percent of those in the school building at the time and only 26 percent of the children who had gone home for the day had moderate or severe symptoms.

In addition to exposure variables, other risk factors include:

- Being female

- Previous trauma exposure

- Preexisting psychiatric disorders

- Parental psychopathology

- Low social support

Parents have been shown to have protective factors (practice parameters). Both parental support and lower levels of parental PTSD have been found to predict lower levels of PTSD in children.

There is less clarity in the findings connecting PTSD with ethnicity and age. While some studies find that minorities report higher levels of PTSD symptoms, researchers have shown that this is due to other factors, such as differences in levels of exposure. It is not clear how a child's age at the time of exposure to a traumatic event affects the occurrence or severity of PTSD. While some studies find a relationship, others do not. Differences that do occur may be due to differences in the way PTSD is expressed in children and adolescents of different ages or developmental levels.

What Does Posttraumatic Stress Disorder Look Like in Children?

As in adults, PTSD in children and adolescence requires the presence of reexperiencing, avoidance and numbing, and arousal symptoms. However, researchers and clinicians are beginning to recognize that PTSD may not present itself in children the same way it does in adults. Criteria for PTSD include age-specific features for some symptoms.

Elementary School-Aged Children

Clinical reports suggest that elementary school-aged children may not experience visual flashbacks or amnesia for aspects of the trauma. However, they do experience "time skew" and "omen formation," which are not typically seen in adults.

"Time skew" refers to a child mis-sequencing trauma-related events when recalling the memory. "Omen formation" is a belief that there were warning signs that predicted the trauma. As a result, children often believe that if they are alert enough, they will recognize the warning signs and avoid future traumas.

School-aged children also reportedly exhibit posttraumatic play or reenactment of the trauma in play, drawings, or verbalizations. Posttraumatic play is different from reenactment in that posttraumatic play is a literal representation of the trauma, involves compulsively repeating some aspect of the trauma, and does not tend to relieve anxiety.

An example of posttraumatic play is an increase in shooting games after exposure to a school shooting. Posttraumatic reenactment, on the other hand, is more flexible and involves behaviorally recreating aspects of the trauma (e.g., carrying a weapon after exposure to violence).

Adolescents and Teens

Posttraumatic stress disorder in adolescents may begin to more closely resemble PTSD in adults. However, there are a few features that have been shown to differ. As discussed above, children may engage in traumatic play following a trauma. Adolescents are more likely to engage in traumatic reenactment, in which they incorporate aspects of the trauma into their daily lives. In addition, adolescents are more likely than younger children or adults to exhibit impulsive and aggressive behaviors.

Besides Posttraumatic Stress Disorder, What Are the Other Effects of Trauma on Children?

Besides PTSD, children and adolescents who have experienced traumatic events often exhibit other types of problems. Perhaps the best information available on the effects of traumas on children comes from a review of the literature on the effects of child sexual abuse.

In this review, it was shown that sexually abused children often have problems with fear, anxiety, depression, anger and hostility, aggression, sexually inappropriate behavior, self-destructive behavior, feelings of isolation and stigma, poor self-esteem, difficulty in trusting others, substance abuse, and sexual maladjustment.

These problems are often seen in children and adolescents who have experienced other types of traumas as well. Children who have experienced traumas also often have relationship problems with peers and family members, problems with acting out, and problems with school performance.

Along with associated symptoms, there are a number of psychiatric disorders that are commonly found in children and adolescents who have been traumatized. One commonly co-occurring disorder is major depression. Other disorders include substance abuse; anxiety disorders, such as separation anxiety, panic disorder, and generalized anxiety disorder (GAD); and externalizing disorders, such as attention deficit hyperactivity disorder (ADHD), oppositional defiant disorder (ODD), and conduct disorder.

> Many people with PTSD have other mental-health conditions, such as depression, anxiety, or even suicidal thoughts or behaviors. Getting treatment for PTSD and any other mental-health conditions will help you get better. Treatment for PTSD works best when you and your doctor know about the effects of other mental-health conditions and take steps to treat them at the same time.
>
> *(Source: "Posttraumatic Stress Disorder," Office on Women's Health (OWH), U.S. Department of Health and Human Services (HHS).)*

How Is Posttraumatic Stress Disorder Treated in Children and Adolescents?

Although some children show a natural remission in PTSD symptoms over a period of a few months, a significant number of children continue to exhibit symptoms for years if untreated. Trauma-focused psychotherapies have the most empirical support for children and adolescents.

Cognitive-Behavioral Therapy

Research studies show that cognitive-behavioral therapy (CBT) is the most effective approach for treating children. The treatment with the best empirical evidence is trauma-focused

CBT (TF-CBT). TF-CBT generally includes the child directly discussing the traumatic event (exposure), anxiety-management techniques, such as relaxation and assertiveness training, and correction of inaccurate or distorted trauma-related thoughts.

Although there is some controversy regarding exposing children to the events that scare them, exposure-based treatments seem to be most relevant when memories or reminders of the trauma distress the child. Children can be exposed gradually and taught relaxation so that they can learn to relax while recalling their experiences. Through this procedure, they learn that they do not have to be afraid of their memories.

Cognitive-behavioral therapy also involves challenging children's false beliefs such as, "the world is totally unsafe." The majority of studies have found that it is safe and effective to use CBT for children with PTSD.

Cognitive-behavioral therapy is often accompanied by psychoeducation and parental involvement. Psychoeducation is education about PTSD symptoms and their effects. It is as important for parents and caregivers to understand the effects of PTSD as it is for children. Research shows that the better parents cope with the trauma, and the more they support their children, the better their children will function. Therefore, it is important for parents to seek treatment for themselves in order to develop the necessary coping skills that will help their children.

Play Therapy

Play therapy can be used to treat young children with PTSD who are not able to deal with the trauma more directly. The therapist uses games, drawings, and other techniques to help the children process their traumatic memories.

Psychological First Aid

Psychological first aid has been used for school-aged children and adolescents exposed to disasters and community violence and can be used in schools and traditional settings. Psychological first aid involves providing comfort and support, normalizing the children's reactions, helping caregivers deal with changes in the child's emotions and behavior, teaching calming and problem-solving skills, and referring the most symptomatic children for additional treatment.

Eye Movement Desensitization and Reprocessing

Another therapy, eye movement desensitization and reprocessing (EMDR), combines cognitive therapy with directed eye movements. While EMDR has been shown to be effective in treating adults, research with children is not as strong. Studies indicate that it is the cognitive component rather than the eye movements that accounts for the change.

Medications

Selective serotonin reuptake inhibitors (SSRI) are approved for use in adults with PTSD. SSRIs are approved for use in children and adolescents with depression and obsessive-compulsive disorder (OCD). Preliminary evidence suggests SSRIs may be effective in treating PTSD, however, there may also be risks, such as irritability, poor sleep, and inattention. At this time, there is insufficient evidence to support the use of SSRIs.

Specialized Interventions

Specialized interventions may be necessary for children exhibiting particularly problematic symptoms or behaviors, such as inappropriate sexual behaviors, extreme behavioral problems, or substance abuse.

Chapter 42

Dissociative Disorders

Dissociation is a psychological state that involves feeling disconnected from reality. A dissociative disorder is a mental-health condition in which the affected person experiences a disconnection from their thoughts, feelings, memories, perceptions, consciousness, or identity.

For many people, dissociation is used as a defense mechanism to block out the memory of extremely stressful or traumatic life experiences, particularly from childhood. Dissociative disorders are often found in individuals who were exposed to physical, emotional, or sexual abuse as children—for instance, and in those who endured such traumatic events as natural disasters, wars, accidents, violent crimes, or the tragic loss of a loved one. Dissociative disorders often manifest themselves during stressful situations in adulthood, which can make it difficult for people affected to deal with the challenges of everyday life.

Research suggests that around two to three percent of people are affected by dissociative disorders. Some of the common symptoms include episodes of memory or sensory loss, feelings of emotional detachment, or a sense of watching oneself from the outside. Dissociative disorders often coincide with other mental-health issues, such as mood swings, attention deficits, drug and alcohol dependence, anxiety, panic attacks, and suicidal tendencies.

According to the American Psychiatric Association's (APA) *Diagnostic and Statistical Manual of Mental Disorders* (*DSM* 5), dissociative disorders take three main forms: Depersonalization/derealization disorder; dissociative amnesia; and dissociative identity disorder.

About This Chapter: "Dissociative Disorders," © 2016 Omnigraphics. Reviewed August 2019.

Forms of Dissociative Disorders
Depersonalization/Derealization Disorder

Depersonalization is a profound sense of detachment or alienation from one's own body, mind, or identity. People with depersonalization disorder may experience an "out of body" sensation, or feel as if they are looking at their own life from an external perspective, like watching a movie. Some people affected by this condition may not recognize their own face in a mirror.

Derealization is the sense that the world does not seem real. People with derealization disorder may report that their surroundings appear hazy, foggy, phony, or far away. Familiar places may seem unfamiliar, and close friends may seem like strangers. In some cases, situations take on a dreamlike quality, and the affected person may feel disoriented and have difficulty determining what is real and what is not.

Dissociative Amnesia

Dissociative amnesia is the inability to remember people, events, or personal information. This memory loss is too substantial to be considered normal forgetfulness, and it is not related to aging, disease, or a head injury. In most cases, people with dissociative amnesia forget a traumatic incident or an extremely stressful period of time. They may also experience smaller lapses in which they forget the content of a conversation or a talent or skill that they have learned.

Dissociative amnesia may be localized, selective, or generalized. In localized amnesia, the memory lapse is concerned with a particular event or span of time. In selective amnesia, the affected person forgets certain parts of a traumatic incident but may remember others. In generalized amnesia, the affected person is unable to remember anything about their own identity or life history. In rare cases dissociative amnesia may take the form of fugue, in which a person travels for hours or days without a sense of their own identity, then suddenly regains awareness and wonders how they got there.

Dissociative Identity Disorder

Dissociative identity disorder (DID), formerly known as "multiple personality disorder," is characterized by a deep uncertainty or confusion about one's identity. People affected by this disorder may feel the presence of other people or alternate identities (known as "alters") within themselves. Each of these alters may have their own name, history, voice, mannerisms, and worldview.

A child who has suffered a severe psychological trauma is more likely to develop a dissociative identity disorder. Since the child's mind lacks the coping mechanisms to process the stressful experience, the still-developing personality may find it easier to dissociate and pretend that it was happening to someone else.

Treatment for Dissociative Disorders

Before diagnosing a dissociative disorder, a doctor may perform tests to rule out physical conditions that may cause similar symptoms, such as a head injury, brain tumor, sleep deprivation, or drug addiction. If no physical cause is found, the patient may be referred to a mental-health professional for further evaluation. The mental-health specialist will likely inquire about childhood trauma and screen the patient for trauma-related conditions, such as anxiety, depression, posttraumatic stress disorder, and substance abuse. Although there is no medication to treat dissociation, antidepressants and antianxiety drugs may provide some relief from the symptoms of associated conditions.

Psychiatrists often treat dissociative disorders with counseling designed to help the patient cope with the underlying trauma. They view dissociation as a normal defense mechanism that the brain may use to adapt to a difficult situation in early life. Dissociation only becomes dysfunctional when it persists into adulthood and governs an individual's response to everyday challenges. In these cases, the patient may benefit from a course of psychotherapy to help them understand and process the traumatic event.

Eye movement desensitization and reprocessing (EMDR) is another technique that can help alleviate symptoms related to psychological trauma. In EMDR, the patient makes side-to-side eye motions, usually by following the movement of the therapist's finger, while recalling the traumatic incident. Although doctors are not sure how EMDR works, it appears to help the brain process distressing memories so that they have less impact on the patient's daily life.

References

1. "Dissociative Disorders," National Alliance on Mental Illness (NAMI), n.d.

2. "Dissociative Disorders," NHS Choices, Gov.UK, 2014.

3. "Dissociation FAQs," International Society for the Study of Trauma and Dissociation (ISSTD), 2014.

Chapter 43

Trauma-Focused Interventions for Youth

This chapter describes different treatments that can be used to help youth heal from trauma. Effective treatments can improve youth's well-being, placement stability, and transition to healthy adulthood. Youth may benefit from different treatments, including therapy and other alternatives to medication.

How Is Treatment Different for Youth Who Have Experienced Trauma?

A trauma-informed approach recognizes trauma symptoms and the impact of trauma on youth's thoughts, feelings, and behaviors. A trauma-informed approach asks "What happened to you?" instead of "What's wrong with you?" Such an approach also helps foster parents, caseworkers, and service providers interact with youth in a way that prevents additional trauma. Trauma-focused (or trauma-specific) treatments look for root causes and not just the resulting symptoms (depression, an inability to concentrate, an eating disorder, etc.). Trauma-focused treatment can help youth understand how trauma affects their emotions and how to cope with related feelings.

Trauma-focused treatment generally supports youth with the following:

- Identifying their feelings and managing anxiety, sadness, anger, and other difficult emotions

About This Chapter: This chapter includes text excerpted from "Supporting Youth in Foster Care in Making Healthy Choices," Child Welfare Information Gateway, U.S. Department of Health and Human Services (HHS), August 5, 2015. Reviewed August 2019.

- Understanding the connection between thoughts, feelings, and behaviors

- Learning to replace hurtful thoughts with more helpful ones

- Reframing traumatic experiences so that they are viewed as only one part of many life experiences

- Learning about personal safety and how to develop healthy boundaries

- Identifying strengths that help them cope with ongoing grief, loss, and uncertainty

You can speak with mental-healthcare providers to find out about what trauma-focused options are appropriate. When programs or providers trained in research-based, trauma-focused treatment are not available in a youth's communities, you can look for other services by professionals who may not be trained in specific research-based treatments yet have an understanding of trauma and its effects.

> Individual trauma results from an event, series of events, or set of circumstances that is experienced by an individual as physically or emotionally harmful or threatening and that has lasting adverse effects on the individual's functioning and physical, social, emotional, or spiritual well-being.
>
> *(Source: "Trauma," Youth.gov)*

How Can Therapy Help?

Approaches other than medication, particularly therapy or counseling, can help youth cope with their thoughts, feelings, and behaviors and contribute to healing. Health and mental-health experts advise that, ideally, therapy should be considered before or at the same time as psychotropic medication.

Therapy can help identify and address the root causes of youth's emotions and behaviors. As previously discussed, trauma-informed therapists can help youth better understand their traumatic experiences and identify ways to manage resulting stress, difficult emotions, and behaviors. Through therapy, youth receive emotional support and encouragement in trying new strategies to build healthy behaviors.

Talk with the mental-health professional and the young person to find the approach (or combination of approaches) that best fit each young person's needs. Also, it will be important to work with treatment providers to ensure the young person receives the help that is sensitive to her or his cultural and sexual identities.

What Other Approaches Can Be Helpful?

In addition to therapy, other helpful approaches may be considered instead of or in addition to medication. Mental-healthcare providers can work with youth to explore appropriate options:

- **Meditation, exercise, and changes in diet.** Exercise for the mind and body can help youth reduce stress and feel calmer. Changes in food and getting enough sleep also may boost mood and energy levels.

- **Self-expression.** Keeping a journal, doing artwork, participating in social media, and similar activities can help youth explore their emotions and identities.

- **Family routines.** Spending time together, creating new traditions, and having fun with other family members can build ties and offer an emotional lift.

- **Clubs or volunteer activities.** Group activities and "giving back" can help youth experience a valuable sense of belonging to a community, group, or cause.

- **Faith and cultural activities.** Cultural practices and being part of a faith community (church, synagogue, mosque, etc.) can help strengthen youth's sense of identity, serve as protective factors, and contribute to healing.

- **Traditional healing approaches.** Youth and their families may have preferences for practices that fit with their cultural beliefs and traditions.

What Is the Possible Role of Psychotropic Medication?

Psychotropic medications are drugs that target the brain and affect a person's mind, emotions, moods, and behaviors. Studies have found them to be effective for specific conditions. Psychotropic medications include antianxiety medications, antipsychotics, antidepressants, mood stabilizers, sleep medications, stimulants, and other medications for attention deficit hyperactivity disorder (ADHD), and others.

Doctors may prescribe such medications to help youth control symptoms and function better at home, in school, and in the community. Sometimes, long-term use of medications is needed to treat specific mental-health disorders, such as schizophrenia. Other times, medications may be used for a short time to lessen symptoms during the healing process. Medication should be only one part of a comprehensive treatment plan.

Psychotropic medications may have serious, mild, or no side effects. Side effects can be very different for different people and may include the following:

- Stomach upset or headaches
- Appetite loss or weight gain
- Sleepiness or sleep problems
- Nervousness, tearfulness, or irritability
- Disturbing thoughts
- Medical problems, such as a racing heart or dizziness
- Long-term illness

Many people have become concerned about the inappropriate use of psychotropic medications among youth for a number of reasons:

- Many youths who may need counseling and other trauma-focused mental-health services do not receive them.
- There are potentially serious side effects to many psychotropic medications.
- The medications have not been tested widely with children and youth.
- Dosages are often higher than might be normally used.
- Monitoring of medications is not always well coordinated across all individuals involved in youth's treatment.
- When prescribers are not aware of all medications youth are taking, some youth may be prescribed several different drugs that have unintended interactions.

The decision to use psychotropic medication should never be made lightly. If a doctor or specialist recommends the use of psychotropic medications for youth, there are important things to consider in making an informed decision. Considerations include benefits, risks, side effects, and youth and family preferences.

Chapter 44

Psychotherapies and Therapeutic Approaches for Victims of Sexual Assault and Abuse

Psychotherapies
Practice Goals

Psychotherapeutic interventions for adult sexual-assault victims are designed to reduce psychological distress, symptoms of posttraumatic stress disorder (PTSD), and rape trauma through counseling, structured or unstructured interaction, training programs, or predetermined treatment plans. Most treatments include individual cognitive-behavioral approaches, such as cognitive-behavioral therapy or insight/experiential therapy. The goals of psychological therapy for victims of sexual assault include:

1. Preventing and reducing PTSD/trauma symptoms, anxiety, depression, and other psychopathologies

2. Improving social adjustment and self-esteem

Target Population

The vast majority of rape and sexual-assault victims are female. The National Crime Victimization Survey (NCVS) found that between 2005 and 2010, there were 2.1 victimizations

About This Chapter: Text under the heading "Psychotherapies" is excerpted from "Psychotherapies for Victims of Sexual Assault," CrimeSolutions.gov, National Institute of Justice (NIJ), September 13, 2013. Reviewed August 2019; Text under the heading "Therapeutic Approaches" is excerpted from "Therapeutic Approaches for Sexually Abused Children and Adolescents," CrimeSolutions.gov, National Institute of Justice (NIJ), August 31, 2015. Reviewed August 2019.

per 1,000 females age 12 and older in the United States. Females who lived in lower-income households and in rural areas reported the highest rates of sexual violence during that time. Psychotherapeutic interventions can be provided to victims of sexual abuse and assault who are experiencing rape trauma or PTSD. Symptoms of PTSD can be categorized into three groups:

1. Re-experiencing intrusive thoughts, emotions, or physiological distress upon exposure to cues of the event

2. Avoidance of thoughts or stimuli that are reminiscent of the event

3. Biological, emotional, or cognitive arousal

Sexual-assault victims also report high rates of depression, difficulty concentrating, uncontrollable grief, low self-esteem, self-destructive behavior, suicidal thoughts, addictive behavior, impaired social and occupational functioning, sexual avoidance, and psychological disorders such as panic attacks.

Practice Components

Psychotherapeutic treatment generally includes two basic components:

1. Development and maintenance of a trusting relationship with a therapist

2. Recounting one's story about the assault in treatment so that the therapist can help the individual overcome the debilitating symptoms resulting from PTSD

In most modalities of psychotherapeutic treatment, therapists attempt to help victims make sense of their memories and reduce or eliminate PTSD symptoms, including thoughts, flashbacks, guilt, and fears associated with the victim's response to the assault. The practice can also teach sexual-assault victims other skills, such as anger management, assertiveness, and communication. Therapists usually focus more on the current situation and its solution, concentrating on a person's views and beliefs about their life.

Therapy models that focus on helping victims recover from trauma can be categorized into three frameworks:

- The cognitive-behavioral model assumes that a person is both the producer and product of her environment; therefore, treatment is aimed at changing a person's behaviors within her environment. The model incorporates cognitive, behavioral, and social learning theory components. Examples of specific cognitive-behavioral approaches include exposure therapy or prolonged exposure, stress inoculation training, eye movement desensitization reprocessing, cognitive-processing therapy, and assertiveness training.

- Psychodynamic psychotherapy focuses on several aspects, such as expression of emotions, exploration of avoidance of distressing emotions, examining past experiences, identification of defense mechanisms, and working through interpersonal relationships. An important part of psychodynamic psychotherapy is bringing the person's conflict and psychic tensions from the unconscious into the conscious to encourage healthier functioning.

- Supportive psychotherapy or supportive counseling may be provided in individual or group settings and allows an individual to share her traumatic experience and the symptoms that resulted from the event. Supportive approaches aim to normalize the experience, instill hope, increase interpersonal learning, and decrease an individual's sense of isolation.

The selection of a specific treatment method depends on the particular characteristics of the victim, such as the extent of PTSD symptoms. The characteristics of treatment (including the duration, number of sessions, treatment setting, and the therapist's experience) will vary depending on the type of therapy.

Therapeutic Approaches
Practice Goals

Therapeutic approaches for sexually abused children and adolescents are designed to reduce the effects of sexual abuse. The effects of sexual abuse can manifest in various ways, such as PTSD, fear, and anxiety. PTSD is the most commonly diagnosed disorder, with estimates suggesting that 37 to 53 percent of sexually abused children eventually develop PTSD. Traumatic reactions may include re-experiencing the abuse through memories or dreams, or actively attempting to avoid situations or stimuli that remind the child of the abuse. Victims may also engage in externalizing behaviors, such as sexual behavioral problems, hyperactivity, and aggression. Alternatively, the effects of sexual abuse can cause children to exhibit internalizing behaviors, such as depression and anxiety.

Sexual abuse can be a single occurrence or can occur over a period of time, sometimes even years. The duration of exposure depends on a range of factors, such as the perpetrator's access to the child or young person and the steps taken to secure the victim's silence, such as threats. Child sexual abuse can be perpetrated within the family, by those known to the children outside of the home, or by strangers. The majority of sexual abuse is committed by people known to the victim, although most are not members of their family. Instead, around one-third of perpetrators are family members.

Overall, therapeutic approaches for sexually abused children and adolescents aim to reduce the developmental consequences that result from this distinct form of maltreatment.

Target Population

Therapeutic approaches to child sexual abuse target children and adolescents aged 18 and under who have experienced sexual abuse. Although males can also experience child sexual abuse and suffer the same consequences, generally females are more often the victims of this specific type of maltreatment. Estimates suggest that between 20 and 32 percent of females experience sexual abuse, whereas approximately 4 to 8 percent of males are victims.

Practice Components

There are a variety of therapeutic approaches that are designed to treat the negative impacts of child sexual abuse, such as cognitive-behavioral therapy (CBT), cognitive-behavioral therapy for sexually abused preschoolers, trauma-focused cognitive-behavioral therapy, child-centered therapy, eye movement desensitization and reprocessing (EMDR), imagery rehearsal therapy, a recovering-from-abuse program, supportive counseling, and stress inoculation training.

Cognitive-behavioral therapy is a well-known treatment approach that can be delivered individually to the victim, or in a group setting. For child victims of sexual abuse, CBT focuses on the meaning of the events for children and their nonoffending parents, addressing the maladaptive cognitions (e.g., being "soiled"), misattributions (e.g., feelings of blame), and low self-esteem. Interventions may also try to address overt behaviors, such as sexualized behavior, externalizing behaviors, or internalizing behaviors.

Cognitive-behavioral therapy is designed to address symptoms, such as emotional distress, anxiety, and behavior problems. CBT helps children to cope effectively with their emotional distress by teaching relaxation techniques and various other skills, such as emotional expression skills and cognitive coping skills. Furthermore, children and their parents are taught how to label feelings and communicate them to others. To reduce anxiety, CBT teaches children and adolescents to recognize the signs of anxiety and the stimuli that trigger it so that they can gradually replace their maladaptive responses with adaptive ones. Finally, to reduce behavior problems, CBT teaches parents how behavior is triggered, shaped, and possibly maintained by consequences. CBT also teaches parents how to improve their child's behavior, and about the impact that the sexual abuse had so that they are better able to understand their child's behavior.

Cognitive-behavioral therapy for sexually abused children and adolescents typically includes short-term structured interventions, lasting about 12 sessions; however, sessions can extend up to 40 sessions depending on the individual's need. Interventions are tailored to the developmental age of the child or adolescent, as well as to their symptoms.

As a type of cognitive-behavioral treatment, imagery rehearsal therapy (IRT) can also be used as a therapeutic approach to child sexual abuse. Given that approximately 70 percent of individuals with PTSD experience chronic nightmares, which most often include reliving their traumatic experiences, IRT is used to help alleviate the posttraumatic nightmares. With IRT, children and adolescents are asked to recall their nightmares and, in time, rewrite the nightmares into less threatening content.

Another therapeutic approach that can be used to treat victims of child sexual abuse is EMDR. The goal of EMDR treatment is to help individuals who have experienced traumatic stress to reprocess and adaptively store traumatic memories. Treatment sessions focus on past experiences that may have caused PTSD or other psychological disorders; the current circumstances that trigger dysfunctional emotions, beliefs, and sensations; and the positive experiences that can improve future adaptive behaviors and mental health.

You can help a friend or family member who was sexually assaulted by listening and offering comfort. Remind this person you believe them. Reinforce the message that she or he is not at fault. A victim never causes sexual assault or "asks for it." You can also explain that it is natural to experience confusion, have problems remembering what happened, or feel angry, numb, or ashamed.

Ask the person whether she would like you to go with her to the hospital or to counseling. If she decides to report the crime to the police, ask whether she would like you to go with her. Let her know that she can get help.

(Source: "Sexual Assault," Office on Women's Health (OWH), U.S. Department of Health and Human Services (HHS).)

Part Four
Prevention, Staying Safe, and Your Legal Rights as a Victim

Chapter 45

Is Your Relationship a Healthy One?

As a teen, you will have relationships with a lot of people. These relationships will probably include friendships and dating relationships. Most of the time, these relationships are fun and healthy, and they make us feel good about ourselves. Sometimes, though, these relationships can be unhealthy. Unhealthy relationships can cause someone to get hurt physically or emotionally. The questions and answers below will help you understand how to spot an unhealthy relationship and how to change a bad situation.

What Is a Healthy Relationship?

In healthy relationships, you and your friend or the person you are dating feel good about each other and yourselves. You do activities together, such as going to the movies or out with other friends, and you talk to one another about how you feel. These relationships can last a few weeks, a few months, or even years.

In healthy relationships, there is respect and honesty between both people. This means that you listen to each other's thoughts and opinions and accept each other's right to say no or to change your mind without giving each other a hard time. You should be able to let the other person know how you are feeling. You might disagree or argue sometimes, but in healthy relationships, you should be able to talk things out to solve problems.

> Relationships are an important part of life and are supposed to be fun and special!

About This Chapter: This chapter includes text excerpted from "In Relationships," girlshealth.gov, Office on Women's Health (OWH), September 22, 2009. Reviewed August 2019.

What Are the Signs That I Am in an Abusive or Unhealthy Relationship?

There are many signs that you could be in an abusive or unhealthy relationship. Take a look at the list of warning signs below and see if any of these describe your relationship.

Your friend or the person you are going out with:

- Gets angry when you talk or hang out with other friends or other dating partners

- Bosses you around

- Often gets in fights with other people or loses her or his temper

- Pressures you to have sex or to do something sexual that you do not want to do uses drugs and alcohol, and tries to pressure you into doing the same thing

- Swears at you or uses mean language

- Blames you for her or his problems or tells you that it is your fault that she or he hurt you

- Insults or tries to embarrass you in front of other people

- Has physically hurt you

- Makes you feel scared of their reactions to things

- Always wants to know where you are going and who you are with

> These are just a few of the signs that you may be in an unhealthy or abusive relationship. Sometimes there are only one or two "warning signs" and sometimes there are many. If any of these signs are a part of your relationship, you should speak to a trusted adult such as a parent/ guardian, teacher, doctor, nurse, or counselor right away!

My Friend Gets Mad If I Hang Out with Other People. What Should I Do?

Be honest and stick to your decision. Tell your friend you like spending time with her or him but that you also want to spend time with other friends and family. Whether you are in a close friendship or a dating relationship, it is important for both of you to stay involved with the activities and interests you enjoyed before you became close. In a healthy relationship, you both need time to hang out with other friends and spend time alone.

What Is Abuse?

Some people think that their relationship is not abusive unless there is physical fighting. There are other types of abuse, though. Below is a list of actions/gestures grouped under different types of abuse:

- **Physical abuse**—when a person touches your body in an unwanted or violent way. This may include:

  - Hitting

  - Kicking

  - Pulling hair

  - Pushing

  - Biting

  - Choking

  - Using a weapon or any other item to hurt you

- **Verbal/emotional abuse**—when a person says something or does something that makes you afraid or feel bad about yourself. This may include:

  - Yelling

  - Name-calling

  - Saying mean things about your family and friends

  - Embarrassing you on purpose

  - Telling you what to do

  - Threatening to hurt you or hurt themselves

  - Pressuring you to use drugs or alcohol

  - Keeping you from spending time with your friends and family

- **Sexual abuse**—any sexual contact that you do not want. You may have said "no" or may be unable to say no because the abuser has threatened you, stopped you from getting out of the situation, or has physically stopped you from leaving. This may include unwanted touching or kissing or forcing you to have sex. Sexual abuse includes date rape.

235

No matter why a person is violent physically, verbally/emotionally, or sexually, it is important for you to know that it is not your fault! You are NOT the reason for the violence. Violence is NEVER okay!

Why Are Some People Violent?

There are many reasons why a person could be violent or abusive to someone in any relationship. For example, a person who has grown up in a violent family may have learned that violence, such as hitting or verbal control, was the way to solve a problem. They may be violent because they feel bad about themselves and think they will feel better if they make someone else feel worse. Others may get pressured by their friends to prove how strong they are. Sometimes people have trouble controlling their anger. Yet, violence NEVER solves problems.

Drugs and alcohol can also play a part in abusive behavior. There are some people who lose control and hurt someone after they have been drinking or taking drugs. But this is no excuse! Just because someone is under the influence of drugs and alcohol or has a bad temper does not mean that their abusive behavior is okay.

What Are Unhealthy Relationships?

In an unhealthy relationship, you usually feel the exact opposite of how you feel when you are in a "healthy relationship." You and your friend do not usually feel good about each other and yourselves. Not all unhealthy relationships are abusive but sometimes they can include verbal, physical, emotional, or sexual abuse. This can involve both people being violent or abusive toward each other or can involve only one person doing this to the other. Many times, a relationship is not unhealthy in the very beginning, but becomes so over time.

Why Do Some People Stay in Unhealthy or Violent Relationships?

Sometimes it may be hard to get out of an abusive relationship, because violent relationships often go in cycles. After a person is violent, she or he may say sorry and promise never to hurt you again. They may even say that they will work on the relationship, and it may be a while before that person acts violently again. These ups and downs can make it hard to leave a relationship.

It is also hard to leave someone you care about. You may be scared or ashamed to admit that you are in an abusive relationship, or you may simply be scared to be alone without that person. You may be afraid that no one will believe you, or that your friend or partner will hurt you more if you tell someone. Whatever the reasons, leaving an unhealthy relationship is hard but it is something you should do.

Leaving an unhealthy relationship will be a lot easier and safer if you have a plan. Here are some tips on making your safety plan:

- Go to your doctor or hospital for treatment if you have been injured.
- Tell a trusted adult such as a parent/guardian, counselor, doctor, teacher, or spiritual or community leader.
- Tell the person who is abusing you over the phone that you do not want to see her or him so they cannot touch you. Do this when a parent or guardian is home so you know you will be safe in your house.
- Use a diary to keep track of the date the violence happened, where you were, exactly what the person you are dating did, and exactly what effects it caused (such as bruises). This will be important if you need the police to order the person to stay away from you.
- Avoid contact with the person.
- Spend time with your other friends, and avoid walking by yourself.
- Think of safe places to go in case of an emergency, such as a police station or a public place such as a restaurant or mall.
- Carry a cell phone, phonecard, or money for a call in case you need to call for help. Use code words on the phone that you and your family decide on ahead of time. If you are in trouble, say the code word on the phone so that your family member knows you cannot talk openly and need help right away.
- Call 911 right away if you are ever afraid that the person is following you or is going to hurt you. Keep domestic violence hotline numbers with you in a safe place or program them into your cell phone. The 24-hour National Domestic Violence Hotline is 800-799-SAFE (800-799-7233) or 800-787-3224 (Toll-Free TDD).

How Do I Get Out of an Unhealthy or Abusive Relationship?

First, if you think that you are in an unhealthy relationship, you should talk to a parent/guardian, friend, counselor, doctor, teacher, coach or other trusted person about your relationship. Tell them why you think the relationship is unhealthy and exactly what the other person has done (hit, pressured you to have sex, tried to control you). If need be, this trusted adult can help you contact your parent/guardian, counselors, school security, or even the police about the violence. With help, you can get out of an unhealthy relationship. Sometimes, leaving an abusive relationship can be dangerous, so it is very important for you to make a safety plan.

Why Should I Leave an Abusive Relationship?

Abusive relationships are very unhealthy for you. You can have trouble sleeping or have headaches or stomach aches. You might feel depressed, sad, anxious or nervous, and you may even lose or gain weight. You may also blame yourself, feel guilty, and have trouble trusting other people in your life. Staying in an abusive relationship can hurt your self-esteem and make it hard for you to believe in yourself. If you are being physically abused, you can be in pain and may suffer permanent damage. You should definitely leave the relationship if you are getting hurt, or if you are being threatened with physical harm in any way.

The most important reason to leave an unhealthy relationship is because you deserve to be in a relationship that is healthy and fun.

What Do I Do If I Am Being Hurt by a Parent/ Guardian or Another Family Member?

Sadly, there are times when different kinds of abuse happen in the home. Child abuse is when any person caring for a child fails to take care of the child, physically hurts the child, or treats the child in a sexual way. No matter what, parents, guardians, and caregivers are supposed to protect and care for their children. The term "child abuse" does not just refer to young children. Child abuse can happen to a child of any age, from infants to teenagers.

What Do I Do If a Friend Tells Me That She or He Is in an Abusive Relationship?

If your friend talks to you about her or his abuse, you can help by:

- Listening without judging or blaming

- Telling your friend that you believe her or him

- Telling your friend that it is NOT her or his fault

- Telling your friend that you are always there to listen if she or he wants to talk about it

- Reminding your friend of all the friends and family who care about her or him

- Letting your friend know that you are worried about her or his safety

- Telling your friend that you want to help her or him talk to a parent/guardian or other trusted adult right away

- Offering to go with your friend to talk to an adult

- Helping your friend make a safety plan

- Sharing the number of the 24-hour National Domestic Violence Hotline: 800-799-SAFE (800-799-7233) or 800-787-3224 (Toll-Free TDD)

- Suggesting your friend take a self-defense class

Be sure not to take this on alone. Talk with a trusted adult, such as a school counselor, about how to help your friend.

Should I Have My Friend Talk about the Abusive Relationship to Her or His Parents/Guardians or Another Adult?

Yes! The most important thing that you can do for your friend is to try to get her or him to talk to an adult right away. This adult could be a parent/guardian, coach, teacher, school counselor, doctor, nurse, or spiritual or community leader. Offer to go with your friend to talk to an adult about the abusive relationship. If your friend is nervous about going to talk to an adult, remind her or him that an adult can:

- Listen and give advice on how to handle the situation

- Help get her or him to a safe place

- Help contact the right people, such as the police, the school principal, or a counselor

What If My Friend Would Not Listen to Me and Wants to Keep the Abuse a Secret?

After you urge your friend to talk to an adult about the abuse, you should also tell an adult. It is too much for you to handle alone. You may think you need to keep your friend's secret, but it is important for you to tell a trusted adult—especially if you are afraid that your friend could get hurt. Your friend will need help even if she or he does not think so.

Do not tell your friend to choose between her or his abusive partner and you. Be supportive, no matter what your friend decides to do. Do not tell your friend's secrets to others.

What Else Do I Need to Know about Relationships?

At least 1 in 10 teens experience physical violence in their relationships. Even if you have not experienced physical, sexual, or verbal and emotional abuse, one of your friends may be in an unhealthy relationship with another friend or dating partner. If you are in an unhealthy relationship, or if your friend is, it is important to get help right away before someone gets hurt!

Chapter 46

Talking to Your Kids about Sexual Assault

To teens, young love can feel all-encompassing. The emotional rush and validation that many experiences from a first love can be exciting, but sometimes, it can turn into codependency. When relationships go from healthy to codependent, abusive behavior can follow.

Knowing that approximately one in three high-school students experience physical or sexual violence by someone they are dating, we need to make sure we talk about these topics with our kids. It is good to start as early as possible. Waiting until your teen is in a relationship may be too late. Here are five tips for talking with your kids about building healthy relationships:

- **Talk early and often.** The key to laying the groundwork for your child to form healthy dating relationships is to have a series of ongoing talks starting when your child is young and continuing through adolescence.

- **Help your kids understand consent.** Make sure younger children understand their body parts, personal boundaries, and drive home the idea of consent. Let them know that no one should touch them without their permission. As your child grows older, discuss how consent works in a sexual relationship. Let them know that consent is a clear "yes" to sexual activity. It means you know and understand what is going on, you know and are able to say what you do and do not want, and you are not under the influence of alcohol or drugs.

- **Bring up less obvious types of abuse.** Adolescents may be familiar with the most extreme types of abuse, such as physical assault or rape. However, they may not recognize

About This Chapter: This chapter includes text excerpted from "Talking to Your Kids about Sexual Assault," Office on Women's Health (OWH), U.S. Department of Health and Human Services (HHS), April 23, 2017.

more subtle forms of abuse, such as emotional and verbal abuse between two people in a relationship.

- **Show them what healthy communication looks like.** Model healthy behaviors at home, and explain that in healthy relationships, people listen well, talk openly and honestly, and treat each other with respect. On the flip side, abusive communication involves name-calling as well as guilting, shaming, and attempting to belittle or control your partner.

- **Keep it short.** These conversations should be casual and short. A conversation as brief as a minute long can still be effective. They can take place in the car or on-the-go. These conversations plant seeds in your child's mind about the behaviors that occur in healthy relationships. By talking about these concepts often but casually, your teen will know they can approach you with questions. It further cements in your teen's mind the behaviors they should seek or avoid in relationships.

If your teen is dating, you may notice that the relationship demands more and more of your child's attention. This is common to an extent, but your teen should know the warning signs of abusive or unhealthy relationships. For example, does their partner demand to check their phone, get angry when they spend time with others, or try to change the way they dress? Does their partner use subtle techniques to coerce or force unwanted sexual activity? To get what they want, an abusive partner may:

- **Threaten to end the relationship:** "If you do not hook up with me, it is over. I am leaving you."

- **Use guilt:** "Come on. You do not mean that. If you really love me, you would show me."

- **Initially respect boundaries but try crossing them again later:** "I know you said that, but that was a few weeks ago. Don't you love me?"

- **Beg until the partner gives in and lets them do what they want, regardless of consent:** "Come on, please. Try this. Pleeease. Come on."

These are all signs of abuse, and they are never okay. Talk to your kids about what to watch out for. Please remember that boys suffer the same emotional and physical abuses but are less likely to seek help.

If you think a young person in your life is feeling unsafe in a relationship, start by visiting loveisrespect.org, call 866-331-9474, or text loveis to 22522. Tell your teen about the Crisis Text Line. By texting HELP to 741741, teens can text with a crisis counselor immediately who can help them find the tools and resources to escape their abusive situation. Finally, teens can call the National Sexual Assault Hotline at 800-656-HOPE (800-656-4673). Help is available—for you and for them.

Impact of Sexual Abuse on Children and Youth

Sexual abuse violates physical and emotional boundaries. Children and youth who have been abused may see the world as unsafe and adults as manipulative and untrustworthy, or they may lack boundaries and be unaware when they are in unsafe situations. Many factors influence how children think and feel about the abuse they experienced, how it affects them, and how they develop resilience.

(Source: "Parenting a Child or Youth Who Has Been Sexually Abused: A Guide for Foster and Adoptive Parents," Child Welfare Information Gateway, U.S. Department of Health and Human Services (HHS).)

Chapter 47

Prevention and Treatment of Domestic Violence and Abuse

Domestic violence often results in physical and emotional injuries. It can also lead to other health problems, reproductive-health challenges, mental-health conditions such as depression, and suicide. Women affected by intimate-partner violence are also more likely to use drugs or alcohol to cope. Domestic violence can even end in death. Women who live in a home with guns are five times more likely to be killed. More than half of women murdered with guns are killed by intimate partners.

(Source: "Signs of Domestic Violence or Abuse," Office on Women's Health (OWH), U.S. Department of Health and Human Series (HHS).)

Understanding and Preventing Violence

Violence is a public-health problem that has a substantial impact on individuals, their families, and entire communities. Each year, millions of people experience the physical, mental, and economic consequences of violence. The good news is that violence is preventable, and the Centers for Disease Control and Prevention (CDC) is committed to stopping violence before it can begin.

The Division of Violence Prevention (DVP) within the CDC's Injury Center works to prevent violence and the injuries and deaths caused by violence, so people can live life to the fullest. As the only federal agency that focuses on stopping violence before it starts, the

About This Chapter: This chapter includes text excerpted from "Understanding and Preventing Violence: Summary of 2016 Research and Surveillance Activities," Centers for Disease Control and Prevention (CDC), July 2017.

DVP monitors and tracks violence trends, conducts research to identify factors that increase or decrease the risk for violence, develops and rigorously evaluates innovative prevention approaches, and supports the widespread use of evidence-based prevention strategies. This critical work helps prevent violence across the lifespan, including child abuse and neglect, youth violence, intimate-partner violence, sexual violence, and suicidal behavior.

This chapter describes the DVP's 2016 research activities in violence prevention and highlights some results from previously funded research and ongoing surveillance activities. This work fills critical knowledge gaps and strengthens our ability to prevent different forms of violence and its consequences. The DVP's research portfolio aligns with its five-year strategic vision for a crosscutting approach to understanding the overlapping causes of violence and factors that protect people and communities from experiencing violence in all its forms.

Examining the Economic Impact of Violence and the Efficiency of Prevention Strategies

Understanding and responding to public-health problems includes recognizing the broad costs of violence and the cost–benefit of prevention strategies. DVP researchers collaborated with health economists in the Injury Center to develop the first national, comprehensive estimate of the societal costs of rape against women and men. The estimates, published in a 2017 report, indicated that the average cost accrued over the course of a rape victim's lifetime was $122,461 per victim. The DVP is also developing an updated national estimate of the societal costs of intimate-partner violence, including estimates of the lifetime costs per case. This research informs understanding of the economic impact of violence and can strengthen the ability to assess returns on investments in prevention.

Testing New and Innovative Prevention Strategies
Preventing Child Abuse and Neglect

Intramural research and new research awards in 2016 will evaluate the effectiveness of policies and programs that provide economic and other support to high-risk families in order to prevent child abuse and neglect.

Preventing Neglect of Children with Special Healthcare Needs

Child maltreatment, particularly neglect, disproportionately affects low-income children with special healthcare needs and has serious short- and long-term consequences. Few evidence-based preventive services exist for such families, particularly within the context of the patient-centered medical home. In 2016, the DVP funded researchers at Boston Medical Center to examine the efficacy of Child Abuse Prevention Problem Solving (CAPPS), a targeted intervention that addresses specific stressors faced by low-income parents and enhances family strengths previously shown to prevent neglect. Specific research aims included decreasing referrals to Child Protective Services for neglect and increasing adherence to recommended medical care; decreasing perceived social isolation, difficulty navigating complex services, and caregiver burden; and enhancing family strengths, social connections, access to support in times of need, and knowledge of parenting and child development.

Strengthening Economic Support Policies

Policies that improve the socioeconomic conditions of families tend to have large impacts on children's development, academic achievements, and health, including exposure to child abuse and neglect. In 2016, DVP researchers reported the effects of paid family leave (PFL) policies on hospital admissions for pediatric abusive head trauma (AHT) by comparing California's 2004 PFL policy with seven comparison states without PFL policies. California's PFL policy showed a significant decrease in abusive head trauma hospital admissions in children less than 2 years old. These promising results underscore the importance of policies that strengthen economic supports for families to help reduce child abuse and neglect.

In 2016, the DVP funded two new rigorous evaluations of economic-support policies for preventing child maltreatment. Researchers at the University of Wisconsin-Madison are examining the impact of Project GAIN (Getting Access to Income Now) on reducing rates of child abuse and neglect among 800 at-risk families in Milwaukee, Wisconsin. Families in the intervention will receive assessments of their economic needs, assistance in identifying and accessing resources, and support with financial decision-making. The second study, conducted by researchers at the University of Kansas-Lawrence, examines whether economic and social safety net policies impact rates of child abuse and neglect. The multiphase study will investigate the association between reports of child neglect and changes in multiple state and county programs (including Temporary Assistance to Needy Families (TANF), Earned Income Tax Credits (EITC), and Supplemental Nutrition Assistance Programs (SNAP)) from 1995 to 2014.

Preventing Youth Violence

Youth violence is a significant problem that negatively impacts youth in urban, suburban, rural, and tribal communities. Research and experience in neighborhoods show individual, family, and community strategies to prevent youth violence. Since 2000, the DVP has supported research investments in academic–community collaborations to advance the science and practice of youth violence prevention. Called "Youth Violence Prevention Centers" (YVPCs), the collaborations rigorously evaluate prevention activities that have community-level impacts on youth violence. The YVPCs have demonstrated substantial success in reducing youth violence in their target communities while also generating a body of generalizable science that can inform prevention activities in other communities.

Evaluating Comprehensive Evidence-Based Approaches to Prevent Youth Violence in High-Risk Communities

From 2010 to 2016, six YVPCs were funded to implement comprehensive prevention strategies with multiple components to impact youth violence at the community level. Components were directed at risk factors at the individual (e.g., delinquency, substance abuse, lack of social skills); relationship (e.g., inadequate parental monitoring, supervision, discipline; peer norms supporting violence); and community (e.g., social disorganization, lack of cohesion, lack of economic or supervised recreational activities for youth) levels. The YVPCs developed multidisciplinary and community partnerships, built community capacity to work collaboratively to prevent violence, and disseminated research findings to build knowledge on youth violence prevention.

The Division of Violence Prevention collaborated with the YVPCs funded from 2010 to 2016 to produce a special issue of the *Journal of Primary Prevention*. The issue shares methods and lessons learned for implementing and evaluating comprehensive evidence-based approaches to prevent youth violence. Articles in the issue emphasize the importance of community partnerships and engagement, collection of youth violence data and indicators at the community level, development of "packages" of evidence-based approaches for youth violence prevention, and design options for evaluating community-level interventions.

Building on the Success of the Youth Violence Prevention Centers

To build upon the success of the YVPCs, the DVP issued new funding opportunity announcements in 2015 and 2016 aimed at filling research gaps in youth violence prevention. These gaps include determining the effectiveness of community- and policy-level prevention strategies to reduce youth violence at the community level; understanding how and why prevention strategies may be effective in preventing youth violence; and examining how community readiness and capacity are related to the selection, implementation, and evaluation of evidence-based youth violence prevention approaches.

Preventing Sexual Violence and Intimate-Partner Violence
Evaluating Primary Prevention Strategies to Build the Evidence Base for Sexual Violence and Intimate-Partner Violence Prevention

Sexual violence and intimate-partner violence are pervasive problems with broad and long-lasting impacts on victims and their family, friends, and communities. The DVP is committed to funding research that builds the evidence base of effective primary prevention programs, policies, and strategies. Ongoing research funded by the DVP in previous years focuses on evaluating strategies that seek to influence social norms around sexual and dating violence by focusing on men and boys, bystander approaches, and community-level interventions. This research includes both adolescent and college-age samples, and holds promise for identifying additional evidence-based programs to prevent sexual and dating violence perpetration at both the relationship and school/community levels. However, gaps remain in our knowledge, particularly related to programs and policies to prevent sexual and intimate-partner violence perpetration that have substantial uptake in practice and are evidence-informed but lack evaluation research evidence.

Evaluating Practice-Based Sexual Violence Primary Prevention Approaches from the Centers for Disease Control and Prevention's Rape Prevention and Education Programs

Numerous prevention approaches are implemented in the practice field to address sexual and intimate-partner violence without being evaluated to establish effectiveness. With this in mind, the DVP funded rigorous evaluations of prevention approaches in the practice field. Through the Rape Prevention and Education (RPE) Program, the CDC funds health departments in all 50 states, the District of Columbia, and four U.S. territories to work with state sexual-assault coalitions, rape crisis centers, and other community-based organizations to advance sexual-violence prevention. The goal of the RPE Program is to strengthen sexual-violence prevention efforts at the local, state, and national levels.

Evaluating the Effectiveness of Teen Dating Violence-Prevention Programs

Each year, approximately 25 percent of U.S. teens sustain physical, psychological, or sexual abuse by dating partners. Many victims of teen dating violence experience a host of devastating consequences, including acute and chronic mental and physical health problems, suicidality, delinquency, risky sexual behavior, substance abuse, and academic failure.

To prevent teen dating violence, the DVP developed Dating Matters®, a comprehensive teen dating violence-prevention program for youth, parents, educators, and communities. The program engages local health departments and reinforces skills taught to parents and youth through evidence-based programs with educator training. A communication campaign supports the program using social media and text messages. Dating Matters® was delivered to nearly 37,000 students in 45 middle schools and over 900 parents across four high-risk, urban communities. The program is being evaluated for effectiveness using a longitudinal cluster randomized controlled trial design. Outcomes include reducing the risk for physical, emotional, and sexual violence among teens in middle and high school. Challenges in evaluating the comprehensive Dating Matters® program include site variability, implementation versus evaluation responsibilities, school retention, parent engagement in research, and working within the context of high-risk urban schools and communities. The implementation phase of the randomized controlled trial concluded with the 2015 to 2016 school year. DVP researchers are working on analyzing the data and examining outcomes on teen dating violence-perpetration and victimization. The DVP will continue to collect follow-up data as the students move to high school through the 2017 to 2018 school year. This work will help guide and strengthen national efforts to stop dating violence.

Preventing Suicide
Preventing Suicide with Connectedness

The Division of Violence Prevention (DVP) is leading efforts to understand whether increasing social connectedness can lower the risk of suicide. The DVP supported researchers at the University of Michigan to evaluate the effectiveness of Links to Enhancing Teens' Connectedness (LET's CONNECT), a community-based mentorship intervention for youth aged 12 to 15 at risk for suicidal behavior due to bullying perpetration/victimization, or low interpersonal connectedness. The intervention was based on a positive youth development framework and involved mentorship from a natural mentor (e.g., family members) and a trained community mentor. Analyses of baseline data from 321 youth in the study revealed that lower levels of social connectedness and higher levels of bullying victimization and perpetration were significantly associated with thinking about and attempting suicide. Researchers also found youth involvement in private religious practices and organizational religiousness were associated with a lower risk of suicidal thoughts. Analysis of the intervention effects over time is still being conducted. However, in the preliminary results, LET's CONNECT was associated with improved social connectedness compared to the control group. Effects for community connectedness, feeling an unmet need to belong, self-esteem, and depression were not significant but in the desired direction (manuscript under review).

Social connections are important determinants of emotional and physical health in later life, and they may be key to preventing suicidal behaviors. The DVP funded researchers at the University of Rochester to evaluate the effectiveness of The Senior Connection (TSC) in addressing risks for suicide, including suicide ideation and social connectedness, among adults over age 60. TSC promotes partnerships between healthcare providers and nonmedical aging service agencies, and links disconnected seniors with peer companions. Preliminary results indicate that after a year, people in TSC had significantly reduced perceived burdensomeness compared to the care as usual (CAU) group with effects most pronounced for people with greater functional impairments. The treatment group also had greater declines in depressive symptoms and anxiety symptoms compared to CAU. Both groups improved in measures of thwarted belongingness and thinking about suicide. Results at the two-year followup are forthcoming.

Technical Packages for Violence Prevention

The Division of Violence Prevention (DVP) released five technical packages in 2016 to 2017 covering the areas of child abuse and neglect, sexual violence, youth violence, suicide, and intimate-partner violence. These technical packages are based on a critical review of the research literature. They describe a collection of strategies that represent the best available evidence to prevent violence. Technical packages are valuable because they allow communities to prioritize interventions that are based on this evidence. The technical packages include strategies (i.e., preventive directions), approaches (i.e., examples of specific ways to advance the strategies through programs, policies, or practices), and the evidence for given approaches. The purpose of these packages is to compile the best available evidence for a given violence topic to be a prevention resource for the field. These packages also help show gaps in knowledge that will inform future research. The topic-specific technical packages include examples of prevention strategies that can have benefits for multiple types of violence. The DVP will be releasing guidance documents to help communities implement the strategies in the technical packages.

251

Chapter 48

How to Help a Friend Who Is Abused at Home

Whether you suspect that a friend or family member is being abused or you witnessed someone being abused, you can take steps to help.

What Are the Signs That Someone May Be Abused?

According to the National Domestic Violence Hotline, some warning signs include the following:

- Their partner insults them in front of other people.
- They are constantly worried about making their partner angry.
- They make excuses for their partner's behavior.
- Their partner is extremely jealous or possessive.
- They have unexplained marks or injuries.
- They have stopped spending time with friends and family.
- They are depressed or anxious, or you notice changes in their personality.

If you think your friend or family member is being abused, be supportive by listening to them and asking questions about how they are doing. The person being abused may not be ready or able to leave the relationship right now.

About This Chapter: This chapter includes text excerpted from "How to Help a Friend Who Is Being Abused," Office on Women's Health (OWH), U.S. Department of Health and Human Services (HHS), September 13, 2018.

How Can I Help Someone Who Is Being Abused?

Knowing or thinking that someone you care about is in a violent relationship can be very hard. You may fear for her/his safety—and maybe for good reason. You may want to rescue her/him or insist she/he leave, but every adult must make her/his own decisions.

Each situation is different, and the people involved are all different too. Here are some ways to help a loved one who is being abused:

- **Set up a time to talk.** Try to make sure you have privacy and would not be distracted or interrupted. Visit your loved one in person if possible.

- **Let her/him know you are concerned about her/his safety.** Be honest. Tell her/him about times when you were worried about her/him. Help her/him see that abuse is wrong. She/he may not respond right away, or she/he may even get defensive or deny the abuse. Let her/him know you want to help and will be there to support her/him in whatever decision she/he makes.

- **Be supportive.** Listen to your loved one. Keep in mind that it may be very hard for her/him to talk about the abuse. Tell her/him that she/he is not alone and that people want to help. If she/he wants help, ask her/him what you can do.

- **Offer specific help.** You might say you are willing to just listen, to help her/him with child care, or to provide transportation, for example.

- **Do not place shame, blame, or guilt on her/him.** Do not say, "You just need to leave." Instead, say something such as, "I get scared thinking about what might happen to you." Tell her/him you understand that her/his situation is very difficult.

- **Help her/him make a safety plan.** Safety planning might include packing important items and helping her/him find a "safe" word. This is a code word she/he can use to let you know she/he is in danger without an abuser knowing. It might also include agreeing on a place to meet her/him if she/he has to leave in a hurry.

- **Encourage her/him to talk to someone who can help.** Offer to help her/him find a local domestic violence agency. Offer to go with her/him to the agency, the police, or the court. The National Domestic Violence Hotline, 800-799-SAFE (800-799-7233); the National Sexual Assault Hotline, 800-656-HOPE (800-656-4673); and the National Teen Dating Abuse Helpline, 866-331-9474, are all available 24 hours a day, 7 days a week. They can offer advice based on experience and can help find local support and services.

- **If she/he decides to stay, continue to be supportive.** She/he may decide to stay in the relationship, or she/he may leave and then go back many times. It may be hard for you to understand, but people stay in abusive relationships for many reasons. Be supportive, no matter what she/he decides to do.

- **Encourage her/him to do things outside of the relationship.** It is important for her/him to see friends and family.

- **If she/he decides to leave, continue to offer help.** Even though the relationship was abusive, she/he may feel sad and lonely once it is over. She/he may also need help getting services from agencies or community groups.

Who Can I Talk to About Leaving an Abusive Relationship?

Many people can help you think about your options to leave an abusive relationship safely. It might be unsafe if an abusive partner finds out you are thinking about leaving. Try to talk only to people who will not tell the abuser about your plans:

- **Your doctor or nurse.** Most people visit the doctor at least once a year for a checkup, so try to visit the doctor or nurse without your partner. If your partner insists on going with you, try to write a note to the office staff saying that you want to see the doctor or nurse alone. Or, tell your partner that you need privacy to speak about a woman's health issue that you are too embarrassed to talk about. Or, tell your partner, where others can hear you, that the doctor's policy is patients only in the exam room.

- **A teacher, counselor, or principal at your child's school.** An adult at your child's school can help connect you to shelters and other safe places in your community. Teachers and others at your child's school want to help the families of the children they teach.

- **Human resources.** If you work outside the home, the human resources (HR) department at your workplace may be able to connect you to an Employee Assistance Program (EAP) or other resources in your community.

- **Family or friends.** Family or friends who knew you before you met an abusive partner might be able to help you. If more than one family member or friend can help you, it might be good for a few people to work together to help.

- **A free 800 telephone hotline.** You can talk to trained advocates at the National Domestic Violence Hotline (800-799-7233), for free 24 hours a day, 7 days a week without giving your name or address. The counselors can help you talk through the steps of leaving an abusive relationship. You can call a hotline as many times as you need to.

(Source: "Leaving an Abusive Relationship," Office on Women's Health (OWH), U.S. Department of Health and Human Services (HHS).)

- **Let her/him know that you will always be there no matter what.** It can be very frustrating to see a friend or loved one stay in an abusive relationship. But if you end your relationship, she/he has one less safe place to go in the future. You cannot force a person to leave a relationship, but you can let them know you will help, whatever they decide to do.

How Do I Report Domestic Violence or Abuse?

If you see or hear domestic violence or child abuse in your neighborhood or in a public place, call 911. Do not worry about whether the couple or person will be angry with you for calling. It could be a matter of life and death, and it is better to be safe than sorry. You do not have to give your name if you are afraid for your own safety.

If you want to report abuse but there is no immediate danger, ask local police or child/adult protective services to make a welfare check. This surprise check-in by local authorities may help the person being abused.

Chapter 49

Promoting Protective Factors for Children Exposed to Domestic Violence

Protective factors are conditions or attributes of individuals, families, communities, or the larger society that, when present, promote well-being and reduce the risk for negative outcomes. These factors may "buffer" the effect of risk exposure and help individuals and families negotiate difficult circumstances and fair better in school, work, and life.

Positive long-term outcomes related to health, school success, and successful transitions to adulthood typically do not occur as the result of single interventions. Focusing on protective factors offers a way to track progress by increasing resilience in the short term and contributing to the development of skills, personal characteristics, knowledge, relationships, and opportunities that offset risk exposure and contribute to improved well-being. In this sense, protective factors associated with the desired longer-term outcomes can be used as interim results for practitioners to monitor progress over time.

At Risk, In Risk, or Both?

The U.S. Department of Health and Human Services (HHS), Administration on Children, Youth and Families (ACYF) serves five vulnerable populations:

- Children exposed to domestic violence

- Homeless and runaway youth

About This Chapter: This chapter includes text excerpted from "Promoting Protective Factors for In-Risk Families and Youth: A Guide for Practitioners," Child Welfare Information Gateway, U.S. Department of Health and Human Services (HHS), September 2015. Reviewed August 2019.

- Pregnant and parenting teens

- Victims of child abuse and neglect

- Youth in and aging out of the foster care system

Many of these children and youth grow up under conditions, such as chronic ill health or poverty, which exposes them to risky and traumatic situations. These populations are clearly at risk for negative outcomes. The populations served by ACYF are considered to be at risk because they already experience one or more of the negative outcomes that prevention programs address.

More than 15 million children in the United States live in homes in which domestic violence has happened at least once. These children are at greater risk for repeating the cycle as adults by entering into abusive relationships or becoming abusers themselves. For example, a boy who sees his mother being abused is 10 times more likely to abuse his female partner as an adult. A girl who grows up in a home where her father abuses her mother is more than six times as likely to be sexually abused as a girl who grows up in a nonabusive home.

Children who witness or are victims of emotional, physical, or sexual abuse are at higher risk for health problems as adults. These can include mental health conditions, such as depression and anxiety. They may also include diabetes, obesity, heart disease, poor self-esteem, and other problems.

(Source: "Effects of Domestic Violence on Children," Office on Women's Health (OWH), U.S. Department of Health and Human Services (HHS).)

Lessons from the Research Literature

To address the broad spectrum of ACYF programs and populations, ACYF commissioned a literature review and expert consultation project to distill findings specifically relevant across the five populations served by ACYF. The findings presented in *Protective Factors for Populations Served by the Administration on Children, Youth and Families: A Literature Review and Theoretical Framework* are based on a thorough review of current research linking protective factors to well-being in the five populations.

Focusing on these in-risk populations has spotlighted specific factors with moderate or strong association with improved well-being. The review highlights the importance of working at multiple levels to impact individual skills and knowledge, focus on nurturing relationships, and increase supports and opportunities available in the broader community. This review also documents the need to enhance the evidence base through further research and practice to better understand the measures for tracking progress and the policy context and strategies that contribute to effective interventions. Protective factor findings were organized into a framework comprising three levels of influence: individual, relationship, and community.

The top ten protective factors with the strongest evidence to date across ACYF populations organized by the three levels of influence are:

- Individual level
    - Self-regulation skills
    - Relational skills
    - Problem-solving skills
    - Involvement in positive activities
- Relationship level
    - Parenting competencies
    - Positive peers
    - Caring adults
- Community level
    - Positive community environment
    - Positive school environment
    - Economic opportunities

Using Protective Factors for Administration on Children, Youth, and Families Populations
Which Individual Skills and Capacities Can Improve Well-Being for Children and Youth?

At the individual level, the evidence is strongest for the protective nature of self-regulation skills, relational skills, and problem-solving skills.

Self-regulation skills refer to a youth's ability to manage or control emotions and behaviors, which can include self-mastery, anger management, character, long-term self-control, and emotional intelligence.

Relational skills refer to a youth's ability to form positive bonds and connections (e.g., social competence, being caring, forming prosocial relationships) and a youth's interpersonal skills (e.g., communication skills and conflict-resolution skills).

Problem-solving skills refer to a youth's adaptive functioning skills and ability to solve problems.

These three important skills are related to positive outcomes, such as resiliency, having supportive friends, positive academic performance, improved cognitive functioning, and better social skills. They are also related to reductions in posttraumatic stress disorder, stress, anxiety, depression, and delinquency. Finally, these skills are related to more satisfaction with out-of-home placements and fewer placement disruptions. Numerous interventions target these three skills and have been evaluated for use with ACYF populations, with promising results. Effective programs include:

- Child and family traumatic-stress intervention

- Multisystemic therapy

- Alternatives for families

- Trauma-focused cognitive-behavioral therapy

- Intensive family preservation services

- Safe dates

In addition to building skills, involvement in positive activities, specifically school connectedness, commitment, and engagement, has strong evidence as a protective factor for ACYF populations. Involvement in positive activities is associated with lower levels of antisocial and general problem behavior, reductions in repeat pregnancies, higher socioeconomic status, and resiliency.

How Can Parents, Guardians, Other Adults, and Peers Contribute to a Child's Well-Being?

For the youth of all ages, the competencies of the parent or guardian include parenting skills (e.g., establishing clear standards and limits, discipline, and proper care) and positive parent–child interactions (e.g., sensitive, supportive, or caring parenting and close relationships between parent and child). These competencies are related to numerous well-being outcomes, such as increases in self-esteem, lower risk of antisocial behavior, lower likelihood of running away and teen pregnancy, reductions in child behavior problems, increases in social skills, better psychological adjustment, and reductions in internalizing behaviors. Also, for children in out-of-home care, improvements in parenting competencies have been associated with family reunification.

The well-being of parents and other caregivers is an important protective factor, especially for younger youth (under the age of 12). The well-being of parents and caregivers primarily refers to the parents' own positive psychological functioning (e.g., lower rates of depression and other mental-health problems of mothers), well-being, and social supports. This protective factor is related to resilience, fewer conduct problems, better social relationships, and better behavioral health outcomes for their children.

The presence of a caring adult is particularly important for teens and young adults. These caring adults are often program staff or home visitors but can also be mentors, advocates, teachers, or extended family members. The presence of a caring adult is related to numerous positive outcomes, including greater resilience, lower stress, less likelihood of arrest, reductions in homelessness, higher levels of employment, less delinquent conduct, favorable health, less suicidal ideation, reductions in rapid repeat pregnancies, and better outcomes for the children of teen mothers.

Positive relationships with peers are another source of protection for in-risk populations and include both support from peers and positive peer norms. Having friendships and support from peers is related to reductions in depressive symptoms, more empathetic parenting attitudes (among teen mothers), and higher self-esteem. The presence of positive peer norms is related to reductions in rapid repeat pregnancies; less alcohol, tobacco and other drug use; lower levels of sexual activity; less antisocial and delinquent behavior; and more success in school. Ensuring that children and youth have positive peers can be achieved by creating groups with positive attitudes and values.

How Can We Create a Community That Promotes Children's Well-Being?

Three community-level factors are particularly important for the populations served by ACYF. A positive school environment, with supportive teachers and staff and specialized school-based programming geared toward improving outcomes, is related to reductions in traumatic stress disorder symptoms, depression, psychosocial dysfunction, and dating violence, as well as improvements in school performance and resilience. Two additional protective factors are a positive community environment, as defined by neighborhood quality and advantage, community safety, social cohesion, and social network support, and economic opportunities, as defined by higher socioeconomic status, employment, and financial support for higher education.

261

Chapter 50

Preventing School Violence

What Is School Violence?

School violence describes violent acts that disrupt learning and have a negative effect on students, schools, and the broader community.

Examples of violent behavior include:

- Bullying

- Fighting (e.g., punching, slapping, and kicking)

- Weapon use

- Cyberbullying

- Gang violence

Places where school violence occurs:

- On school property

- On the way to or from school

- During a school-sponsored event

- On the way to or from a school-sponsored event

About This Chapter: This chapter includes text excerpted from "Preventing School Violence," Centers for Disease Control and Prevention (CDC), June 27, 2019.

How Big Is the Problem?

According to the Centers for Disease Control and Prevention's (CDC) nationwide Youth Risk Behavior Survey (YRBS):

- Nearly 9 percent of high-school students had been in a physical fight on school property one or more times during the 12 months before the survey.

- About 6 percent of students had been threatened or injured with a weapon (for example, a gun, knife, or club) on school property one or more times during the 12 months before the survey.

- About 7 percent of students had not gone to school at least 1 day during the 30 days before the survey because they felt they would be unsafe at school or on their way to or from school.

- Most school-associated violent deaths occur during transition times—immediately before and after the school day and during lunch.

- Violent deaths are more likely to occur at the start of each semester.

- Nearly 50 percent of homicide perpetrators gave some type of warning signal, such as making a threat or leaving a note, before the event.

- Firearms used in school-associated homicides and suicides came primarily from the perpetrator's home or from friends or relatives.

- Homicide is the second leading cause of death among youth aged 5 to 18. Data from this study indicate that between 1 percent and 2 percent of these deaths happen on school grounds or on the way to or from school. These findings underscore the importance of preventing violence at school as well as in communities.

(Source: "School-Associated Violent Death Study," Centers for Disease Control and Prevention (CDC).)

How Can We Prevent Violence in Schools?

All students have the right to learn in a safe school environment. The good news is that school violence can be prevented. No one factor in isolation causes school violence. Preventing school violence requires addressing factors at all levels of the social ecology—the individual, relational, community, and societal levels. Research shows that prevention efforts by teachers, administrators, parents, community members, and even students can reduce violence and improve the school environment.

"A Comprehensive Technical Package for the Prevention of Youth Violence and Associated Risk Behaviors" by the CDC helps communities and states prioritize prevention strategies based on the best available evidence. The strategies and approaches in the technical package are intended to shape individual behaviors as well as the relationship, family, school, community, and societal factors that influence risk and protective factors for violence. They are meant to work together and to be used in combination in a multilevel, multisector effort to prevent violence. The strategies are as follows:

- Promote family environments that support healthy development
  - Early childhood home visitation
  - Parenting skills and family relationship programs
- Provide quality education early in life
  - Preschool enrichment with family engagement
- Strengthen youth's skills
  - Universal school-based programs
- Connect youth to caring adults and activities
  - Mentoring programs
  - After-school programs
- Create protective community environments
  - Modify the physical and social environment
  - Reduce exposure to community-level risks
  - Street outreach and community norm change
- Intervene to lessen harms and prevent future risk
- Treatment to lessen the harms of violence exposures
  - Treatment to prevent problem behavior and further involvement in violence
  - Hospital–community partnerships

Chapter 51

Preventing Teen Dating Violence

The ultimate goal of education about youth violence is to stop teen dating violence before it begins. During the preteen and teen years, young people are learning the skills they need to form positive, healthy relationships with others, and it is, therefore, an ideal time to promote healthy relationships and prevent patterns of teen dating violence that can last into adulthood.

In addition to teaching relationship skills, prevention programs can focus on promoting protective factors—that is, characteristics of a teen's environment that can support healthy development—and positive youth development. These can also be fostered by a teen's home and community. For example, higher levels of bonding to parents and enhanced social skills can protect girls against victimization. Similarly, for boys, high levels of parental bonding have been found to be associated with less externalizing behavior, which in turn is associated with less teen dating violence victimization.

Most of the handful of programs that have been empirically investigated are school-based and use a group format. Program length varies from less than a day to more than 20 sessions. A few programs frame the issue using a feminist perspective, while others use a more skills-based and gender-neutral approach. Teen dating violence prevention programs tend to focus on attitudes about violence, gender stereotyping, conflict management, and problem-solving skills. Activities aimed at increasing awareness and dispelling myths about violence in relationships are often included in the curriculum.

About This Chapter: This chapter includes text excerpted from "Prevention Programs," Youth.gov, February 7, 2012. Reviewed August 2019.

> ## February is Teen Dating Violence Awareness and Prevention Month
>
> Teen dating violence can be prevented when teens, families, organizations, and communities work together to implement effective prevention strategies.
>
> Teaching healthy relationship skills and changing norms about violence can help prevent teen dating violence. Talk to teens now about the importance of developing healthy, respectful relationships.
>
> *(Source: "Teen Dating Violence," Centers for Disease Control and Prevention (CDC).)*

Teen Dating Violence-Prevention Programs
The Safe Dates Project

The Safe Dates Project is an intervention that includes school activities (e.g., a theater production performed by peers, a curriculum of ten 45-minute sessions taught by health and physical education teachers, and a poster contest) and community activities (e.g., services for adolescents in abusive relationships and service provider training). A 4-year follow-up study found reductions in the likelihood of being a victim or a perpetrator of moderate psychological and physical violence as well as sexual violence among the eighth- and ninth-grade students from North Carolina who had participated in the Safe Dates Project; however, there were no reductions in the likelihood of being a victim of severe physical or psychological violence. Further, findings showed that those students involved in the Safe Dates Project reported less acceptance of dating violence and traditional gender roles, a stronger belief in the need for help, and more awareness of services available in the community.

Break the Cycle's Ending Violence Curriculum

Ending Violence is a curriculum designed for high-school students that focuses on educating youth about the legal repercussions and protections for perpetrators and victims of dating violence. An evaluation of Break the Cycle's Ending Violence curriculum with a sample of predominately Latino teens from a large urban school district found that the youth demonstrated improved knowledge of the laws related to dating violence, less acceptance of female-on-male aggression, and increased perception of the likelihood and helpfulness of seeking assistance from various sources after they had completed the program.

The 4th R

The 4th R, an interactive classroom curriculum for ninth-grade students, aims to reduce youth dating violence by addressing youth violence and bullying, unsafe sexual behavior, and substance use. Researchers found that the rate of physical dating violence for a random sample of Canadian students who participated in the curriculum was significantly lower than the control group (9.8% versus 7.4%). Significance was not maintained for those who had been dating in the previous year. However, boys in the intervention group were significantly less likely than boys in the control group to engage in dating violence (2.7%, compared to 7.1%). Girls in both groups showed the same rates of dating violence (11.9% versus 12%). This was also true when the previously dating subsample was analyzed.

The Youth Relationships Project

The Youth Relationships Project is a prevention program focused on addressing the emotional, behavioral, and cognitive factors that allow youth to strengthen the expression of positive interactions with dating partners and reduce the probability of power-assertive and violent behavior. The project educates youth about gender-based violence, and helps them to develop skills and social actions, such as personal responsibility, communication, and community participation. An experimental study that randomly assigned 14- to 16-year-olds from child protective services to control or to the Youth Relationship Project curriculum found that the intervention was effective in reducing incidents of physical and emotional abuse and symptoms of emotional distress over time for the youth in the intervention. Specifically, youth in the intervention showed significantly greater declines in the use of coercive tactics within the dating relationship and enhanced motivation, interest, and understanding of the content of the program.

Shifting Boundaries

Shifting Boundaries, a school-based dating violence prevention program for middle-school students (sixth and seventh grades), had positive effects on reducing dating violence within a randomized experimental study in a large urban school district. The study looked at the effectiveness of a classroom curriculum, a school intervention at the building level, and a combination of the two. The classroom intervention included six sessions in which there was an emphasis on the consequences of perpetrating teen dating violence (including state laws and penalties), the construction of gender roles, and healthy relationships. The building-based intervention included the use of temporary school-based restraining orders, higher levels of faculty and security presence in areas identified through student mapping of safe/unsafe "hot spots," and the use of posters to increase awareness and reporting of teen dating violence to school personnel. Compared to a control group, the students who participated in the building-only interventions and those who experienced both the building interventions and the classroom interventions were more knowledgeable about the consequences of perpetrating teen dating violence, more likely to avoid areas where teen dating violence is likely to occur, and more likely to intervene as a bystander six months postintervention. The combination also resulted in reduced incidences of sexual and physical dating violence by as much as 50 percent up to six months after the intervention. The classroom-only intervention did not prove effective.

Programs and evidence to support programs will continue to evolve. To find the most up-to-date evidence-based programs related to teen dating violence, go to CrimeSolutions.gov and search "teen dating violence" or related terms.

Chapter 52

Suicide Prevention

Suicide is a major public-health concern. Over 47,000 people died by suicide in the United States in 2017; it is the 10th leading cause of death overall. Suicide is complicated and tragic, but it is often preventable. Knowing the warning signs for suicide and how to get help can help save lives.

- Suicide was the second leading cause of death among individuals between the ages of 10 and 34, and the fourth leading cause of death among individuals between the ages of 35 and 54.
- There were more than twice as many suicides (47,173) in the United States as there were homicides (19,510).
- Suicide rate is based on the number of people who have died by suicide per 100,000 population. Because changes in population size are taken into account, rates allow for comparisons from one year to the next.

(Source: "Suicide," National Institute of Mental Health (NIMH).)

Identifying People at Risk for Suicide

- **Universal screening:** Research has shown that a three-question screening tool helps emergency room personnel identify adults at risk for suicide. Researchers found that screening all patients—regardless of the reason for their emergency room visit—doubled the number of patients identified as being at risk for suicide. The researchers estimated

About This Chapter: This chapter includes text excerpted from "Suicide Prevention," National Institute of Mental Health (NIMH), July 2019.

that suicide-risk screening tools could identify more than three million additional adults at risk for suicide each year.

- **Predicting suicide risk using electronic health records:** Researchers from NIMH partnered with the U.S. Department of Veterans Affairs (VA) and others to develop computer programs that could help predict suicide risk among veterans receiving VA healthcare. Other healthcare systems are beginning to use data from electronic health records to help identify people with suicide risk as well.

No one person (parent, teacher, counselor, administrator, mentor, etc.) can implement suicide prevention efforts on their own. The participation, support, and active involvement of families, schools, and communities are essential.

(Source: "Preventing Youth Suicide," Youth.gov)

Treatments and Therapies
Brief Interventions

- **Safety planning:** Personalized safety planning has been shown to help reduce suicidal thoughts and actions. Patients work with a caregiver to develop a plan that describes ways to limit access to lethal means, such as firearms, pills, or poisons. The plan also lists coping strategies and people and resources that can help in a crisis.

- **Follow-up phone calls:** Research has shown that when at-risk patients receive further screening, a Safety Plan intervention, and a series of supportive phone calls, their risk of suicide goes down.

Psychotherapies

Multiple types of psychosocial interventions have been found to help individuals who have attempted suicide. These types of interventions may prevent someone from making another attempt.

- **Cognitive-behavioral therapy (CBT)** can help people learn new ways of dealing with stressful experiences through training. CBT helps individuals recognize their thought patterns and consider alternative actions when thoughts of suicide arise.

- **Dialectical behavior therapy (DBT)** has been shown to reduce suicidal behavior in adolescents. DBT has also been shown to reduce the rate of suicide in adults with borderline personality disorder, a mental illness characterized by an ongoing pattern of varying moods, self-image, and behavior that often results in impulsive actions and problems in relationships. A therapist trained in DBT helps a person recognize when her or his feelings or actions are disruptive or unhealthy, and teaches the skills needed to deal better with upsetting situations.

Medication

Some individuals at risk for suicide might benefit from medication. Doctors and patients can work together to find the best medication or medication combination, as well as the right dose. Because many individuals at risk for suicide often have a mental illness and substance use problems, individuals might benefit from medication along with psychosocial intervention.

Clozapine is an antipsychotic medication used primarily to treat individuals with schizophrenia. To date, it is the only medication with a specific U.S. Food and Drug Administration (FDA) indication for reducing the risk of recurrent suicidal behavior in patients with schizophrenia or schizoaffective disorder.

If you are prescribed a medication, be sure you:

- Talk with your doctor or a pharmacist to make sure you understand the risks and benefits of the medications you are taking.

- Do not stop taking a medication without talking to your doctor first. Suddenly stopping a medication may lead to "rebound" or worsening of symptoms. Other uncomfortable or potentially dangerous withdrawal effects also are possible.

- Report any concerns about side effects to your doctor right away. You may need a change in the dose or a different medication.

- Report serious side effects to the FDA MedWatch Adverse Event Reporting program online or by phone at 800-332-1088. You or your doctor may send a report.

Other medications have been used to treat suicidal thoughts and behaviors, but more research is needed to show the benefit of these options.

Collaborative Care

Collaborative Care has been shown to be an effective way to treat depression and reduce suicidal thoughts. A team-based Collaborative Care program adds two new types of services to usual primary care: behavioral healthcare management and consultations with a mental-health specialist.

The behavioral healthcare manager becomes part of the patient's treatment team and helps the primary care provider evaluate the patient's mental health. If the patient receives a diagnosis of a mental-health disorder and wants treatment, the care manager, primary-care provider, and patient work together to develop a treatment plan. This plan may include medication, psychotherapy, or other appropriate options.

Later, the care manager reaches out to see if the patient likes the plan, is following the plan, and if the plan is working or if changes are needed to improve management of the patient's disorders. The care manager and the primary-care provider also regularly review the patient's status and care plan with a mental-health specialist, like a psychiatrist or psychiatric nurse, to be sure the patient is getting the best treatment options and improving.

If You Know Someone in Crisis

Call the National Suicide Prevention Lifeline (Lifeline) at 800-273-TALK (800-273-8255), or text the Crisis Text Line (text HELLO to 741741). Both services are free and available 24 hours a day, seven days a week. The deaf and hard of hearing can contact the Lifeline via TTY at 800-799-4889. All calls are confidential. Contact social media outlets directly if you are concerned about a friend's social media updates or dial 911 in an emergency.

Chapter 53

Conflict Resolution

Conflict is a normal, natural part of human relationships. People will not agree about everything all the time. In and of itself, conflict is not necessarily a negative thing. When handled constructively it can help people to stand up for themselves and others, and work together to achieve a mutually satisfactory solution. But if the conflict is handled poorly, it can cause anger, hurt, divisiveness, and more serious problems. This chapter discusses how to deal with conflict in a constructive manner.

Sources of Conflict

There can be many causes or reasons for conflict. However, some of the most common include:

- Personal differences, such as values, ethics, personalities, age, education, gender, social and economic status, cultural background, temperament, health, religion, political beliefs, etc.

- A clash of ideas, choices, or actions. For instance, conflict can occur when people have incompatible goals when they are in direct competition, or even when they have different work styles.

- Finally, poor communication or miscommunication is one of the biggest causes of conflict.

About This Chapter: This chapter includes text excerpted from "Conflict Resolution," National Oceanic and Atmospheric Administration (NOAA), U.S. Department of Commerce (DOC), October 14, 2012. Reviewed August 2019.

Preventing Conflict

While it is not possible to prevent all conflict, there are steps that you can take to try to keep conflict to a minimum. One way to manage conflict is to prevent it from occurring in the first place. Preventing conflict is not the same as avoiding conflict. Preventing conflict means behaving and communicating in a way that averts needless conflicts.

Consider the following tips:

- **Respect differences.** Many conflicts arise from differences in gender, generations, cultures, values, etc. We live in an increasingly diverse world. Learn to respect and celebrate peoples' differences and their opinions.

- **Treat others as you would like to be treated.** Regardless of your personal opinion of someone, be professional, courteous, respectful, and tolerant, even when you are frustrated. If a person treats you disrespectfully, calmly tell them you do not appreciate it. Do not exacerbate the situation by retaliating with inappropriate behavior or comments.

- **Keep negative opinions to yourself**—Most people are put off by hearing negative comments about others—especially if it is about a personal issue. In the workplace, this may lead to disciplinary action. Friends and acquaintances may be equally "turned off" by negative comments about someone, particularly if they feel they are being drawn into a conflict or being asked to take sides. If you need to vent about a personal issue, do so outside of the workplace, keep it to a close, trusted friend or a loved one and keep it to a minimum.

- **Keep your distance**—Unfortunately, this is often easier said than done. Often the conflicts arise with those who are closest to us. It is often easier to get along if you respect one another's privacy and boundaries. Taking a break from each other can go along way in keeping the peace.

Resolving Conflict

Sometimes, conflict cannot—or should not—be avoided. Knowing how to deal with conflict is important for anyone. However, often people have not been given the tools to effectively deal with conflict. Consider the following tips:

- **Address the issue early.** The longer you let an issue fester, the more time you waste and the greater chance you have of it spiraling into other problems.

- **Address the issue privately.** Set up a time to talk in a private place, where you would not be overheard or interrupted. Speak to the person with whom you have the conflict and try to resolve the issue one-on-one before involving others.

- **Expect discomfort.** You may have to say up front: "Although this is uncomfortable for me, if I do not address this, I am afraid we will not meet our goal."

- **Be specific and objective.** Identify the specific issue at hand and the effect it is having. Avoid generalizing statements such as "always," "ever" or "never." Stick to the subject; try not to digress into broad personality issues or revive past issues.

- **Focus on the outcome.** Do not dwell on problems or blame. Keep the spotlight on finding solutions and how you will reach the desired outcomes. "In order to reach the goal of X, I think we need to do Y."

- **Be open.** Doing so establishes an atmosphere of mutual respect and cooperation. Listen to and consider others' opinions, points of view, and ideas. Understand and appreciate that they think differently than you and may bring a greater, or different, understanding to the table that will help resolve the problem more quickly and effectively.

- **Respond constructively.** Let the other person know you value what she or he is saying, even if you do not agree. Try to avoid responding negatively or directively, for example, criticizing, ridiculing, dismissing, diverting (talking about yourself rather than about what the other person has said), or rejecting the other person or what they are saying.

- **Know your triggers.** Learn to recognize your personal warning signs for anger and figure out the ways that work best for you to constructively control your anger.

- **Maintain a sense of humor.** Be willing to laugh, including at yourself. Maintaining a sense of humor can relieve stress and tension, and help get you and others through a difficult time.

- **Learn to compromise.** Compromise is important in any relationship. If you disagree on an issue, discuss the problem calmly, allow each person to explain her or his point of view, and look for ways to meet each other in the middle.

- **Do not attempt to resolve conflict when tempers are flaring.** During an argument, often no one can agree on a reasonable solution. If that is the case, agree to take a break and come back to the problem later, when you have had time to settle down and think about the issue.

- **Know when to retreat.** The conflict resolution process will not always work. The level of the skills of some people may not be at the point where they can be full partners in this process. For example, you may have a spouse who does not want to, or know how to solve the problem. You may also have a conflict with a coworker, boss or higher-ups who is known for irrational outbursts. You must take all these factors into consideration and know when it may be more appropriate for you to cut your losses and retreat.

- **Practice forgiveness.** There may be times when someone makes a mistake or says or does something hurtful—whether intentionally or unintentionally. While it is okay to be angry, it is also important to let go of the anger and move on. On a personal level, it is healthier to let go of negative emotions like stress and anger. And it is difficult to maintain a good relationship if you cannot get past these feelings.

Mutual Conflict Resolution

In most cases, you should be able to resolve conflicts by working with others involved. Here are some steps to consider:

- **Step one:** Identify the purpose and importance of the conflict—and your mutual desire to solve it.

- **Step two:** Takes turns listening to each other's side. This is a very important step and one that requires good listening skills.

- **Step three:** Once all the issues are discussed, repeat and summarize what was said. It may help to write this down or even create "minutes" to document issues discussed.

- **Step four:** Ask questions as needed and encourage others to do the same. Do you understand their point of view? Are you sure they understand yours? Clarify as needed.

- **Step five:** No matter how intense the conflict, you should always find issues or points that you agree upon: For instance, "We agree that our goal is to increase sales by 10 percent this year." Or, "We agree that we need to cut our household costs, we just do not agree on what costs we can cut."

- **Step six:** Next, list all solutions—even those that may seem unrealistic, unreasonable, or wrong.

- **Step seven:** Review all the possible solutions and highlight those you find mutually acceptable. Hopefully, you will have at least one or two that you agree upon.

- **Step eight:** Choose the one (or few) that you agree will work best.

- **Step nine:** Put a plan into action. What steps will you take to implement? How will you review progress?

By creating step-by-step guidelines and mutually agreed upon solutions and action plans, you should be able to minimize conflict and achieve desired goals.

Conflict resolution uses a variety of approaches to manage and resolve concerns, disagreement, and conflict.

Key Behaviors

- Invites others to express their points of view
- Identifies and takes steps to prevent potential situations that could result in unpleasant confrontations
- Expresses disagreements in a way that does not attack or disparage others
- Helps uncover underlying and unstated issues causing the conflict
- Brings disagreements into the open and addresses them
- Expands areas of agreement and narrows areas of disagreement
- Facilitates the development of creative solutions to conflict
- Identifies the truth in criticisms
- Knows when to compromise and when to stand firm

(Source: "Conflict Resolution," Office of Human Resources, U.S. Department of Health and Human Services (HHS).)

Dealing Constructively with Anger

Conflict can result in anger. Anger is a normal human emotion ranging from annoyance to absolute rage. Each person's anger "triggers" are different. Some may get angry at a friend's behavior; other causes of anger can be more serious—such as personal problems or a previous traumatic experience.

In and of itself, anger is not necessarily a problem—when focused appropriately it can help people to stand up for themselves and others. But if anger is channeled in negative, inappropriate ways it can cause problems. Consider the following ideas to help deal constructively with anger:

- **Anger** is a strong emotion, and is not always easy to control. Two crucial skills in managing anger are self-awareness and self-control. Try to recognize and identify your feelings, especially anger. Once the feeling is identified you can then think about the appropriate response.

  - **Self-awareness** is being conscious of thoughts and feelings. Examine how and why you are feeling angry to better understand and manage these feelings. For example, ask yourself questions such as "Why am I angry?" or "What is making me feel this way?" to assist in self-analysis.

- **Self-control** means stopping and considering actions before taking them. Learn to stop and think before you act or speak in anger. For example, envision a stop sign when you are angry—and to take the time to think about how to react. Explore techniques to calm down such as counting backward from 10 to 1, deep breathing, or just walking away.

- **Relax.** Try relaxation exercises, such as breathing deeply from the diaphragm (the belly, not the chest) and slowly repeating a calming word or phrase like "take it easy." Or to think of relaxing experiences, such as sitting on a beach or walking through a forest.

- **Think positively.** Remind yourself that no one is out to get you, you are just experiencing some of the rough spots of daily life.

- **Problem-solve.** Identify the specific problem that is causing the anger and approach it head-on—even if the problem does not have a quick solution.

- **Communicate with others.** Angry people tend to jump to conclusions and speak without thinking about the consequences of what they are saying. Slow down and think carefully about what you want to say. Listen carefully to what the other person is saying.

- **Manage stress.** Set aside personal time to deal with the daily stresses of work, activities, and family. Ideas include: listening to music, writing in a journal, exercising, meditating, or talking about your feelings with someone you trust.

- **Change the scene.** A change of environment may help reduce angry feelings. For example, if your coworkers or friends are angry frequently and/or make you angry, consider spending time with people who may contribute more to your self-confidence and well-being.

- **Find a distraction.** If you cannot seem to let your anger go, it can help to do something distracting, for example, read or watch television or a movie.

- **Set a good example.** If you are teaching your child to control their anger, make sure you practice what you preach. Show by example how you manage your own anger.

When to Seek Help

There may be times when, despite your best efforts, you may not be able to resolve a conflict on your own. If so, get help.

If the conflict is work-related, you may need to speak to your manager or human resources department, particularly if the situation is affecting your work or impeding your chances of achieving goals.

In any conflict, if the conflict is so severe that it is leading to serious relationship problems, or creates a danger of physical harm and/or emotional or psychological damage, seek immediate help. Consider the following sources of assistance:

- Your employee assistance program (EAP)

- Medical practitioner

- Mental-health professionals, such as psychiatrists, psychologists, social workers, or mental-health counselors, etc.

- Community mental-health resources

Chapter 54

Staying Safe While Having Fun

As a teen, your family may give you more responsibilities and the chance to spend more time with your friends. This extra time with your friends may put you in new or different social situations and places. With your parents not around as much, you are making more choices for yourself and will need to keep yourself safe. If you forget about your safety, your fun can quickly turn into danger. Check out these questions and answers to learn how to stay safe on the go.

How Do You Keep Yourself Safe at a Party?

New social settings such as parties are a fun way for you to spend time with your friends. Most of the time parties are safe, but sometimes things can happen that can make a party a dangerous place to be. It is important to know what to do if a party gets out of control and how to keep yourself safe.

- Never walk away with strangers

- Never be alone with someone who has been drinking or taking drugs

- Do not drink alcohol or do drugs

- Tell your parents and friends where you are going

- Never get in a car with someone who has been drinking or doing drugs

About This Chapter: This chapter includes text excerpted from "Having Fun and Staying Safe," girlshealth.gov, Office on Women's Health (OWH), September 22, 2009. Reviewed August 2019.

What If Someone Offers You Alcohol or Drugs

You are more likely to be offered alcohol or drugs by a friend than a stranger. It is okay to say no to friends. Many people are focused on themselves, so they would not be as worried about what you are doing as you may think. Below are eight great ways to turn down an offer:

1. No, thanks.

2. I am not into that.

3. Alcohol is not my thing.

4. I do not feel like it—do you have any soda?

5. I am okay. Thanks.

6. No, I am training for _____.

7. No, I am on the _____ team so I do not want to risk it.

8. No. I gotta go soon.

You can set an example for others by staying away from drugs and alcohol. You might be worried about not being "cool" if you do not try drugs or alcohol, but you can start a different, more real kind of "cool" by being looked up to like someone who makes confident choices for you.

How Can You Make a Safety Plan for Different Social Situations?

No matter what the situation is, you can create a plan to help keep yourself safe. Read the following list and create your safety plan right now!

- Tell your parents where you are going, who you will be with, and when you will be back. This may sound lame, but you will be safer for doing so.

- Carry money, a phonecard, or a cell phone in case you need to make an emergency phone call. Do not forget to keep emergency numbers and the phone number of a taxi service in your wallet or backpack or program them into your cell phone.

- Stay in well lit public places.

- Stick with another person or a group of your friends.

- Be aware that drugs used for sexual assault often are slipped into drinks. Open your own drinks and keep your own drink with you at all times.

- Try to avoid strangers. If you talk to them, do not share information about yourself.

- Use code words on the phone that you and your family decide on ahead of time. If you are in trouble, say the code word so that your family member knows you cannot talk openly and need to be picked up right away.

What Do You Do If You Are Walking in a Neighborhood You Do Not Know Well?

There are certain things that you can do to keep yourself safe until you are near home.

- Walk with another person whenever possible.

- Walk on the sidewalks of main streets and stay where it is well lit.

- Do not walk with headphones so that you can hear what is going on around you.

- If you think that you are being followed, cross the street to see if the person does the same. Do not be afraid to start running if you need to—do not wait until the person is very close to you to do this. Go to the nearest store, restaurant, or police station.

- Walk quickly and confidently.

- If someone grabs your purse or bag, just let go. Do not struggle with them to try to get it back. If you fight, you risk getting hurt. Money and other stuff can be replaced—your safety is the most important thing. Run in the opposite direction of the person and go to the nearest police station or store to call for help.

- If you are in trouble, yell! This will bring attention from the people around you.

Keep in Mind

Mixing fun and safety will ALWAYS make you a winner! Someone else might think you are worrying too much or your brother or sister might tell you there is nothing to worry about. But checking out the situation and planning ahead is the best way to keep bad things from happening. Being the worrywart is not such a bad thing when it keeps you and your buddies out of emergency rooms and on the field or in activities.

(Source: "Having Fun and Staying Safe," Centers for Disease Control and Prevention (CDC).)

What Do You Do If You Are Out and Someone That You Do Not Know Comes Up to You?

When you were younger, your parents probably taught you never to talk to strangers. This is a good rule for children, but in your teenage years, it does not always seem to fit. There are lots of times when you might need to talk to someone that you do not know. Most strangers are nice people, but it is important that you do not trust everyone that you meet right away.

Know the warning signs and how to protect yourself:

- **Be aware** of anyone in a car who stops to talk to you or ask you for directions if you are walking down the street, even if you are in a familiar neighborhood. Try to keep your distance from the car and never offer to get in the car—even if the stranger is going in the same direction that you are headed, or the stranger says there is an emergency.

- **Be assertive.** If a person that you do not know comes up to you to start a conversation, you do not have to talk to them if you do not feel comfortable. Do not be afraid to sound rude if someone keeps bothering you. Stay calm and firmly say "No."

- **Be street smart.** Not all dangerous strangers are rude or forceful right away when you first meet them. It is important that you are aware of strangers, both men and women, who seem nice—the ones who make conversation easily and get important information about you without you even realizing it. Remember that you do not have to share any information. If a stranger tells you where she or he lives, it does not mean that you have to tell her or him where you live.

- **Be careful who you trust.** Keep your distance from a new person until you have had the chance to get to know her or him. Do not trust someone who follows you around or will not leave you alone if you ask them to. You can make up code words with your family that they will use if there is an emergency at home. This way, if a stranger comes up to you and says that there is an emergency and that you need to leave with them, you can ask for the code words that only you and your parents know. If you are worried or nervous, you can go to police officers or security guards with name tags and badges. You will also find people who may be able to help you at information desks and customer service desks at public places such as the mall; restaurant or store managers may also be able to help you.

- **Be prepared.** Check out self-defense classes in your town. Your local police department or school might offer classes that can teach you how to protect yourself and how to handle uncomfortable situations. Thinking ahead and planning for your safety is a way to feel powerful and confident!

You do not have to be afraid every time you leave the house. But, it is important that you take some responsibility for your own safety. Trust your instincts, pay attention to what is going on around you, and protect yourself. Remember, being safe will not take away from your fun. Being safe will make sure that you can keep having it!

Talking with Teens about Online Safety

Recognize Both the Benefits and Risks of the Internet

The Internet may be foreign to parents who did not grow up with it. But most teens are digital natives and see it as just another part of their world. Like all parts of life, it has both benefits and risks.

Recognize Links between Online and Offline Behavior

Teens who are most vulnerable to risky behaviors online tend to be the same teenagers who have difficulty in other parts of their lives as well. In other words, teens who are generally making healthy, positive choices in other areas of their lives are most likely to be making positive choices online. The skills, values, and attitudes you develop in your family will also help to guide them in their online activities. On the other hand, if you have concerns about your teen's behavior offline, be aware that these patterns could be a problem online as well. Teens who engage in risky behaviors offline are more likely to engage in risky online behaviors too.

About This Chapter: This chapter includes text excerpted from "Talking with Teens about Online Safety: How You Make a Difference," Office of Adolescent Health (OAH), U.S. Department of Health and Human Services (HHS), July 2, 2019.

Potential Benefits of Being Online
- Socialization and communication
- Enhanced learning opportunities
- Useful health and sexuality information
- Self-expression and creativity
- Cross-cultural communication
- Involvement in civic issues and causes

Potential Risks of Being Online
- Cyberbullying and harassment, usually by peers
- Sharing sexually explicit photographs
- Inaccurate or harmful health and sexuality information
- Exposure to inappropriate and illegal content
- Sharing too much information
- Sexual solicitations

Be a Good Role Model

In 2012, 1 in 5 teens ages 13 to 17 wished their parents would spend less time using mobile phones and other devices.

Empower Your Child to Navigate the Digital World

Equally important is educating and empowering youth so they learn to navigate digital worlds safely and are equipped with strategies to use when they do encounter challenges. Teens who are educated about the importance of online safety are more likely to take steps to keep themselves safe online than teens who are not educated.

Help Your Teen Learn to Critique Online Information

There is a lot of great information available online for young people to use while doing homework, caring for pets, doing hobbies, investigating private health or sexuality issues, and many other topics. But there is also bad information. Help your teen become a critical user of information by teaching skills for evaluating what is online. Here are some questions to ask about things your teen finds on the Internet:

- What authority, expertise, or credentials does the information provider have? Is the site generally a widely trusted site? Is it clear who is behind the site, or is that hidden?

- What can you tell about the accuracy of the information? Is it current? Does it refer to trusted research sources or other sources of expertise? Is the information consistent with what you find on trusted sites?

- Is there an agenda behind the information that is being posted? Is the site primarily promoting a particular product, point of view, or cause? Is a bias evident? Is it clear and straightforward, or does it seek to manipulate through its words, graphics, or interactive features?

- Does the site design enhance or distract from your understanding? Is it well organized, or do you have to really look to find what you need?

Set Appropriate Boundaries on Internet Use

Options to consider Internet boundaries include:

- Limit daily Internet use. If using the Internet becomes the single biggest activity in your teen's life or if it interferes with other activities (such as schoolwork, sports, physical exercise, family time, or other relationships), it is important to investigate. Excessive use may suggest problems in other areas of life (such as social isolation or loneliness) that may require immediate action.

- Know the legal age restrictions for social media and other sites. The U.S. Children's Online Privacy Protection Act (COPPA) prohibits websites from collecting information on those younger than 13 years old without parental permission.

- Consider using filtering, blocking, or monitoring software, but recognize its limits. Software solutions help some with blocking exposure to certain online content. But, if they want, teens can find many ways around these barriers, such as using a different computer, using a smartphone, or figuring out the password. So installing and using software can be useful, but it should be seen as only a part of an overall strategy for keeping your child safe online.

Educate Yourself and Teens about Online Scams and Fraud

Whether through e-mail, social networking sites, or on websites, scammers continue to look for ways to coax people into revealing personal and financial information. Others may simply be promoting inaccurate information, such as urban legends. Ask your teen to follow specific guidelines, such as:

- Check with a parent before giving anyone personal information, such as your name, address, school, phone number, or picture of yourself.

- Never provide bank account information or a Social Security number (SSN) unless you are 100 percent confident in the website (such as your own bank) and its security.

- Always use caution before providing personal or financial information online, and teach teens to do the same.

- Be skeptical of any websites that offer prizes or giveaways.

- Do not enter an area of a website that charges for service without first checking with a parent.

Do not post your photo on the Internet or send it to someone you do not know. Do not post or send personal information, including:

- Full name
- Address
- Phone number
- Login name, IM screen name, passwords
- School name
- School location
- Sports teams
- Clubs
- Social Security number
- Financial information (credit card numbers and bank account numbers)
- Where you work or hang out
- Names of family members

(Source: "Safety in Online Communities," girlshealth.gov, Office on Women's Health (OWH).)

Develop an Online Exit Strategy

If teens ever feel threatened online by a bullying friend or a predatory adult, what should they do? Talk about this in advance so they have options in mind if there should ever be a need. For example, they can end the interaction immediately and block the person. Insist that they tell you or another trusted adult if they have any concerns about someone they meet online or about any of the activities they are encountering, such as bullying or sexting. If the person keeps trying to contact the youth or continues with threatening behaviors, the situation should be reported to the police or other appropriate authorities.

Chapter 56

How the Child Welfare System Works

The child welfare system is a group of services designed to promote the well-being of children by ensuring safety, achieving permanency, and strengthening families to care for their children successfully. While the primary responsibility for child welfare services rests with the states, the federal government plays a major role in supporting states in the delivery of services through the funding of programs and legislative initiatives.

The primary responsibility for implementing federal child and family legislation rests with the Children's Bureau, within the Administration on Children, Youth and Families, Administration for Children and Families, U.S. Department of Health and Human Services (HHS). The Children's Bureau works with state and local agencies to develop programs that focus on preventing child abuse and neglect by strengthening families, protecting children from further maltreatment, reuniting children safely with their families, or finding permanent families for children who cannot safely return home.

Most families first become involved with their local child welfare system because of a report of suspected child abuse or neglect (sometimes called "child maltreatment"). Child maltreatment is defined by CAPTA as serious harm (neglect, physical abuse, sexual abuse, and emotional abuse or neglect) caused to children by parents or primary caregivers, such as extended family members or babysitters. Child maltreatment also can include harm that a caregiver allows to happen or does not prevent from happening to a child. In general, child welfare agencies do not intervene in cases of harm to children caused by acquaintances or strangers. These cases are the responsibility of law enforcement.

About This Chapter: This chapter includes text excerpted from "How the Child Welfare System Works," Child Welfare Information Gateway, U.S. Department of Health and Human Services (HHS), February 2013. Reviewed August 2019.

The child welfare system is not a single entity. Many organizations in each community work together to strengthen families and keep children safe. Public agencies, such as departments of social services or child and family services, often contract and collaborate with private child-welfare agencies and community-based organizations to provide services to families, such as in-home family preservation services, foster care, residential treatment, mental-health care, substance-abuse treatment, parenting skills classes, domestic-violence services, employment assistance, and financial or housing assistance.

Child welfare systems are complex, and their specific procedures vary widely by state. This chapter gives a brief overview of the purposes and functions of child welfare from a national perspective. Child welfare systems typically:

- Receive and investigate reports of possible child abuse and neglect

- Provide services to families that need assistance in the protection and care of their children

- Arrange for children to live with kin or with foster families when they are not safe at home

- Arrange for reunification, adoption, or other permanent family connections for children leaving foster care

The Child Abuse Prevention and Treatment Act

The Child Abuse Prevention and Treatment Act (CAPTA), originally passed in 1974, brought national attention to the need to protect vulnerable children in the United States. CAPTA provides federal funding to states in support of prevention, assessment, investigation, prosecution, and treatment activities as well as grants to public agencies and nonprofit organizations for demonstration programs and projects. Additionally, CAPTA identifies the federal role in supporting research, evaluation, technical assistance, and data collection activities. CAPTA also sets forth a minimum definition of child abuse and neglect. Since it was signed into law, CAPTA has been amended several times. It was amended and reauthorized on December 20, 2010, by the CAPTA Reauthorization Act of 2010.

What Happens When Possible Abuse or Neglect Is Reported

Any concerned person can report suspicions of child abuse or neglect. Most reports are made by "mandatory reporters"—people who are required by state law to report suspicions of child abuse and neglect. As of August 2012, statutes in approximately 18 states and Puerto Rico require any person who suspects child abuse or neglect to report it. These reports are generally received by Child Protective Services (CPS) workers and are either "screened in" or "screened out." A report is screened in when there is sufficient information to suggest an investigation is warranted. A report may be screened out if there is not enough information on which to follow up or if the situation reported does not meet the state's legal definition of abuse or neglect. In these instances, the worker may refer the person reporting the incident to other community services or law enforcement for additional help.

What Happens after a Report Is "Screened In"

Child Protective Services caseworkers often called "investigators" or "assessment workers," respond within a particular time period, which may be anywhere from a few hours to a few days, depending on the type of maltreatment alleged, the potential severity of the situation, and requirements under state law. They may speak with the parents and other people in contact with the child, such as doctors, teachers, or child care providers. They also may speak with the child, alone or in the presence of caregivers, depending on the child's age and level of risk. Children who are believed to be in immediate danger may be moved to a shelter, a foster home, or a relative's home during the investigation and while court proceedings are pending. An investigator also engages the family, assessing strengths and needs and initiating connections to community resources and services.

Some jurisdictions now employ an alternative, or differential response system.

In these jurisdictions, when the risk to the children involved is considered low, the CPS caseworker focuses on assessing family strengths, resources, and difficulties and on identifying supports and services needed, rather than on gathering evidence to confirm the occurrence of abuse or neglect.

At the end of an investigation, CPS caseworkers typically make one of two findings—unsubstantiated (unfounded) or substantiated (founded). These terms vary from state to state. Typically, a finding of unsubstantiated means there is insufficient evidence for the worker to conclude that a child was abused or neglected, or what happened does not meet the legal definition of child abuse or neglect. A finding of substantiated typically means that an incident of child abuse or neglect, as defined by state law, is believed to have occurred. Some states have additional categories, such as "unable to determine," that suggest there was not enough evidence to either confirm or refute that abuse or neglect occurred.

The agency will initiate court action if it determines that the authority of the juvenile court (through child protection or dependency proceeding) is necessary to keep the child safe. To protect the child, the court can issue temporary orders placing the child in shelter care during the investigation, ordering services, or ordering certain individuals to have no contact with the child. At an adjudicatory hearing, the court hears evidence and decides whether maltreatment occurred and whether the child should be under the continuing jurisdiction of the court. The court then enters a disposition, either at that hearing or at a separate hearing, which may result in the court ordering a parent to comply with the services necessary to alleviate the abuse or neglect. Orders can also contain provisions regarding visitation between the parent and the child, agency obligations to provide the parent with services, and services needed by the child.

What Happens in Substantiated (Founded) Cases

If a child has been abused or neglected, the course of action depends on state policy, the severity of the maltreatment, an assessment of the child's immediate safety, the risk of continued or future maltreatment, the services available to address the family's needs, and whether the child was removed from the home and a court action to protect the child was initiated. The following general options are available:

- **No or low risk**—The family's case may be closed with no services if the maltreatment was a one-time incident, the child is considered to be safe, there is no or low risk of future incidents, and any services the family needs will not be provided through the child welfare agency but through other community based resources and service systems.

- **Low to moderate risk**—Referrals may be made to community-based or voluntary in-home child welfare services if the CPS worker believes the family would benefit from these services and the child's present and future safety would be enhanced. This may happen even when no abuse or neglect is found, if the family needs and is willing to participate in services.

- **Moderate to high risk**—The family may again be offered voluntary in-home services to address safety concerns and help reduce the risks. If these are refused, the agency may seek intervention by the juvenile dependency court. Once there is a judicial determination that abuse or neglect occurred, juvenile dependency court may require the family to cooperate with in-home services if it is believed that the child can remain safely at home while the family addresses the issues contributing to the risk of future maltreatment. If the child has been seriously harmed, is considered to be at high risk of serious harm, or the child's safety is threatened, the court may order the child's removal from the home or affirm the agency's prior removal of the child. The child may be placed with a relative or in foster care.

What Happens to Parents

Caregivers who are found to have abused or neglected a child are generally offered support and treatment services or are required by a juvenile dependency court to participate in services that will help keep their children safe. In cases of low risk, in-home services and supports may be provided, including parent education, child care, counseling, safety planning, and more.

In more severe cases or fatalities, police are called on to investigate and may file charges in criminal court against the perpetrators of child maltreatment. In many states, certain types of abuse, such as sexual abuse and serious physical abuse, are routinely referred to law enforcement.

Whether or not criminal charges are filed, the name of the person committing the abuse or neglect may be placed on a state child maltreatment registry if abuse or neglect is confirmed. A registry is a central database that collects information about maltreated children and individuals who are found to have abused or neglected those children. These registries are usually confidential and used for internal child protective purposes only. However, they may be used in background checks for certain professions that involve working with children to protect children from contact with individuals who may mistreat them.

What Happens to Children

Depending on the severity of the case, children may remain at home or be removed into foster care.

In-Home

In low-risk cases, children may remain in their own homes with their families, and the families may receive in-home services and supports. These may include parent education, safety planning, counseling, and more. Families may also be connected with community services that provide concrete help (e.g., housing, food) as well as services, such as therapy, parent training, and support groups.

Out-of-Home

Most children in foster care are placed with relatives or foster families, but some may be placed in a group or residential setting. While a child is in foster care, she or he attends school and should receive medical care and other services as needed. The child's family also receives services to support their efforts to reduce the risk of future maltreatment and to help them, in most cases, be reunited with their child. Visits between parents and their children and between siblings are encouraged and supported, following a set plan.

Every child in foster care should have a permanency plan. Families typically participate in developing a permanency plan for the child and a service plan for the family, and these plans guide the agency's work. Family reunification, except in unusual and extreme circumstances, is the permanency plan for most children. In some cases, when prospects for reunification appear less likely, a concurrent permanency plan is developed. If the efforts toward reunification are not successful, the plan may be changed to another permanent arrangement, such as adoption or transfer of custody to a relative.

Federal law requires the court to hold a permanency hearing, which determines the permanent plan for the child, within 12 months after the child enters foster care and every 12 months thereafter. Many courts review each case more frequently to ensure that the agency is actively pursuing permanency for the child.

Whether or not they are adopted, older youth in foster care should receive support in developing some form of permanent family connection, in addition to transitional or independent-living services, to assist them in being self-sufficient when they leave foster care between the ages of 18 and 21.

Chapter 57

Understanding Child Welfare and the Courts

Involvement with Child Protective Services often includes the court system, especially if your child is removed from the home or at risk for removal. In most states, if a case requires court involvement, it will come before either a juvenile or a family court.[1] The court experience can be intimidating or overwhelming. This chapter is designed to answer parent and caregiver concerns about the court process and provide resources regarding legal action and parental rights.

[1]*Most cases dealing with children and youth under age 18 come before juvenile or family courts. Tribal citizen children are treated separately and come under the jurisdiction of the Indian Child Welfare Act, which empowers the child's Tribe and family in decisions affecting the child.*

A Parent's Rights and Responsibilities

When a parent or caregiver is contacted by Child Protective Services (CPS) because of alleged child abuse or neglect, they may be asked to answer questions and attend court to determine the best course of action. The court decides whether the child will stay in the home or be removed. The child may be allowed to stay home if services can be provided or if other actions can be taken to ensure the child's safety. It is important to remember that as a parent or primary caregiver, you have certain rights and responsibilities while your child-welfare case is being investigated. It is also helpful to keep in mind that most cases do not result in a child being removed from the home and that services may be available to help your family.

About This Chapter: This chapter includes text excerpted from "Understanding Child Welfare and the Courts," Child Welfare Information Gateway, U.S. Department of Health and Human Services (HHS), October 2016. Reviewed August 2019.

> Child welfare laws vary by state. It may be helpful to consult Child Welfare Information Gateway's State Statute Search for your State's specific requirements (www.childwelfare.gov/systemwide/laws_policies/state).

Many court systems offer an alternative to traditional court proceedings, referred to as mediation. This may allow you to settle the issues and avoid court.

Your rights include the following:

- In most states, the right to an attorney (appointed by the court or hired by you)

- The right to notice, which is a legal term referring to your right to be informed about the reason you are being investigated, the outcome of the investigation, and details regarding upcoming court hearings

- The right to ask questions (e.g., "Why am I being investigated?")

- The right to a hearing

- The right to play an active role in planning for your case

- The right to suggest a relative or other placement if your child cannot remain in your care

- The right to appeal decisions within a certain timeframe

A directory of attorneys in each state and extensive legal resources are available on the American Bar Association's (ABA) website at apps.americanbar.org/legalservices/findlegal-help/home.cfm.

Your responsibilities include the following:

- Asking questions to help you understand your role and the court process, including whether your area provides parent partners or peer advocates who have been in your position and can help you understand and navigate the legal process

- Attending and being well prepared for all appointments and court hearings (bring documentation, keep a personal journal of your progress during the case, etc.)

- Cooperating with the case plan you help develop and communicating any difficulties you may be experiencing

Consult your caseworker or lawyer—or parent partner, if relevant—if you have specific questions about your case or the court process. Remember that asking for help is a sign of strength. A list of State parent advocacy groups is available on the Child Welfare Information Gateway website at www.childwelfare.gov/organizations/?CWIGFunctionsaction=rols:main.dspROL&rolType=Custom&RS_ID=138.

Court Hearings in Child Welfare Cases

The primary role of a juvenile or family court in child welfare cases is to protect children and help their parents provide a safe environment. This is a civil court, not a criminal court, and the hearings are often less formal than those you might have seen on TV. In most cases, everyone in court has the same goal—to make sure the child is safe.

The case planning and court hearing processes work together to determine what changes need to be made to return a child home or reach some other goal, such as placement with a relative. Parents might be ordered to partake in specific services before children can be returned to their care. These services may include mental health or substance use treatment. It may be challenging, but these services are designed to enable you to keep your child safe and ultimately back at home.

After a child welfare agency receives a report of suspected child abuse, neglect, or abandonment—also referred to as "maltreatment"—the legal process typically progresses through the following steps:

1. **Court order.** After a petition has been filed on behalf of a child, a court order is issued in most jurisdictions to investigate suspected or reported abuse or neglect—but a court order is not required in all jurisdictions to launch an investigation.

2. **Emergency protection order.** If the initial investigation finds that the child is unsafe, the court files this order to temporarily remove the child from the home.

3. **Preliminary protective, emergency removal, or shelter hearing.** The investigator will present evidence regarding the suspected abuse or neglect. The parents can also present their own evidence to challenge the petition. Based on this information, the judge will either allow the child to stay or return home until the trial or determine a temporary out-of-home placement, such as with a family member or with a foster family.

4. **Fact-finding hearing or adjudicatory trial.** This is a trial to determine whether enough evidence exists to conclude that the reported abuse or neglect has occurred. The judge may decide to dismiss the case based on lack of evidence or decide that enough ("sufficient") evidence exists to suggest there was maltreatment.

5. **Dispositional hearing.** This hearing will determine whether the child can remain at home and, if not, where the child will live. If the home is found unsafe, the child may be placed in the custody of the agency and then placed with family members or in foster care. The judge will determine a visitation plan for the parents or caregivers, and the case manager will work with them to draft a case plan.

6. **Review hearings.** Review hearings are held at least every six months to determine case plan progress and assess whether the child can return home safely. The parents or guardians must successfully complete the case plan before they are allowed to regain custody of the child(ren).

7. **Permanency hearing.** After 12 to 18 months, the court will determine the child's permanent living situation, which can be a return to the parent(s) and/or caregiver (referred to as "reunification"), guardianship, permanent placement with a relative, or the termination of parental rights (TPR) and adoption.

8. **Termination of parental rights hearing.** After a reasonable amount of time (12 to 24 months), parental rights may be terminated. This may be based on specific conduct or failure to meet case plan goals. Parents may also opt to voluntarily give up their parental rights. In some states, this will release the child for adoption. The TPR hearing may happen sooner in instances of very serious maltreatment, often called "aggravated circumstances."

The length of time between each of these steps varies by state. You can familiarize yourself with your state's specific rules by consulting Gateway's State Statute series at www.childwelfare.gov/systemwide/laws_policies/state.

Who Should Attend Court Hearings and Reviews?

Parents and caregivers are strongly encouraged to attend every hearing and be well-prepared to share their story with the judge and the court. If you are being investigated, it is important to work closely with your lawyer and caseworker. Children and youth should attend permanency hearings and reviews whenever possible and appropriate. Older children may wish to share thoughts or concerns, and judges may wish to observe the well-being of young children. Some judges may ask to speak with youth and children in private to see how they are doing and to make sure they understand the process and why decisions are being made.

Grandparents and involved relatives or caregivers—as well as family acquaintances—may be encouraged to attend court hearings. In addition to supporting the children and/or their parents in court, family members and other caregivers can provide an important view of the situation, and the hearings can help them to better understand the court's decisions.

Parents should consult their attorney if they feel that other supportive contacts—such as close friends, work colleagues, teachers, their child's sports coach, mentor, or pastor—might help their case in court. If a child is in out-of-home care, it is a good idea for parents to build a relationship with the child's caregivers so they can be a support to the parents as the case proceeds.

Parents who maintain physical custody of their child(ren) but who have an active court case—as well as those whose children have been placed in out-of-home care—will be notified of the hearings and are expected to attend. As mentioned earlier, children may be required or encouraged to attend, depending on their age. Child care arrangements should be made for young children not involved in the investigation.

How to File an Appeal

Parents or youth may file an appeal in child maltreatment and TPR cases with the assistance of an attorney or guardian ad litem (GAL) if they believe the judge has acted in error. Appeal procedures differ by state, and a GAL or attorney will be able to explain the appeal process to you. Every state also has a judicial board with the authority to investigate complaints of judicial misconduct and impose discipline and removal if appropriate. Contact information for each state office is available through the clerk of the court. State-specific contact information is available at www.justice.gov/usao/find-your-united-states-attorney.

Chapter 58

Your Legal Rights as a Victim of Sexual Assault or Domestic Abuse

Any type of violence is illegal. Laws about violence against women give additional support to women and families affected by violence. The most significant laws related to violence against women are the Violence Against Women Act (VAWA) and the Family Violence Prevention and Services Act (FVPSA).

Violence against Women Reauthorization Act of 2013

The main federal law against violence against women is the Violence Against Women Reauthorization Act of 2013. Domestic violence and abuse are already against the law. This law provides services and support for victims of domestic violence and sexual assault.

The direct services provided for individual women by the Violence Against Women Reauthorization Act of 2013. include:

- Free rape exams

- No charge for prosecution or civil protection orders in domestic violence

- Programs to meet the needs of immigrant women and women of different races and ethnicities

- Programs and services for women with disabilities

About This Chapter: Text in this chapter begins with excerpts from "Laws on Violence against Women," Office on Women's Health (OWH), U.S. Department of Health and Human Services (HHS), October 11, 2018; Text beginning with the heading "What Are the Federal Crimes?" is excerpted from "Federal Domestic Violence Laws," U.S. Department of Justice (DOJ), December 6, 2017.

- Legal aid for survivors of violence

- Services for children and teens

- Protections for victims who are evicted from their homes because of events related to domestic violence or stalking

The Family Violence Prevention and Services Act

The Family Violence Prevention and Services Act (FVPSA) helps victims of domestic violence and their children by providing shelters and resources. Under the FVPSA, the Administration for Children and Families, part of the U.S. Department of Health and Human Services (HHS), funds national, state, and community programs, such as state domestic-violence coalitions and the Domestic Violence Resource Network. The Domestic Violence Resource Network includes national resource centers on domestic violence and the National Domestic Violence Hotline (800-799-7233).

Local Laws about Violence against Women

Each community has slightly different laws about violence. But no one ever has the right to hurt you physically. In all communities, you should call 911 if you are in immediate danger. Violence is a criminal act. You must contact the local police to report violence and be protected by the law. Some communities have outdated or limited local laws about sexual assault. The legal definition of rape in your local community may be slightly different than what you expect. The U.S. Department of Justice (a federal agency) defines rape as "the penetration, no matter how slight, of the vagina or anus with any body part or object, or oral penetration by a sex organ of another person, without the consent of the victim." The federal government uses this legal definition to collect information about rape from local police.

Even though local laws can be slightly different from community to community, do not be afraid to report violence to the police. The police will file a report, which is the start of a legal process to get help and protection under the law.

What Are the Federal Crimes?

All the federal domestic violence crimes are felonies.

It is a federal crime under the Violence Against Women Act ("VAWA"):

- To cross state lines or enter or leave Indian country and physically injure an "intimate partner";

- To cross state lines to stalk or harass or to stalk or harass within the maritime or territorial lands of the United States (this includes military bases and Indian country); and

- To cross state lines to enter or leave Indian country and violate a qualifying protection order.

It is a federal crime under the Gun Control Act:

- To possess a firearm and/or ammunition while subject to a qualifying protection order; and

- To possess a firearm and/or ammunition after conviction of a qualifying misdemeanor crime of domestic violence.

In a VAWA case, the Court must order restitution to pay the victim the full amount of loss. These losses include costs for medical or psychological care, physical therapy, transportation, temporary housing, child-care expenses, loss of income, attorney's fees, costs incurred in obtaining a civil protection order, and any other losses suffered by the victim as a result of the offense.

In a Gun Control Act case, the Court may order restitution. Please keep a record of all expenses caused by the domestic violence crime.

What Is a Qualifying Domestic Violence Misdemeanor?

Possession of a firearm and/or ammunition after conviction of a "qualifying" domestic violence misdemeanor is a federal crime under Section 922(g)(9). Generally, the misdemeanor will "qualify" if the conviction was for a crime committed by an intimate partner, parent or guardian of the victim that required the use of attempted use of physical force or the threatened use of a deadly weapon. The United States Attorney's Office will examine your case and determine whether the prior domestic violence misdemeanor conviction qualifies according to the law.

Who Is an Intimate Partner?

Generally, the federal law recognizes an intimate partner as a spouse, a former spouse, a person who shares a child in common with the victim, or a person who cohabits or has cohabited with the victim.

Can My Concerns Be Heard in a Federal Court?

A victim in a VAWA case shall have the right to speak to the judge at a bail hearing to inform the judge of any danger posed by the release of the defendant. Any victim of a crime of violence shall also have the right to address the Court in person at the time of sentencing.

Victims' Rights

1. A federal domestic violence victim has the following rights under 42 U.S.C. Section 10606(b): The right to be treated with fairness and with respect for the victim's dignity and privacy;

2. The right to be reasonably protected from the accused offender;

3. The right to be notified of court proceedings;

4. The right to be present at all public court proceedings related to the offense, unless the court determines that testimony by the victim would be materially affected if the victim heard other testimony at the trial;

5. The right to confer with the attorney for the government in the case;

6. The right to restitution;

7. The right to information about the conviction, sentencing, imprisonment, and release of the offender.

Chapter 59

Bullying and the Law

Although no federal law directly addresses bullying, in some cases, bullying overlaps with discriminatory harassment when it is based on race, national origin, color, sex, age, disability, or religion. When bullying and harassment overlap, federally funded schools (including colleges and universities) have an obligation to resolve the harassment. When the situation is not adequately resolved, the U.S. Department of Education's (ED) Office for Civil Rights (OCR) and the U.S. Department of Justice's (DOJ) Civil Rights Division may be able to help.

Are There Federal Laws That Apply to Bullying?

At present, no federal law directly addresses bullying. In some cases, bullying overlaps with discriminatory harassment which is covered under federal civil rights laws enforced by the ED and the DOJ. No matter what label is used (e.g., bullying, hazing, teasing), schools are obligated by these laws to address conduct that is:

- Severe, pervasive, or persistent

- Creates a hostile environment at school. That is, it is sufficiently serious that it interferes with or limits a student's ability to participate in or benefit from the services, activities, or opportunities offered by a school

- Based on a student's race, color, national origin, sex, disability, or religion

  - Although the ED, under Title VI of the Civil Rights Act of 1964 does not directly cover religion, often religious-based harassment is based on shared ancestry of ethnic

About This Chapter: This chapter includes text excerpted from "Federal Laws," StopBullying.gov, U.S. Department of Health and Human Services (HHS), September 26, 2017.

characteristics which is covered. The U.S. Department of Justice has jurisdiction over religion under Title IV of the Civil Rights Act of 1964.

What Are the Federal Civil Rights Laws U.S. Department of Education and U.S. Department of Justice Enforce?

- A school that fails to respond appropriately to harassment of students based on a protected class may be violating one or more civil rights laws enforced by the ED and the DOJ, including:

  - Title IV and Title VI of the Civil Rights Act of 1964

  - Title IX of the Education Amendments of 1972

  - Section 504 of the Rehabilitation Act of 1973

  - Titles II and III of the Americans with Disabilities Act

  - Individuals with Disabilities Education Act (IDEA)

Do Federal Civil Rights Laws Cover Harassment of Lesbian, Gay, Bisexual, and Transgender Youth?

- Title IX and Title IV do not prohibit discrimination based solely on sexual orientation, but they protect all students, including students who are LGBT or perceived to be LGBT, from sex-based harassment.

- Harassment based on sex and sexual orientation are not mutually exclusive. When students are harassed based on their actual or perceived sexual orientation, they may also be subjected to forms of sex discrimination recognized under Title IX.

What Is an Example of a Case Where Harassment Based on Sex and Sexual Orientation Overlap?

- A female high-school student was spit on, slammed into lockers, mocked, and routinely called names because she did not conform to feminine stereotypes and because of her sexual orientation. The student had short hair, a deep voice, and wore male clothing. After the harassment started, she told some classmates she was a lesbian, and the harassment worsened. The school described the harassment as "sexual orientation harassment" in its incident reports and did not take any action.

• In this case, the student was harassed based on her nonconformity to gender stereotypes. In this case, then, although the school labeled the incident as "sexual orientation harassment," the harassment was also based on sex and covered under Title IX.

Things You Can Say to Someone Who Bullies

It can be hard to know what to say to a person who bullies. You might want to practice what you will say with an adult. Of course, do not try talking back to someone who seems dangerous. Remember to try to keep your tone calm and cool even if you are upset.

You could keep your reply short, so you do not give the person too much attention. You might try something like, "Okay, good to know," "Thanks for sharing that," "Nice try," or "So?" You could also try to lighten the mood by playfully agreeing if that seems like it might fit the situation.

You could try something like, "That was kind of funny, but now it is time to stop."

You also might take the bully by surprise and just say what you think is true: "You are acting like a bully, and it is not cool." "What you said is pretty ridiculous." "You know, that is not really funny. Please stop."

(Source: "If You Are Bullied," girlshealth.gov, Office on Women's Health (OWH).)

What Are a School's Obligations Regarding Harassment Based on Protected Classes?

Anyone can report harassing conduct to a school. When a school receives a complaint they must take certain steps to investigate and resolve the situation.

• Immediate and appropriate action to investigate or otherwise determine what happened

• Inquiry must be prompt, thorough, and impartial

• Interview targeted students, offending students, and witnesses, and maintain written documentation of investigation

• Communicate with targeted students regarding steps taken to end harassment

• Check in with targeted students to ensure that harassment has ceased

- When an investigation reveals that harassment has occurred, a school should take steps reasonably calculated to:

  - End the harassment

  - Eliminate any hostile environment

  - Prevent harassment from recurring

  - Prevent retaliation against the targeted student(s) or complainant(s)

What Should the School Do to Resolve a Harassment Complaint?

- Appropriate responses will depend on the facts of each case.

- School must be an active participant in responding to harassment and should take reasonable steps when crafting remedies to minimize burdens on the targeted students.

- Possible responses include:

  - Develop, revise, and publicize:

    - Policy prohibiting harassment and discrimination

    - Grievance procedures for students to file harassment complaints

    - contact information for Title IX/Section 504/Title VI coordinators

- Implement training for staff and administration on identifying and addressing harassment

- Provide monitors or additional adult supervision in areas where harassment occurs

- Determine consequences and services for harassers, including whether discipline is appropriate

- Limit interactions between harassers and targets

- Provide harassed student an additional opportunity to obtain a benefit that was denied (e.g., retaking a test/class)

- Provide services to a student who was denied a bene

Are There Resources for Schools to Assist with Resolving Harassment Complaints?

The DOJ's Community Relations Service is the Department's "peacemaker" for community conflicts and tensions arising from differences of race, color, and national origin and to prevent and respond to violent hate crimes committed on the basis of gender, gender identity, sexual orientation, religion, disability, race, color, and national origin. It is a free, impartial, confidential, and voluntary Federal Agency that offers mediation, conciliation, technical assistance, and training.

What If the Harassment Continues

If harassment persists, consider filing a formal grievance with the district and contacting the U.S. Department of Education's (ED) Office for Civil Rights (OCR) and from the DOJ Civil Rights Division.

Part Five
If You Need More Information

Chapter 60

Abuse and Violence: A Statistical Summary

Youth Violence

Thousands of people experience youth violence every day. While the magnitude and types of youth violence vary across communities and demographic groups, youth violence negatively impacts youth in all communities—urban, suburban, rural, and tribal.

- **Youth violence is common.** Nearly 1 in 5 high-school students reported being bullied on school property in the last year, and about 1 in 7 were electronically bullied (texting, Instagram, Facebook, or other social media).

- **Youth violence kills and injures.** Homicide is the third leading cause of death for young people ages 10 to 24. Each day, about 14 young people are victims of homicide and about 1,300 are treated in emergency departments for nonfatal assault-related injuries.

About This Chapter: Text under the heading "Youth Violence" is excerpted from "Preventing Youth Violence," Centers for Disease Control and Prevention (CDC), February 26, 2019; Text under the heading "Intimate Partner Violence" is excerpted from "Preventing Intimate Partner Violence," Centers for Disease Control and Prevention (CDC), February 26, 2019; Text under the heading "Teen Dating Violence" is excerpted from "Preventing Teen Dating Violence," Centers for Disease Control and Prevention (CDC), 2019; Text under the heading "School Violence" is excerpted from "Preventing School Violence," Centers for Disease Control and Prevention (CDC), June 27, 2019; Text under the heading "Bullying" is excerpted from "Facts about Bullying," StopBullying.gov, U.S. Department of Health and Human Services (HHS), June 10, 2019; Text under the heading "Injury- and Violence-Related Deaths" is excerpted from "Key Injury and Violence Data," Centers for Disease Control and Prevention (CDC), May 8, 2017.

- **Youth violence is costly.** Youth homicides and nonfatal physical assault-related injuries result in more than $21 billion annually in combined medical and lost productivity costs alone, not including costs associated with the criminal justice system, psychological and social consequences for victims, perpetrators and their families, or costs incurred by communities.

Intimate Partner Violence

Intimate partner violence (IPV) is common. It affects millions of people in the United States each year. Data from the Centers for Disease Control and Prevention's (CDC) National Intimate Partner and Sexual Violence Survey (NISVS) indicate:

- About 1 in 4 women and nearly 1 in 10 men have experienced contact sexual violence, physical violence, and/or stalking by an intimate partner during their lifetime and reported some form of IPV-related impact.

- Over 43 million women and 38 million men experienced psychological aggression by an intimate partner in their lifetime.

- Nearly about 1 in 5 women and 1 in 7 men report having experienced severe physical violence from an intimate partner in their lifetime.

- About 1 in 5 women and 1 in 12 men have experienced contact sexual violence by an intimate partner.

- 10 percent of women and 2 percent of men report having been stalked by an intimate partner.

Teen Dating Violence

Teen dating violence (TDV) is common. It affects millions of teens in the United States each year. Data from the CDC's Youth Risk Behavior Survey (YRBS) and NISVS indicate that:

- Nearly 1 in 11 female teens and about 1 in 15 male high-school students report having experienced physical dating violence in the last year.

- About 1 in 9 female and 1 in 36 male high-school students report having experienced sexual dating violence in the last year.

- 26 percent of women and 15 percent of men who were victims of contact sexual violence, physical violence, and/or stalking by an intimate partner in their lifetime first experienced these or other forms of violence by that partner before age 18.

- The burden of TDV is not shared equally across all groups—sexual minority groups are disproportionately affected by all forms of violence, and some racial/ethnic minority groups are disproportionately affected by many types of violence.

School Violence

According to the CDC's nationwide YRBS:

- Nearly 9 percent of high-school students had been in a physical fight on school property one or more times during the 12 months before the survey.

- About 6 percent of students had been threatened or injured with a weapon (for example, a gun, knife, or club) on school property one or more times during the 12 months before the survey.

- About 7 percent of students had not gone to school at least 1 day during the 30 days before the survey because they felt they would be unsafe at school or on their way to or from school.

Bullying
Been Bullied

- The 2017 School Crime Supplement (SCS) (National Center for Education Statistics (NCES) and Bureau of Justice) indicates that, nationwide, about 20 percent of students ages 12 to 18 experienced bullying.

- The 2017 Youth Risk Behavior Surveillance System (YRBSS) (Centers for Disease Control and Prevention (CDC)) indicates that, nationwide, 19 percent of students in grades 9 to 12 report being bullied on school property in the 12 months preceding the survey.

Bullied Others

- Approximately 30 percent of young people admit to bullying others in surveys.

Seen Bullying

- 70.6 percent of young people say they have seen bullying in their schools.

- 70.4 percent of school staff have seen bullying. 62 percent witnessed bullying two or more times in the last month and 41 percent witness bullying once a week or more.

- When bystanders intervene, bullying stops within 10 seconds 57 percent of the time.

Been Cyberbullied

- The 2017 School Crime Supplement (NCES and Bureau of Justice) indicates that, among students ages 12 to 18 who reported being bullied at school during the school year, 15 percent were bullied online or by text.

- The 2017 YRBSS (CDC) indicates that an estimated 14.9 percent of high-school students were electronically bullied in the 12 months prior to the survey.

How Often Bullied

- In one large study, about 49 percent of children in grades 4 to 12 reported being bullied by other students at school at least once during the past month, whereas 30.8 percent reported bullying others during that time.

- Defining "frequent" involvement in bullying as occurring two or more times within the past month, 40.6 percent of students reported some type of frequent involvement in bullying, with 23.2 percent being the youth frequently bullied, 8.0 percent being the youth who frequently bullied others, and 9.4 percent playing both roles frequently.

Types of Bullying

- The most common types of bullying are verbal and social. Physical bullying happens less often. Cyberbullying happens the least frequently.

- According to one large study, the following percentages of middle schools students had experienced these various types of bullying: name calling (44.2 %); teasing (43.3 %); spreading rumors or lies (36.3%); pushing or shoving (32.4%); hitting, slapping, or kicking (29.2%); leaving out (28.5%); threatening (27.4%); stealing belongings (27.3%); sexual comments or gestures (23.7%); e-mail or blogging (9.9%).

Where Bullying Occurs

- Most bullying takes place in school, outside on school grounds, and on the school bus. Bullying also happens wherever kids gather in the community. And of course, cyberbullying occurs on cell phones and online.

- According to one large study, the following percentages of middle-schools students had experienced bullying in these various places at school: classroom (29.3%); hallway or lockers (29.0%); cafeteria (23.4%); gym or PE class (19.5%); bathroom (12.2%); playground or recess (6.2%).

How Often Adult Notified

- Only about 20 to 30 percent of students who are bullied notify adults about the bullying.

Injury- and Violence-Related Deaths

Each year 214,000 people die from injury—1 person every 3 minutes. But these deaths are on the tip of the iceberg. Each year, millions of people are injured and survive. They are faced with life-long mental, physical, and financial problems.

- 2.8 million people were hospitalized due to injuries in 2015.

- 27.6 million people were treated in an emergency department for injuries in 2015.

Injury and violence also have an alarming economic toll. The total costs of injuries and violence in the United States was $671 billion in 2013. The costs associated with fatal injuries was $214 billion while nonfatal injuries accounted for over $457 billion.

Injury and Violence in the United States—by the Numbers

- Every year 214,000 people die from injuries and violence in the United States.

- Total cost from injuries and violence estimates $671 billion which includes medical and work loss costs.

- For every person that dies 13 are hospitalized and 129 are treated in an emergency room.

- More than 33,700 people died in motor vehicle crashes.

- More than 14,800 people died from prescription opioid overdoses.

- 2,791,000 older people treated in emergency rooms for fall injuries each year.

- 325,000 kids treated for sports and recreation-related concussion in an emergency room.

Chapter 61

Directory of Abuse and Violence Resources

Hotlines

IMAlive

Toll-Free: 800-SUICIDE (800-784-2433)
Website: www.imalive.org
E-mail: volunteer@imalive.org

National Domestic Violence Hotline (NDVH)

P.O. Box 161810
Austin, TX 78716
Toll-Free: 800-799-SAFE (800-799-7233)
Phone: 512-453-8117
Toll-Free TTY: 800-787-3224
Website: www.thehotline.org
E-mail: hotline.requests@ndvh.org

National Runaway Safeline (NRS)

3141B N. Lincoln
Chicago, IL 60657
Toll-Free: 800-RUNAWAY (800-786-2929)
Phone: 773-880-9860
Fax: 773-929-5150
Website: www.1800runaway.org
E-mail: info@1800runaway.org

Resources in this chapter were compiled from several sources deemed reliable; all contact information was verified and updated in August 2019.

Domestic Violence Organizations

National Coalition Against Domestic Violence (NCADV)
600 Grant
Ste. 750
Denver, CO 80203
Phone: 303-839-1852
Website: www.ncadv.org
E-mail: mainoffice@ncadv.org

National Resource Center on Domestic Violence (NRCDV)
6041 Linglestown Rd.
Harrisburg, PA 17112
Toll-Free: 800-537-2238
Website: nrcdv.org
E-mail: nrcdvTA@nrcdv.org

Pennsylvania Coalition Against Domestic Violence (PCADV)
3605 Vartan Way
Ste. 101
Harrisburg, PA 17110
Phone: 717-545-6400
Website: www.pcadv.org

Teen Dating Violence

Break the Cycle
P.O. Box 811334
Los Angeles, CA 90081
Phone: 424-265-7346
Website: www.breakthecycle.org
E-mail: info@breakthecycle.org

Girls Inc.
National Office
120 Wall St.
18th Fl.
New York, NY 10005-39021
Phone: 212-509-2000
Website: www.girlsinc.org
E-mail: communications@girlsinc.org

Peace over Violence

Metro Headquarters
1015 Wilshire Blvd.
Ste. 200
Los Angeles, CA 90017
Phone: 213-955-9090
Fax: 213-955-9093
Website: www.peaceoverviolence.org
E-mail: info@peaceoverviolence.org

Lesbian, Gay, Bisexual, Transgendered, Queer (LGBTQ) Youth

Community United Against Violence (CUAV)

427 S. Van Ness Ave.
San Francisco, CA 94103
Phone: 415-777-5500
Fax: 415-777-5565
Website: www.cuav.org
E-mail: info@cuav.org

Parents, Families, and Friends of Lesbians and Gays (PFLAG)

National Office
1828 L. St., N.W.
Ste. 660
Washington, DC 20036
Phone: 202-467-8180
Fax: 202-467-8194
Website: pflag.org
E-mail: info@pflag.org

Sexual Assault

FaithTrust Institute

2414 S.W. Andover St.
Ste. D208
Seattle, WA 98106
Phone: 206-634-1903
Website: www.faithtrustinstitute.org
E-mail: info@faithtrustinstitute.org

Office on Violence Against Women (OVW)

U.S. Department of Justice (DOJ)
145 N. St., N.E.
Ste. 10W.121
Washington, DC 20530
Phone: 202-307-6026
TTY: 202-307-2277
Fax: 202-305-2589
Website: www.justice.gov/ovw
E-mail: ovw.info@usdoj.gov

Rape Abuse and Incest National Network (RAINN)

1220 L. St., N.W.
Ste. 505
Washington, DC 20005
Toll-Free: 800-656-HOPE (800-656-4673)
Phone: 202-544-1034
Website: www.rainn.org
E-mail: info@rainn.org

Additional Abuse and Violence Resources

American Bar Association (ABA)

Chicago Headquarters
321 N. Clark St.
Chicago, IL 60654
Toll-Free: 800-285-2221
Website: www.americanbar.org
E-mail: service@americanbar.org

American Humane

1400 16th St., N.W.
Ste. 360
Washington, DC 20036
Toll-Free: 800-227-4645
Website: www.americanhumane.org
E-mail: info@americanhumane.org

Child Welfare Information Gateway

Children's Bureau/Administration on Children, Youth and Families (ACYF)
330 C. St., S.W.
Washington, DC 20201
Toll-Free: 800-394-3366
Website: www.childwelfare.gov
E-mail: info@childwelfare.gov

Internet Crimes Against Children (ICAC) Task Force Program

Toll-Free: 877-798-7682
Website: www.icactaskforce.org

The Kempe Foundation

The Gary Pavilion at Children's Hospital Colorado, Anschutz Medical Campus
13123 E., 16th Ave.
Ste. B390
Aurora, CO 80045
Toll-Free: 844-CO-4-KIDS (844-264-5437)
Phone: 303-864-5300
Website: www.kempe.org
E-mail: questions@kempe.org

National Center for Missing and Exploited Children® (NCMEC)

333 John Carlyle St.
Ste. 125
Alexandria, VA 22314-5950
Toll-Free: 800-THE-LOST (800-843-5678)
Phone: 703-224-2150
Fax: 703-224-2122
Website: www.missingkids.com

National Center for Victims of Crime (NCVC)

P.O. Box 101207
Arlington, VA 22210
Phone: 202-467-8700
Fax: 202-467-8701
Website: victimsofcrime.org

National Center on Elder Abuse (NCEA)

c/o University of Southern California (USC) Keck School of Medicine
1000 S. Fremont Ave.
Unit 22, Bldg. A-6
Alhambra, CA 91803
Toll-Free: 855-500-ELDR (855-500-3537)
Fax: 626-457-4090
Website: ncea.acl.gov
E-mail: ncea-info@aoa.hhs.gov

Office for Victims of Crime (OVC)

810 Seventh St., N.W.
Second Fl.
Washington, DC 20531
Phone: 202-307-5983
Website: www.ovc.gov

Prevent Child Abuse America (PCAA)

228 S. Wabash Ave.
10th Fl.
Chicago, IL 60604
Toll-Free: 800-CHILDREN (800-244-5373)
Phone: 312-663-3520
Fax: 312-939-8962
Website: preventchildabuse.org
E-mail: info@preventchildabuse.org

Start Strong

Futures Without Violence
100 Montgomery St.
The Presidio
San Francisco, CA 94129
Phone: 415-678-5500
Website: startstrong.futureswithoutviolence.org
E-mail: info@startstrongteens.org

Chapter 62

Victims of Abuse and Violence: Where to Go for Help

Child Abuse

Childhelp
4350 E. Camelback Rd.
Bldg. F250
Phoenix, AZ 85018
Toll-Free: 800-4-A-CHILD (800-422-4453)
Phone: 480-922-8212
Website: www.childhelp.org

Childsafe
House 89B St., 103
Phnom Penh
Cambodia
Phone: 855-23-986-601
Website: www.thinkchildsafe.org
E-mail: info@thinkchildsafe.org

Resources in this chapter were compiled from several sources deemed reliable; all contact information was verified and updated in August 2019.

Prevent Child Abuse America® (PCAA)

228 S., Wabash Ave.
10th Fl.
Chicago, IL 60604
Toll-Free: 800-CHILDREN (800-244-5373)
Phone: 312-663-3520
Fax: 312-939-8962
Website: preventchildabuse.org
E-mail: info@preventchildabuse.org

Child Sexual Abuse

Stop It Now!

351 Pleasant St.
Ste. B-319
Northampton, MA 01060
Toll-Free: 888-PREVENT (888-773-8368)
Phone: 413-587-3500
Website: www.stopitnow.org
E-mail: info@stopitnow.org

Washington Coalition of Sexual Assault Programs (WCSAP)

4317 Sixth Ave., S.E.
Ste. 120
Olympia, WA 98503
Phone: 360-754-7583
TTY: 360-709-0305
Fax: 360-786-7807
Website: www.wcsap.org

Family Violence

National Domestic Violence Hotline (NDVH)

P.O. Box 161810
Austin, TX 78716
Toll-Free: 800-799-SAFE (800-799-7233)
Phone: 512-453-8117
Toll-Free TTY: 800-787-3224
Website: www.thehotline.org
E-mail: hotline.requests@ndvh.org

Missing/Abducted Children

Child Find of America, Inc.
P.O. Box 277
New Paltz, NY 12561-0277
Toll-Free: 800-I-AM-LOST (800-426-5678)
Phone: 845-883-6060
Website: childfindofamerica.org
E-mail: information@childfindofamerica.org

National Center for Missing And Exploited Children® (NCMEC)
333 John Carlyle St.
Ste. 125
Alexandria, VA 22314-5950
Toll-Free: 800-THE-LOST (800-843-5678)
Phone: 703-224-2150
Fax: 703-224-2122
Website: www.missingkids.com

Operation Lookout Cannabidiol
6320 Evergreen Way
Ste. 201
Everett, WA 98203
Toll-Free: 877-543-7335
Fax: 425-348-4411
Website: www.operationlookout.org

Rape/Incest

Rape And Incest National Network (RAINN)
1220 L. St., N.W.
Ste. 500
Washington, DC 20005
Toll-Free: 800-656-HOPE (800-656-4673)
Phone: 202-544-1034
Website: www.rainn.org

Youth In Trouble/Runaways

National Runaway Safeline (NRS)

3141B N. Lincoln
Chicago, IL 60657
Toll-Free: 800-RUNAWAY (800-786-2929)
Phone: 773-880-9860
Fax: 773-929-5150
Website: www.1800runaway.org
E-mail: info@1800RUNAWAY.org

Crime Victims

National Center for Victims of Crime (NCVC)

P.O. Box 101207
Arlington, VA 22210
Phone: 202-467-8700
Fax: 202-467-8701
Website: victimsofcrime.org

Chapter 63

How and Where to Report Child Abuse

There are ways you can help if you suspect or know that a child is being abused or neglected. If you or someone else is in immediate and serious danger, you should call 911. National and local resources are available to provide assistance and information about reporting suspected maltreatment.

How Do I Report Suspected Child Abuse or Neglect?

Contact your local Child Protective Services office or law enforcement agency.

Who Can Report Child Abuse or Neglect?

Anyone can report suspected child abuse or neglect. Reporting abuse or neglect can protect a child and get help for a family.

All U.S. states and territories have laws identifying persons who are required to report suspected child abuse or neglect. Mandatory reporters may include social workers, teachers and other school personnel, child-care providers, physicians and other healthcare workers, mental-health professionals, and law-enforcement officers. Some states require any person who suspects child abuse or neglect to report.

About This Chapter: This chapter includes text excerpted from "How to Report Suspected Child Maltreatment," Child Welfare Information Gateway, U.S. Department of Health and Human Services (HHS), December 13, 2014. Reviewed August 2019. The appended list of additional resources in this chapter were compiled from several sources deemed reliable; all contact information was verified and updated in August 2019.

What Do I Report?

Provide a complete, honest account of what you observed that led you to suspect the occurrence of child abuse or neglect. Any reasonable suspicion is sufficient.

What Will Happen after I Make a Report of Child Abuse or Neglect?

After you make a report, it will be sent to Child Protective Services (CPS). When CPS receives a report, the CPS worker reviews the information and determines if an investigation is needed. The CPS worker may talk with the family, the child, or others to help determine what is making the child unsafe. The CPS worker can help parents or other caregivers get services, education, or other assistance.

Other Child Abuse Reporting Numbers

The following organizations are among many that have information on child abuse reporting numbers. Inclusion on this list is for information purposes and does not constitute an endorsement by Child Welfare Information Gateway or the Children's Bureau. For the most current information, please refer to the National Organizations section of Child Welfare Information Gateway at www.childwelfare.gov/organizations.

State toll-free numbers and websites for specific agencies designated to receive and investigate reports of suspected child abuse and neglect.

Alabama
Website: dhr.alabama.gov/services/Child_Protective_Services/Abuse_Neglect_Reporting.aspx
Visit the website above for information on reporting or call Childhelp (800-422-4453) for assistance.

Alaska
Toll-Free: 800-478-4444
Fax: 907-269-3939
Website: dhss.alaska.gov/ocs/Pages/default.aspx
To report via e-mail: ReportChildAbuse@alaska.gov

Arizona

Toll-Free: 888-SOS-CHILD (888-767-2445)
Website: dcs.az.gov
Arizona's Online Reporting Service for Mandated Reporters via the secure website in nonemergency cases: dcs.az.gov/report-child-abuse

Connecticut

Toll-Free: 800-842-2288
Toll-Free TDD: 800-624-5518
Website: portal.ct.gov/DCF/1-DCF/Reporting-Child-Abuse-and-Neglect

Delaware

Toll-Free: 800-292-9582
Website: kids.delaware.gov
Online reporting: kids.delaware.gov/fs/fs_iseethesigns.shtml

District of Columbia

Phone: 202-671-SAFE (202-671-7233)
Website: cfsa.dc.gov/service/report-child-abuse-and-neglect

Georgia

Toll-Free: 855-GA-CHILD (855-422-4453)
Website: dfcs.dhs.georgia.gov/child-abuse-neglect
Visit the website above for information on reporting or call Childhelp (800-422-4453) for assistance.

Guam

Phone: 671-987-9567 or 671-987-8829

Hawaii

Phone: 808-832-5300
Toll-Free: 888-380-3088
Website: humanservices.hawaii.gov/ssd/home/child-welfare-services

Indiana

Toll-Free: 800-800-5556
Website: www.in.gov/dcs/2398.htm

Iowa

Toll-Free: 800-362-2178
Website: dhs.iowa.gov/report-abuse-and-fraud

Kansas

Toll-Free: 800-922-5330
Website: www.dcf.ks.gov/Pages/Report-Abuse-or-Neglect.aspx
Online reporting for mandated reporters in nonemergency situations: www.dcf.ks.gov/services/PPS/Pages/KIPS/KIPSWebIntake.aspx

Kentucky

Toll-Free: 877-KYSAFE1 (877-597-2331)
Website: chfs.ky.gov/agencies/dcbs/dpp/cpb/Pages/default.aspx

Louisiana

Toll-Free: 855-4LA-KIDS (855-452-5437)
Website: dss.louisiana.gov/index.cfm?md=pagebuilder&tmp=home&pid=109
Online reporting portal for mandated reporters in nonemergency situations: mr.dcfs.la.gov/c/MR_PortalApp.app

Maine

Toll-Free: 800-452-1999
Toll-Free TTY: 711-452-1999
Website: www.maine.gov/dhhs/ocfs/hotlines.htm

Massachusetts

Toll-Free: 800-792-5200
Website: www.mass.gov/how-to/report-child-abuse-or-neglect

Michigan

Toll-Free: 855-444-3911
Website: www.michigan.gov/dhs/0,1607,7-124-5452_7119---,00.html

Minnesota

Website: mn.gov/dhs/report-abuse
Visit the website above for information on reporting or call Childhelp (800-422-4453) for assistance.

Mississippi

Toll-Free: 800-222-8000
Phone: 601-432-4570
Website: www.mdcps.ms.gov/report-child-abuse-neglect
Report on child abuse: reportabuse.mdcps.ms.gov
Reporting via the online system or by downloading the MDCPS Report Child Abuse mobile app: www.mdcps.ms.gov/report-child-abuse-neglect

Missouri
Toll-Free: 800-392-3738
Toll-Free TTY: 800-735-2466
Website: dss.mo.gov/cd/can.htm
Visit the website above for information on reporting or call Childhelp (800-422-4453) for assistance. Online reporting for mandated reporters in nonemergency situations: dss.mo.gov/cd/keeping-kids-safe/can.htm

Montana
Toll-Free: 866-820-5437
Website: www.dphhs.mt.gov/cfsd/index.shtml

Nevada
Toll-Free: 833-803-1183
Website: dcfs.nv.gov/Programs/CWS/CPS/CPS
Visit the website above for information on reporting or call Childhelp (800-422-4453) for assistance.

New Hampshire
Toll-Free: 800-894-5533
Phone: 603-271-6562
Website: www.dhhs.nh.gov/dcyf/cps/stop.htm

New Jersey
Toll-Free: 877-NJ-ABUSE (877-652-2873)
Toll-Free TDD/TTY: 800-835-5510
Website: www.nj.gov/dcf/reporting/hotline

New Mexico
Toll-Free: 855-333-SAFE (855-333-7233)
Website: cyfd.org/child-abuse-neglect

New York
Toll-Free: 800-342-3720
Toll-Free TDD/TTY: 800-638-5163
Website: ocfs.ny.gov/main/cps/Default.asp

North Carolina
Toll-Free: 800-CHILDREN (800-244-3736)
Website: www.ncdhhs.gov/divisions/social-services/child-welfare-services/child-protective-services/about-child-abuse-and
Visit the website above for information on reporting or call Childhelp (800-422-4453) for assistance.

North Dakota
Website: www.nd.gov/dhs/services/childfamily/cps/#reporting
Visit the website above for information on reporting or call Childhelp (800-422-4453) for assistance.

Oklahoma
Toll-Free: 800-522-3511
Website: www.ok.gov/health/Family_Health/Family_Support_and_Prevention_Service/Oklahoma_Child_Abuse_Hotline/index.html

Oregon
Toll-Free: 855-503-SAFE (855-503-7233)
Website: www.oregon.gov/dhs/children/child-abuse/Pages/Reporting-Numbers.aspx
Visit the website above for information on reporting or call Childhelp (800-422-4453) for assistance.

Pennsylvania
Toll-Free: 800-932-0313
Website: www.dhs.pa.gov/citizens/reportabuse/index.htm#.Vr4FO032aM8
Online reporting portal for mandated reporters in nonemergency situations: www.compass.state.pa.us/cwis/public/home

Puerto Rico
Toll-Free: 800-981-8333
Phone: 787-749-1333

Rhode Island
Toll-Free: 800-RI-CHILD (800-742-4453)
Website: www.dcyf.ri.gov/child-protective-services

South Carolina
Website: dss.sc.gov/abuseneglect/report-abuse-and-neglect
Visit the website above for information on reporting or call Childhelp (800-422-4453) for assistance.

South Dakota

Toll-Free: 877-244-0864

Website: dss.sd.gov/childprotection/reporting.aspx

Visit the website above for information on reporting or call Childhelp (800-422-4453) for assistance.

Tennessee

Toll-Free: 877-237-0004

Website: www.tn.gov/dcs/program-areas/child-safety/reporting/child-abuse.html

Online reporting: apps.tn.gov/carat

U.S. Virgin Islands

Website: www.dhs.gov.vi/contact/index.html

Vermont

Toll-Free: 800-649-5285

Website: dcf.vermont.gov/protection/reporting

Virginia

Toll-Free: 800-552-7096

Phone: 804-786-8536

Website: www.dss.virginia.gov/family/cps/index.cgi

Washington

Toll-Free: 866-END-HARM (866-363-4276)

Website: www.dcyf.wa.gov/contact-us

West Virginia

Toll-Free: 800-352-6513

Website: dhhr.wv.gov/bcf/Services/Pages/Centralized-Intake-for-Abuse-and-Neglect.aspx

Wisconsin

Website: dcf.wisconsin.gov/reportabuse

Visit the website above for information on reporting or call Childhelp (800-422-4453) for assistance.

Wyoming

Website: dfsweb.wyo.gov/programs-and-services/social-services/child-protective-services

Visit the website above for information on reporting or call Childhelp (800-422-4453) for assistance.

Index

Index

Page numbers that appear in *Italics* refer to tables or illustrations. Page numbers that have a small 'n' after the page number refer to citation information shown as Notes. Page numbers that appear in **Bold** refer to information contained in boxes within the chapters.